WORKSHOPS IN COMPUTING
Series edited by C. J. van Rijsbergen

Also in this series

Women into Computing: Selected Papers 1988–1990
Gillian Lovegrove and Barbara Segal (Eds.)

3rd Refinement Workshop (organised by BCS-FACS, and sponsored by IBM UK Laboratories, Hursley Park and the Programming Research Group, University of Oxford), Hursley Park, 9–11 January 1990
Carroll Morgan and J. C. P. Woodcock (Eds.)

Designing Correct Circuits, Workshop jointly organised by the Universities of Oxford and Glasgow, Oxford, 26–28 September 1990
Geraint Jones and Mary Sheeran (Eds.)

Functional Programming, Glasgow 1990,
Proceedings of the 1990 Glasgow Workshop on Functional Programming, Ullapool, Scotland, 13–15 August 1990
Simon L. Peyton Jones, Graham Hutton and Carsten Kehler Holst (Eds.)

4th Refinement Workshop, Proceedings of the 4th Refinement Workshop, organised by BCS-FACS, Cambridge, 9–11 January 1991
Joseph M. Morris and Roger C. Shaw (Eds.)

AI and Cognitive Science '90, University of Ulster at Jordanstown, 20–21 September 1990
Michael F. McTear and Norman Creaney (Eds.)

Software Re-use, Utrecht 1989, Proceedings of the Software Re-use Workshop, Utrecht, The Netherlands, 23–24 November 1989
Liesbeth Dusink and Patrick Hall (Eds.)

Z User Workshop, 1990, Proceedings of the Fifth Annual Z User Meeting, Oxford, 17–18 December 1990
J.E. Nicholls (Ed.)

IV Higher Order Workshop, Banff 1990
Proceedings of the IV Higher Order Workshop, Banff, Alberta, Canada, 10–14 September 1990
Graham Birtwistle (Ed.)

ALPUK91 Proceedings of the 3rd UK Annual Conference on Logic Programming, Edinburgh, 10–12 April 1991
Geraint A.Wiggins, Chris Mellish and Tim Duncan (Eds.)

Specifications of Database Systems,
1st International Workshop on Specifications of Database Systems, Glasgow, 3–5 July 1991
David J. Harper and Moira C. Norrie (Eds.)

7th UK Computer and Telecommunications Performance Engineering Workshop,
Edinburgh, 22–23 July 1991
J. Hillston, P.J.B. King and R.J. Pooley (Eds.)

Logic Program Synthesis and Transformation,
Proceedings of LOPSTR 91, International Workshop on Logic Program Synthesis and Transformation, University of Manchester, 4–5 July 1991
T.P. Clement and K.-K. Lau (Eds.)

Declarative Programming, Sasbachwalden 1991
PHOENIX Seminar and Workshop on Declarative Programming, Sasbachwalden, Black Forest, Germany, 18–22 November 1991
John Darlington and Roland Dietrich (Eds.)

Building Interactive Systems:
Architectures and Tools
Philip Gray and Roger Took (Eds.)

Functional Programming, Glasgow 1991,
Proceedings of the 1991 Glasgow Workshop on Functional Programming, Portree, Isle of Skye, 12–14 August 1991
Rogardt Heldal, Carsten Kehler Holst and Philip Wadler (Eds.)

Object Orientation in Z
Susan Stepney, Rosalind Barden and David Cooper (Eds.)

Code Generation – Concepts, Tools, Techniques
Proceedings of the International Workshop on Code Generation, Dagstuhl, Germany, 20–24 May 1991
Robert Giegerich and Susan L. Graham (Eds.)

Z User Workshop, York 1991, Proceedings of the Sixth Annual Z User Meeting, York, 16–17 December 1991
J.E. Nicholls (Ed.)

continued on back page...

Tim Denvir, Ros Herman and R.W. Whitty (Eds.)

Formal Aspects of Measurement

Proceedings of the BCS-FACS Workshop on Formal Aspects of Measurement, South Bank University, London, 5 May 1991

Published in collaboration with the British Computer Society

Springer-Verlag
London Berlin Heidelberg New York
Paris Tokyo Hong Kong
Barcelona Budapest

Tim Denvir, MA, CEng, MIEE, MBCS
Translimina Ltd
37 Orpington Road
Winchmore Hill
London N21 3PD, UK

Rosalind Herman, MA, MSc
Humanities Programme
Imperial College
180 Queen's Gate
London SW7 2BZ, UK

Robin Whitty, BSc, PhD, C.Math, FIMA
Centre for Systems and Software Engineering
South Bank University
103 Borough Road
London SE1 0AA, UK

ISBN 3-540-19788-5 Springer-Verlag Berlin Heidelberg New York
ISBN 0-387-19788-5 Springer-Verlag New York Berlin Heidelberg

British Library Cataloguing in Publication Data
A catalogue record for this book is available from the British Library

Library of Congress Cataloging-in-Publication Data
A catalog record for this book is available from the Library of Congress

Apart from any fair dealing for the purposes of research or private study, or criticism or review, as permitted under the Copyright, Designs and Patents Act 1988, this publication may only be reproduced, stored or transmitted, in any form or by any means, with the prior permission in writing of the publishers, or in the case of reprographic reproduction in accordance with the terms of licences issued by the Copyright Licensing Agency. Enquiries concerning reproduction outside those terms should be sent to the publishers.

©British Computer Society 1992
Printed in Germany

The use of registered names, trademarks etc. in this publication does not imply, even in the absence of a specific statement, that such names are exempt from the relevant laws and regulations and therefore free for general use.

The publisher makes no representation, express or implied, with regard to the accuracy of the information contained in this book and cannot accept any legal responsibility or liability for any errors or omissions that may be made.

Typesetting: Camera ready by authors

34/3830-543210 Printed on acid-free paper

Preface

This book contains the eight invited papers presented at the workshop on Formal Aspects of Measurement held at South Bank University on 5th May 1991, organised by the British Computer Society's Special Interest Group on Formal Aspects of Computer Science (FACS). In addition, there are five papers which have been included because of their relevance to the subject of the workshop.

The book represents something of a landmark in software engineering research. The British Computer Society's Special Interest Group on Formal Aspects of Computer Science (FACS) has an established reputation among researchers in formal methods of software specification, design and validation. These researchers have not in the past paid much attention to software measurement. Perhaps software measurement research was felt to have emphasised its management potential at the expense of proper scientific foundations? At any rate, for the FACS group to host a workshop in this field is recognition of the significant body of formal measurement theories and techniques which has now become available to software engineers.

The workshop was also a landmark in bringing together nearly all the leading researchers in formal aspects of software measurement. These are among the people who have done most to bring into the field the techniques of measurement theory, axiomatic measurement, and experimental design, all of which are themes which recur often in the pages of this book. They are also the people at the heart of the debate about the exact role for formalism in software measurement. It must be a healthy sign that the discussion on "Software measurement: a mathematical or empirical science?", which ended the workshop, had primarily an air of pragmatism. No danger here of formalism becoming a refuge from scientific common sense.

The workshop was timed to coincide with the fifth meeting, at City University, of the so-called 'Grubstake Group' which was founded with NATO funding in 1988 to promote formal methods in software measurement. There is a significant contribution to this book from the Grubstake Group, including a statement of its philosophy (the final paper in section 1). Overall, the papers are split roughly fifty-fifty between Europe and the US. We were very lucky to be able to achieve such a balance for a one-day meeting.

We have arranged the book to reflect four different formal aspects of measurement: section 1, on principles of measurement, contains three papers which discuss the scientific motivation behind current approaches to software measurement; section 2 on formal measurement in practice, contains four papers which illustrate how the principles are reflected in the design and implementation of actual measurements; section 3 contains two papers on measurement validation and verification; finally section 4 contains four papers discussing the mathematical and logical foundations which are an underlying theme in all the preceding sections.

The workshop was very smoothly supported by BCS-FACS and we would like to thank John Cooke and Brian Monahan in particular for their help and encouragement. Dr Fuchs' attendance was supported by ESPRIT Project 2686 (COSMOS) and Dr Zuse's by ESPRIT Project 2384 (METKIT); Dr Bieman, Dr Gustafson and Dr Melton were supported by NATO Collaborative Research Grant 0343/88. We would like to record our thanks to the referees of the non-invited papers: John Bainbridge, Preetham Kumari, Robert Lockhart, Tien Chu Chung and Julian Rose. Special thanks go to Akungwa Nwagbara, Research Administrator at the CSSE, for all the effort she has put in to preparing the final copy of this book.

May 1992

Tim Denvir
Translimina Ltd, London

Ros Herman
Imperial College, London

Robin Whitty
South Bank University, London

Contents

1. Principles of Measurement

Software Measurement: Why a Formal Approach?
(Invited Paper)
N. Fenton 3

Never Mind the Metrics What About the Numbers!
(Invited Paper)
B. Kitchenham 28

Moving from Philosophy to Practice in Software Measurement
*J.M. Bieman, N. Fenton, D.A. Gustafson, A. Melton
and R. Whitty* 38

2. Formal Measurement in Practice

Deriving Measures of Software Reuse in Object Oriented
Systems (Invited Paper)
J.M. Bieman 63

Language Independent Definition of Axiomatic Metrics
N. Fuchs and S. Stainer 84

Complexity Measures on Trees
M.D. Rice 108

Multi-dimensional Software Metrics
R. Whitty 116

3. Measurement Validation/Verification

A Critique of Validation/Verification Techniques for Software
Development Measures
*D.A. Gustafson, R.M. Toledo, R.E. Courtney
and N. Temsamani* 145

Algebraic Models and Metric Validation (Invited Paper)
M. Shepperd 157

4. Foundations

Properties of Software Measures (Invited Paper)
D.A. Gustafson and B. Prasad 179

Specifying Internal, External, and Predictive Software Metrics (Invited Paper)
A. Melton 194

The Mathematics of Measurement in Software Engineering
M. Russell 209

Measurement Theory and Software Measures (Invited Paper)
H. Zuse and P. Bollmann-Sdorra 219

Author Index 261

1. Principles of Measurement

SOFTWARE MEASUREMENT: WHY A FORMAL APPROACH?

Norman Fenton
Centre for Software Reliability
City University
London, UK

Abstract

As a discipline software measurement has suffered from a fragmented approach and a lack of a rigorous foundation. We show that the observation of some very simple, but fundamental principles of measurement can have an extremely beneficial effect in the field of software measurement. Simply interpreting the formal definition of measurement in the software context leads to: (i) rationalizing and relating the various diverse software metrics activities, (ii) practical help in constructing and validating software measures, and (iii) the exposure of inconsistencies of some existing approaches in software measurement.

Any measurement involves an obligation to identify the entities of interest and the attributes of these to be measured. In software the entities may be classified as products, processes, and resources, while the attributes may be classified as internal or external to the entities. Next comes an obligation to determine whether measurement is being used for assessment or prediction.

We look at some well-known approaches to software measurement within this framework, exposing both the good points and bad points. We also describe the relevance of measurement theory to software measurement.

1 Introduction to measurement

1.1 Measurement in everyday life

Measurement lies at the heart of many systems which govern our lives. Measurements in economic systems determine price and pay increases. Measurements in radar systems enable us to detect aircraft through clouds. Measurements in medical systems enable the diagnosis of specific illnesses. Measurements in atmospheric systems are the basis for weather prediction. Without measurement, technology could scarcely have begun.

But measurement is not solely the domain of professional technologists. We all use it in everyday life. We can calculate the total bill in a shop to make sure we are given the right change. We can measure the height of our children to make sure we buy the right size clothes. When we go on a journey by car, we can work out how far we will be travelling by using a map, and then use this to predict how long the journey will take (since we can measure our speed on a speedometer), or how much petrol we need to buy.

1.2 What is measurement?

The examples we have mentioned make up a varied collection of measurement activities. What is it that they all have in common? How do we define the process of measurement? The formal definition is:

> *Measurement* is the process by which numbers or symbols are assigned to attributes of entities in the real world in such a way as to describe them according to clearly defined rules.

So measurement is concerned with capturing information about *attributes* of *entities*. But what does all this mean? An *entity* may be an object, such as a person or a room, or an event such as a journey or the testing phase of a software project. The *attribute* is the feature or property of the entity which we are interested in, such as the height or blood pressure (of a person), the area or colour (of a room), the cost (of a journey), or the time (of the testing phase). Thus it is wrong to say that we 'measure things' or that we 'measure attributes'; in fact we measure attributes of things. It is ambiguous to say that we 'measure a room', since we could measure its length, area, or temperature. Equally it is ambiguous to say that we 'measure the temperature', since we measure the temperature of a specific geographical location under specific conditions.

Measurement assigns *numbers* or *symbols* to these attributes of entities in order to *describe* them. Hence when we are measuring the heights of people we will always assign bigger numbers to the taller people, although the numbers themselves will differ according to whether we use metres, inches, or feet. The number is a useful and important abstraction. If we have never met Hermann but are told that he is 7 feet tall, then we can imagine how tall Hermann is in relation to ourselves, and we will know that he will have to stoop when he enters the door of our house.

Many people think that measurement is a clear-cut concept. In fact there are many different authoritative views about it, which lead to different interpretations about what is and what is not measurement. This leads to many difficult questions which need to be answered. For example:

- We noted above that colour was an attribute of a room. In a room with blue walls, is 'blue' a measure of the colour of the room?

- We all agree that height of people can be measured, but what about intelligence as measured say by an IQ test score? Or wine quality measured by ratings of experts?

- Proposed measures of intelligence of humans or quality of wine appear to have likely error margins. Is this a reason to reject them?

- There is an error margin in measuring the best understood physical attributes using the most sophisticated measuring devices. In our height example, we could get vastly different measures for the same person depending on whether we make allowances for the shoes being worn or of the standing posture. So how do we decide which error margins are acceptable and which are not?

- We saw that we can measure height in terms of metres, inches, or feet. These are all different *scales*. What makes these scales acceptable and others not. How do we know if a new scale for an attribute is acceptable?

- What kind of manipulations can we apply to the results of measurement? For example why is it acceptable to say that Fred is twice as tall as Joe, but not acceptable to say that it is twice as hot today as it was yesterday?

To answer these and many other questions which are especially pertinent to software measurement, we have to look at the science of measurement. Without such a rigorous approach we will never know what, if anything, we have achieved with any proposed measurements.

1.3 Measurement in software engineering

1.3.1 Software engineering: solution to a crisis

'Software engineering' is the term used to describe the collection of techniques concerned with applying an engineering approach to the construction of software products. By 'engineering' approach we mean managing, costing, planning, modelling, analysing, designing, implementing, testing and maintaining. These activities, together with tools and techniques to support and integrate them, have long been seen as the solution to the so-called 'software crisis': poor quality systems delivered late and over-budget. Any text book on software engineering begins by quoting frightening figures about the increasing costs of software development and the unacceptable number of failed projects. But although the software engineering solution was proposed over two decades ago, the software crisis remains and software 'engineering' is little more than an unrealized ideal.

Did something go wrong or did we expect too much too soon? Perhaps a little of both is true. More rigorous approaches to the construction of software systems have certainly been adopted; without these it is unlikely that many of the largest systems developed today (for all their imperfections) would have been possible. But methodological improvements alone do not make an engineering discipline.

1.3.2 Engineering disciplines need measurement

Engineering disciplines need methods which are underpinned by models and theories. In designing electrical circuits we appeal to theories like Ohm's law which describes the relationship between resistance, current and voltage in the circuit. But these theories have evolved out of the classical scientific method in which measurement is the basis. In addition to its role in developing the theories, we use measurement to enable us to apply them. Thus to build a circuit with a specific current and resistance we know what voltage is required and we have instruments which enable us to measure whether we have such a voltage in a given battery.

1.3.3 Neglect of measurement in software engineering

It would be difficult to imagine how the disciplines of electrical, mechanical and civil engineering could have evolved without a central role for measurement. But it has been almost totally ignored within mainstream software engineering. More often than not:

1) We still fail to set measurable targets when developing software products. For example we promise they will be 'user-friendly', 'reliable', and 'maintainable' without specifying what these mean in measurable terms.

2) We fail to measure the various components which make up the real costs of software projects. For example we usually do not know how much time was really spent on design compared with testing.

3) We do not attempt to quantify the quality (in any sense) of the products we produce. Thus, for example, we cannot tell a potential user how reliable a product will be in terms of likelihood of failure in a given period of use, or how much work will be needed to port the product to a different machine environment.

4) We still rely on purely anecdotal evidence to convince us to try yet another revolutionary new development technology or tool. (see Figure 1).

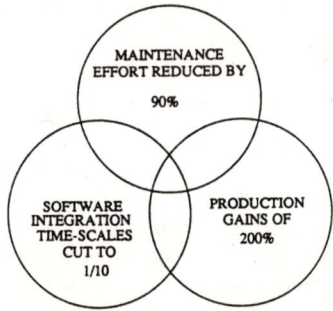

Typical extracts from publicity material promoting courses and tools on *formal methods* for software development. We have grave doubts about the scientific basis for these claims. Were any real measurements taken within properly constructed experiments?

Figure 1: *Measurement as the vehicle for promoting a new technique or tool*

What little measurement that is performed is done infrequently, inconsistently, and incompletely. Moreover it is often quite detached from the normal scientific view of measurement. We do see reports which make claims like '80% of all software costs are on maintenance' or that 'there are on average 55 bugs in every 1000 lines of software code'. But we are not told how these results were obtained, how experiments were designed and executed, which entities were measured and how, and what are the realistic error margins. Without these we cannot objectively repeat the measurements in our own environments to get realistic comparisons with industry standards. Thus problems due to insufficient measurement are compounded by a lack of a rigorous approach to measurement.

All of this is disappointing because the idea of a central role for rigorous measurement is not new to computing. In addition to the traditional work concerned with measuring computer hardware performance, the measurement of algorithmic complexity [16] has for many years been a key component of computer science. Unfortunately, whereas this kind of measurement tells us much about small programs, it does not address the problems of large complex systems which are the domain of software engineering.

Unless we are prepared to accept a more central role for measurement the software crisis may well be with us for many years to come.

1.3.4 Objectives for software measurement

So software production is in a crisis. It suffers from excessive *costs* (especially the proportion spent on maintenance activities), low *productivity*, and continued poor *quality*. In summary software production is often *out of control*. It has been suggested that software production is out of control because we do not *measure*. In his book [9], which presents a powerful argument in support of the need for measurement in software development, Tom DeMarco asserts that:

'You cannot control what you cannot measure.'

This argument is fine as far as it goes, but it is not complete. Often where measurement does take place the specific motivations for doing so are either unclear or, worse, do not exist. It is not enough to assert that we must measure 'in order to gain control'. Measurement activities must have clear objectives or goals, and it is these which will determine the kinds of entities and attributes which must be measured. Objectives will differ according to the kind of personnel involved at various levels in software development and use.

The following outline suggests a coherent shopping list of the kind of things that need to be measured in order to meet various objectives. It is presented from the viewpoint of managers and engineers:

Managers:

- Need to measure the *cost* of various processes within software production. For example, the process of developing a whole software system from the listing requirements stage to maintenance after delivery has a cost which must be known in order to determine its *price* for suitable profit margins.

- Need to measure the *productivity* of staff in order to determine pay settlements for different divisions.

- Need to measure the *quality* of the software products which are developed, in order to compare different projects, make predictions about future ones, and establish baselines and set reasonable targets for improvements.

- Need to define measurable targets for projects like how much test coverage should be achieved and how reliable the final system should be.

- Need to measure repeatedly particular process and resource attributes in order to determine which factors affect cost and productivity.

- Need to evaluate the efficacy of various software engineering methods and tools, in order to determine whether it would be useful to introduce them to the company.

Engineers:

- Need to monitor the quality of evolving systems by making process measurements. These might include the changes made during design, or errors found during different reviewing or testing phases.

- Need to specify quality and performance requirements in strictly measurable terms, in order that such requirements are testable. For example a requirement that a system be 'reliable' might be replaced by 'the mean time to failure must be greater than 15 elapsed hours of CPU time'.

- Need to measure product and process attributes for the purpose of *certification*. For example certification may require measurable properties of the product e.g. 'less than 20 reported errors per β-test site', 'no module more than 100 lines long', or of the development processes e.g. 'unit testing must achieve 90% statement coverage'.

- Need to measure attributes of existing products and current processes to make predictions about future ones. For example i) measures of 'size' of specifications can be used to predict 'size' of the target system, ii) predictions about future maintenance 'blackspots' can be made by measuring structural properties of the design documents, and iii) predictions about the reliability of software in operational use can be made by measuring reliability during testing.

1.3.5 Measurement for assessment and prediction

Studying the above list of measurement objectives and activities we can see that there are two broad purposes of software measurement. On the one hand we have those measurements which are used for *assessment*. These help to keep track of a particular software project. On the other hand we have those measurements which are used primarily for *predicting* important characteristics of projects. But it is important not to exaggerate the potential of such predictions, and it is certainly not true, as some believe, that software measurement is *only* about prediction. Even worse some people are led to believe that by applying an appropriate model or tool, accurate prediction should even be possible with a minimal amount of measurement (or even no measurement whatsoever). In this sense, the expectations for measurement when used for predictive purposes, are unrealistic.

2 Introduction to measurement theory

2.1 Measurement and measures

From the formal definition of measurement in Section 1, we may define:

> A *measure* is an empirical objective assignment of a number (or symbol) to an entity to characterize a specific attribute.

Thus *measurement* is the general activity in question — we shall describe the formal techniques for this below — and a *measure* is an actual assignment of numbers. Such an assignment is also referred to as the *measurement mapping*. Thus a measure is not in itself a *number* but a defined *mapping* for the entities and attribute in question. However even measurement theorists sometimes deliberately relax the distinction. The following simple example from software measurement should make these ideas clear.

Example 1 Suppose we wish to measure the attribute of *length* for source code programs. Then a possible candidate measure for length is the mapping of source code programs to the *number of executable source statements* (defined in an appropriately formal way).

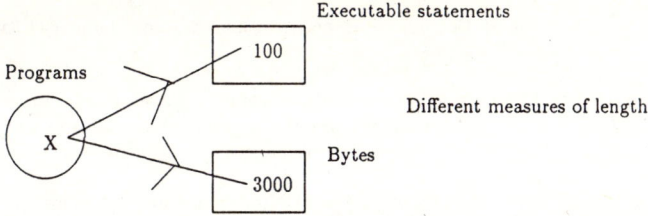

A different candidate measure for length is the mapping of source code programs onto the *number of bytes of computer storage*. For a specific program X we might also talk about the measure of length of X being 100 executable source statements, but this is really a relaxation of the terminology and is only done when the mapping in question is absolutely clear. If the only choice was between the two mappings described here then it is unambiguous which measure we were referring to. However there may be a number of alternative ways to define the mapping to executable source statements and in such situations we cannot simply talk about X having 100 executable statements without reference to the chosen mapping.

To measure something we must know what entities are being measured and we must have some idea of the attribute (property) of the entity which we are attempting to capture numerically. Although this point seems obvious, it is ignored surprisingly often in many data-collection activities.

Once we have identified an attribute and a means of measuring it, we can begin to accumulate data. Analysing the results of this process normally leads to the clarification and re-evaluation of the attribute. This in turn leads to improvements in the accuracy of measurement and as we shall see, an improved *scale*. In [26] Finkelstein cites the history of development of thermometry from simple devices and concepts to the modern thermodynamic definition of temperature as an example of this.

2.2 Direct and indirect measurement

We can measure some attributes such as mass and length without reference to any other attribute. On the other hand, measuring attributes such as density involves measuring other attributes (namely mass and length). To make clear these distinctive types of measurement we define:

> *Direct measurement* of an attribute is measurement which does not depend on the measurement of any other attribute. *Indirect measurement* of an attribute is measurement which involves the measurement of one or more other attributes.

Some attributes, for example temperature, can be measured in terms of just one other attribute (in this case *length* of a mercury column). Note however that such measurement is still indirect.

Direct and indirect measurement refer to the measurement mapping rather than to the attributes themselves. The representational theory of measurement as described in the next section is initially concerned with direct measurement of attributes. Where no previous measurement has been performed, this constitutes a natural process of understanding the attribute and the entities which possess it. It does not preclude the possibility that more accurate measurement will subsequently be achieved indirectly. In the case of software attributes, many of which are poorly understood, this approach is particularly pertinent.

2.3 Measurement theory

2.3.1 The issues addressed

In addition to the questions posed in Section 1.1, we intend to use measurement theory to answer the following more concrete types of questions:

1. How much do we need to know about some attribute before it is reasonable to consider measuring it? For example, do we know enough about 'complexity' of programs to be able to measure it?

2. How do we know if we have really measured the attribute we wanted to measure? For example, does a count of the number of 'bugs found' in a system during integration testing measure the *reliability* of the system? If not what does it measure?

3. Using measurement, what kind of statements can we make about an attribute and the entities which possess it which are *meaningful*? For example is it meaningful to talk about a 20% increase in design *quality*?

4. What kind of operations can we perform on measures which are meaningful? For example can we meaningfully compute the average level of productivity for a group of personnel?

The framework for answering the first two questions is provided by the *representation condition* for measurement. The answers to the last two questions come out of an understanding of the notion of *scales* of measurement. We need to know what the different scale types are, and if and when we are measuring on an appropriate scale.

2.3.2 The representational approach

The representational theory of measurement as described in [14, 20] is based on sets, relations, axioms, and functions. It is beyond the scope of this paper to describe the details, but we can summarize the key components as follows:

Direct measurement of a particular attribute possessed by a set of entities must be preceded by intuitive understanding of that attribute. This intuitive understanding leads to the identification of empirical relations between entities. The set of entities, together with the set of empirical relations, is called an *empirical relation system* for the attribute in question. Thus the attribute of 'height' of people gives rise to relations like 'is tall', 'taller than', and 'much taller than'. We also observe properties or axioms which hold for certain relations. For example, the binary relation 'taller than' satisfies the axiom of *transitivity*. Thus, if we have already observed that A is taller than B and that B is taller than C, then we may infer that A is taller than C, without further observation of A and C.

To measure the attribute we need to have corresponding relations in some number system. This means identifying an appropriate *numerical relation system*. Then measurement is a mapping from the empirical to the numerical relation system in which entities are mapped to numbers (or symbols) and empirical relations are mapped to numerical relations, in such a way that all empirical relations are preserved. Thus, for example, if person A above is mapped to the real number x and B to y then, provided that the relation 'taller than' is mapped to the relation '>', we must have $x > y$. This is the so-called *representation condition*, and the mapping which satisfies it is called a *representation*. The representation condition insists that the correspondence between empirical and numerical relations is two way. Suppose, for example that the binary relation R is mapped by M to the numerical relation $<$. Then, not only does xRy imply $M(x) < M(y)$ but also $M(x) < M(y)$ implies xRy.

There may in general be many ways of assigning numbers which satisfy the representation condition for a given empirical relation system. However, it will also be the case that any two mappings are related in a very specific way. For example, suppose M and M' are two different mappings which represent the accepted notion of height of people; say M is in inches and M' is in centimetres. Then we can always find a constant $c > 0$ such that $M = cM'$ (in this case $c = 2.54$). This transformation from one valid representation into another is called an *admissible transformation*. Thus, in the case of height, every admissible transformation is a scalar multiplication. In general, the class of admissible transformations determines the *scale type* for the attribute. Where the admissible transformations all have the form of scalar multiplication, then the scale type is called *ratio*. This is a sophisticated scale of measurement which reflects a very rich empirical relation system. Suppose that for an attribute like 'criticality' of software failures our empirical relation system only identifies different classes of failures and a binary relation 'is more critical than'. Then in this case, any two representations are related by a monotonically increasing transformation. With this class of admissible transformations, we have an *ordinal* scale type.

There are 5 well known scale types: In order of sophistication these are: *nominal, ordinal, interval, ratio,* and *absolute*. Each of these is characterized by the class of admissible transformations. Note that it is the empirical relation system for an attribute which determines the scale type; any measure, that is a mapping which satisfies the representation condition, must be on the given scale. This formal definition of scale type appears daunting to many who feel they understand the concepts intuitively. However, this is the only definition of scale type for a measure which enables us to determine rigorously what kind of statements we can meaningfully make using the measure.

Formally, a statement involving measurement is *meaningful* if its truth or falsity remains unchanged under any admissible transformation of the measures involved. Thus, for example, it is meaningful to say that 'Hermann is twice as tall as Peter'; if the statement is true (false) when we measure height in inches, it will remain true (false) when we measure height in any constant multiple of inches. On the other hand the statement 'Failure x is twice as critical as failure y' is not meaningful if we only have an ordinal scale empirical relation system for failure criticality. This is because a valid ordinal scale measure M might define $M(x) = 6$, $M(y) = 3$, while another valid ordinal scale measure M' might define $M(x) = 10,$; $M(y) = 9$. In this case the statement is true under M but false under M'.

The notion of meaningfulness also enables us to determine what kind of operations we can perform on different measures. For example, it is meaningful to compute *means* for ratio scale measures, but not for ordinal measures, and we can compute *medians* for ordinal scale measures but not for nominal scale measures.

As our understanding of an attribute increases so does the richness of our empirical relation system. This leads to the possibility of measurements on more sophisticated scales. In considering how to move on to improved measures it is important that such measurements develop as we have described above. At the same time we must be true to the basic intent. One of the principal problems of scientific method is to ensure that the measurement procedure established for an attribute yields measures which always describe the entity in a manner which corresponds to generally accepted views about the attribute as given by the empirical relation system. What must be avoided is the temptation to *define* a poorly understood, but intuitively recognizable, attribute in terms of some numerical assignment. Many have argued that equating intelligence of people with their scores on IQ tests is one such example of the dangers of this approach. It is equally worrying that, in software engineering, some people equate program 'complexity' with a 'measure' like McCabe's cyclomatic number.

The really serious mathematical aspects of measurement theory are largely concerned with theorems which assert conditions under which certain scales of direct measurement are possible for certain relation systems. A typical example of such a theorem, due to Cantor, gives necessary and sufficient conditions for ordinal measurement when we have a countable set C of entities and a binary relation R on C:

Cantor's Theorem: The empirical relation system (C, R) has an *ordinal* scale representation if and only if R is a strict weak order.

R being a 'strict weak order' means that the relation is:
i) *asymmetric* meaning that if x is related to y then it follows that y is *not* related to x, and
ii) *negatively transitive* meaning that if x is related to y then for every z, either x is related to z or z is related to y.

We can use this apparently abstract result to illustrate why it is pointless to attempt to find a (single) 'metric' (real-valued function) to characterize program 'complexity'. In fact we will show that it is impossible even to find a metric to characterize complexity of *flowgraphs* which model program control structure. Let C be the set of all program flowgraphs. It is claimed that the notion of 'complexity' leads to an intuitive relation R on program flowgraphs. Specifically, two programs x, y are in the relation R precisely when 'x is more complex than y'. Broadly speaking, complexity metrics are mappings of flowgraphs into real numbers which are supposed to preserve the relation R. It follows from Cantor's theorem that these are (ordinal) measures of 'complexity' if and only if the relation R is a strict weak order. It is our contention that no general notion of complexity can give rise to such an order because negative transitivity is not a reasonable expectation. In Figure 2 it seems plausible that xRy but that neither xRz nor zRy.

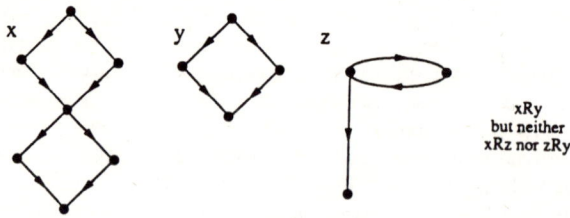

Figure 2: *Complexity relation not negatively transitive?*

However, taking say McCabe's cyclomatic number [23] M, we find that

$$M(x) = 3, \text{ and } M(y) = M(z) = 2$$

Now if M really was a valid measure of complexity, then it follows that xRz, that is, the definition of M *forces* x to be more 'complex' than z, which does not concur with our understanding of R.

Although Cantor's theorem thus appears to suggest that single real-valued measures of general software complexity are not feasible, it does not exclude the possibility of ordinal measurement in some number system which is not the real numbers. However, a more valuable approach is to identify specific attributes which contribute toward complexity. For example, the maximum depth of nesting, distribution of primes in the decomposition tree, and the number of paths of various types, can all be measured rigorously and automatically[11].

We have been careful to talk about representation in a *number system* rather than restricting ourselves to the special case of the real numbers. Examples of the use of the complex numbers in electrical engineering should dispel the notion that the real numbers are the only useful number system for measurement. As a software example, it is shown in [10] that, with regard to measuring algorithmic efficiency, we are only able to achieve true measurement when we drop the restriction to the real numbers. Moreover, classification of a set of entities is a special form of measurement and we will certainly wish to use many types of symbols other than numbers for this purpose.

More detailed accounts of measurement theory in the context of software measurement are contained in [11, 28].

2.4 Measures and software metrics

Proper measurement principles have rarely been adhered to in software engineering. This is evident from the confusion surrounding the terms metric and measure. The term *metric* has been used in the following distinct ways in the software engineering/metrics literature (among others):

1. A number derived from a product, process or resource. For example one hears about the 'metric' *number of function points* or the 'metric' *Lines of Code (LOC) per programmer month*.

2. A scale of measurement. For example one hears about a proposed nominal scale (classification) of software failures as a 'metric'.

3. An identifiable attribute. For example one hears about the 'metric' *portability* of programs or the 'metric' *coupling* in designs, even though no number or function is necessarily attached.

4. A theoretical or data driven *model* describing a dependent variable (such as 'effort') as a function of independent variables (such as program 'size'), with the intention that the model is used for prediction purposes. For example one hears about the 'COCOMO metric'.

It is also worth noting that there have been attempts to distinguish the notions of *metric* and *measure* in software in the following way:

- 'metrics numerically characterise "simple" attributes like length, number of decisions, number of operators (for programs), or number of bugs found, cost, and time (for processes)'

- 'measures are "functions" of metrics which can be used to assess or predict more "complex" attributes like cost or quality'

We shall show that all of the above ideas may be accommodated within the framework of scientific measurement, using the well-defined terms and notions which have long been established there. For example the above proposed informal distinction between 'measure' and 'metric' can be formally captured by the distinction between direct measures on the one hand and indirect measures on the other. Thus we shall try not to use the term 'metric' at all because of its different meaning to different people. However we expect people familiar with software measurement will be able to find the activity or activities which they feel are synonymous with metrics appearing somewhere within our unified framework!

3 Framework for software measurement

3.1 A classification of software measures

Using the philosophy of Section 2 we know that the first obligation in any software measurement activity is to identify the entities and attributes of interest which we wish to measure. In software, there are three classes of entities whose attributes we may wish to measure. These are:

- *Processes* which are any software related activities; these normally have a time factor.
- *Products* which are any artefacts, deliverables or documents which arise out of the processes.
- *Resources* which are the items which are inputs to processes.

Anything that we are ever likely to want to measure or predict in software is an attribute of some entity of the above three classes.

We make a distinction between attributes which are *internal* and *external*:

- *Internal attributes* of a product, process, or resource are those which can be measured purely in terms of the product, process, or resource itself.
- *External attributes* of a product, process, or resource are those which can only be measured with respect to how the product, process, or resource relates to its environment.

Table 1 describes the framework, and provides examples of the various types of attributes.

External attributes tend to be the ones that software managers and software users would most like to measure and predict. For example software managers would like to know the *cost-effectiveness* of some process or the *productivity* of their personnel, while users would like to know the *usability, reliability,* or *portability* of a system they are looking to purchase. Unfortunately, external attributes are, by their very nature, the most difficult to measure. Moreover, there are normally no agreed definitions; attributes like *quality* are so general that they are almost meaningless. Thus we are forced to make contrived definitions of the attributes in terms of some other attributes which *are* measurable. For example some people define quality of a software system (an external product attribute) in terms of *the number of bugs found during formal testing* (an internal process attribute). Invariably it seems that we need internal attributes to support the measurement of external attributes.

There is a relationship between internal and external attributes on the one hand and direct and indirect measurement on the other. It follows from our definitions that internal attributes can in principle be measured directly. However, as we already stressed, this does not preclude the possibility that more accurate measurement can be achieved indirectly. External attributes cannot be measured directly.

3.2 Measures, predictions and models

We have already seen that we can use measurement either for assessment or prediction. In software engineering we are particularly interested in using measurement for prediction. For

ENTITIES	ATTRIBUTES	
Products	Internal	External
Specifications	size, reuse, modularity, redundancy functionality, syntactic correctness	comprehensability maintainability ....
Designs	size, reuse, modularity, coupling cohesiveness, functionality	quality, complexity maintainability ....
Code	size, reuse, modularity, coupling functionality, algorithmic complexity control-flow structuredness....	reliability, usability maintainability ....
Test Data	size, coverage level, ...	quality ....
Processes		
Constructing specification	time, effort, number of requirements changes	quality, cost stability ....
Detailed design	time, effort, number of specification faults found	cost-effectiveness cost ....
Testing	time, effort, number of bugs found	cost-effectiveness stability, cost ....
....	....	....
Resources		
Personnel	age, price, ...	productivity, experience, intelligence ....
Teams	size, communication level, structuredness,....	productivity, quality ....
Software	price, size,....	usability, reliability ....
Hardware	price, speed, memory size	reliability, ...
Offices	size, temperature, light	comfort, quality ....
....	....	....

Table 1: *Components of software measurement*

example, although we can only truly assess the reliability of a software system once it is operational, we also try to predict its likely reliability on the basis of our knowledge of the system when under development.

We want to formalize the distinction between these notions of measurement. Let us define:

> A *model* is an abstract representation of an object.

This definition is very general, and suggests correctly that there are a multitude of different classes of models. There are essentially two different types of models which are of interest in software measurement:

- Models which are abstract representations of the various products, processes and resources. We need these in order to define measures unambiguously. Such models must capture the attributes being measured; for example a flowgraph model of source code can capture certain attributes relating to program control structure. Note that even to define a measure of an apparently simple and well-understood attribute like program source-code length, we require a formal model of program source code.

- Models which are abstract representations of relationships between attributes of entities. These models normally relate two or more measures in a mathematical formula.

Let us look more closely at the latter case. *Indirect* measures are models in this sense.

Example 2 A very simple model of this kind is:

$$m = x/a$$

where x is a variable representing a measure of source-code program length (in Lines of Code), m is a measure of number of hard copy pages for source-code programs, and a is a constant.

The extent to which such a model is being used for *assessment*, as opposed to solving a *prediction* problem depends on how much is known about the parameters of the model.

In Example 2, suppose a is known to be 55 in a specific environment. If a program exists with a known x, then the indirect measure of hard copy pages computed by the formula cannot really be claimed to be solving a prediction problem (except in a very weak sense), particularly if the hard copy already exists! However, if we have only a *specification* for a program and we wish to know roughly how many hard copy pages the final implementation will involve, then we *would* be using the model to solve a *prediction problem*. In this case we would need some kind of prediction procedure for determining the unknown value of x based on our knowledge of the program specification.

This simple example illustrates a very important point which is pertinent to many models in software measurement: *The model alone is not enough to perform the required prediction. Additionally we need some means of determining the model parameters, and a procedure to interpret the results*. To formalize this Littlewood [22] has made the following definition:

> A *prediction system* consists of a mathematical model together with a set of prediction procedures for determining unknown parameters, and interpreting results.

Using the same model will generally yield different results if we use different prediction procedures.

There is often enormous confusion about whether a proposed software measure is really being used for assessment or prediction. Since it is generally accepted that the ultimate goal of software measurement is in *prediction*, proponents of particular measures have often claimed that their measure is part of some prediction system, when in fact it might simply (and usefully) be a measure of some specific attribute.

Example 3 Albrecht has defined the notion of *function points* (FPs) [2]. The idea is that we examine a system specification, looking for things like types of inputs, outputs, and internal files. The number of FPs is computed as an indirect measure of these. It seems that FPs may be a reasonable measure of the attribute of *functionality* in specification documents. To show that it is such a (product) measure, in the sense of Section 2, would require confirmation that it captures (at least) the intuitive order of specifications with regard to functionality; i.e. if specification S_1 has more functionality than specification S_2 then the FP count for S_1 must be greater than that for S_2. A measure of such an important product attribute would be very welcome. However, to the best of our knowledge nobody has ever attempted to 'validate' the FP measure in this way. In fact FPs are not used in this way at all; they are used as part of a prediction system for *effort*.

A model defines an association between attributes. It is possible to have useful prediction systems based on models in which we have not determined the full functional form of the relationship:

Example 4 In a major study of software design measures Kitchenham *et al.* [18] confirmed an association between large values of certain program structure and size measurements and large values of measures of fault-proneness, change-proneness, and subjective complexity. As a result of their study a special type of prediction system was constructed. This had two components:
1) A procedure for defining what was meant by a "large" value for each measure;
2) A statistical technique for confirming that programs with large values of size and structure measures were more likely to have a large number of faults, and/or changes, and/or to be regarded as complex, than programs that did not have large values.
Kitchenham *et al.* concluded that their procedure of identifying programs with large values of size and/or structure could be used to assist project managers to reduce potential project risks by identifying a group of programs or modules which were likely to benefit from additional software development, for example re-design or additional testing.

3.3 We must know what we are measuring

Anything that we might wish to measure (either for assessment or prediction) about 'software' can be classified as an identifiable attribute of either some product, process or resource.

Many misunderstandings surrounding software measures are due to the failure to make clear the distinction between a) product/process/resource attributes and measures, and b) internal and external attributes and measures. The following example of such a misunderstanding should explain why we took great care in the preceding material to define clearly where these distinctions lie and to emphasize the precision in making them.

Example 5 In one of the few books on software metrics [8], Conte *et al.* suggest that it is often the case that a measure is *both* a process and product measure. Their example is: *number of defects discovered during formal testing*. Let us call this measure D. In our terminology it is clear that D is a process measure – it is a count of the number of incidents, in this case defects found, during the process of formal testing. Assuming that no other form of testing has been performed it might also be argued that it is an absolute measure of a rather trivial attribute of the code, namely *the number of known errors*. However Conte *et al.* claim it is product measure because it is a measure of *the number of errors in the code*, E. We argue that E is quite different to D. E is certainly an absolute measure of the internal code attribute of *errors resident*. The problem of computing E is known to be intractable for all but the smallest programs, and it is for this reason that practitioners seek to propose other more easily obtainable *process* measures as predictors of it.

Thus what is really meant when it is claimed that D is a measure of E is that there is a hypothesized high correlation between D and E. Specifically this must involve the construction of a theory.

In reality, the measure D may be more closely correlated to a measure of the internal process attribute of *duration of formal testing* or to some measures which capture the external resource attribute of *experience of tester* than it is to E. What is most likely is that a more accurate prediction of E would be obtained by considering all of these (and other) process measures.

It is also interesting to note that the measure D has been used in industry to characterize both *quality* and *reliability* of the product. The argument above should forewarn the reader of the possible pitfalls of this approach. Additionally, Adams [1] has shown that there is no simple correlation between the number of faults in a software product (which might be found during testing) and the number of failures of the system in operation.

At the heart of the problem we observe that certain product attributes are accepted as being more important and hence more worth measuring than others. These are invariably external attributes like quality, reliability and maintainability. However, we cannot measure these directly from the product alone. Normally we are forced to resort to using process measures as approximate measures for the product attribute. For example a proposed measure of maintainability is *mean time to repair a bug* (MTTR) or *number of bugs repaired* in a specific time interval. A proposed measure of *reliability* is *mean time to failure* MTTF; like MTTR this is a process measure – you have to observe the software in operation and time the failures occurring.

Although MTTF is definitely an internal process measure it is not a product measure because it does not measure an attribute of a product. However there is no reason why the product attribute of reliability might not be *approximated* by this measure.

In fact, software reliability is normally *defined* in terms of probability of failure free operation. This is an example of where a proposed (process-type) measure of the product attribute may become sufficiently well used that it assumes the role of a standard definition for the attribute. It is accepted in this case because there is a reasonable *consensus* about the definition of software reliability. Recall from Section 2 that rigorous measurement of any attribute evolves out of just such a consensus.

What is unacceptable (and leads to more confusion) is to *define* certain external product attributes in terms of measures of specific internal attributes without any kind of consensus. The literature abounds with 'measures of complexity' where complexity, a poorly understood external attribute, is normally re-defined in terms of some specific internal attribute e.g. *number of control-flow program paths*. Similar 'definitions' have been proposed for attributes like *maintainability* and *readability*.

It is not difficult to understand why so much confusion about software measurement exists. We need only look at one of the original theses on the subject which can be said to have been its catalyst. This is Halstead's 'software science' [15]:

Example 6 Halstead's software science:
We start by listing some of Halstead's definitions and theories:
A Program P is a collection of *tokens*, classified as either *operators* or *operands*. Basic 'metrics' are:

μ_1 = number of unique operators μ_2 = number of unique operands
N_1 = total occurrences of operators N_2 = total occurrences of operands

The *length* of P is $N = N_1 + N_2$. The *vocabulary* of P is $\mu = \mu_1 + \mu_2$. The *volume* of a program ('number of mental comparisons needed to write a program of length N') is $V = N \times \log \mu$.
The *program level* of a program P of volume V is $L = V^*/V$ where V^* is the *potential volume* – the volume of the minimal size implementation of P. The inverse of level is the *difficulty* $D = 1/L$.

Theory: An estimate $\hat{L}$ of L is given by: $\hat{L} = \frac{1}{\hat{D}} = \frac{2}{\mu_1} \times \frac{\mu_2}{N_2}$

Theory: Estimated program length: $\hat{N} = \mu_1 \times \log \mu_1 + \mu_2 \times \log \mu_2$.

The **effort** for P is given by

$$E = \frac{V}{\hat{L}} = \hat{D} \times V = \frac{\mu_1 N_2 N \log \mu}{2\mu_2}.$$

where the unit of measurement of E is *elementary mental discriminations*.

Theory: A psychologist, John Stroud claimed that the human mind is capable of making a limited number β of elementary discriminations per second. He asserted that $5 \leq \beta \leq 20$. Halstead claimed that $\beta = 18$, hence, the programming time T of a program of effort E is $T = E/18$ seconds.

Software science impinges on several different aspects of the software measurement problem. However, the way this is presented in the literature – as a definitive collection of 'metrics' – gives no real indication of its proper role and the relationship between different components of the theory. Nor is it clear in what sense the 'metrics' are measures or prediction systems.

Using the conceptual framework described above it becomes clear how the Halstead components fit in:

The only product on which any attributes are measured or predicted is the *source code* for an imperative language. As a prerequisite for any measurement there must actually be a model; in this case what is required is a model of source code which is sufficiently precise to identify unambiguously the *operators* and *operands* as objects and *occurrences of these*. There are four internal attributes which are measured, and each of these is measured on an absolute scale. These are the number of distinct operators, μ_1 (corresponding to the source code attribute of 'having operators'), the number of distinct operands, μ_2, and total number of respective occurrences of these N_1 and N_2.

The formula $N = N_1 + N_2$ is a proposed measure of the internal program attribute of *length*. From a measurement theory viewpoint this is a reasonable measure of length of actual code (i.e. without comments) since it does not contradict any intuitively understood relations between programs in respect of this attribute. A similar argument applies to the formula for the internal program attribute of *vocabulary*. The program attribute *volume* is supposed to correspond to the amount of computer storage necessary for a uniform binary encoding; the assumption of a uniform encoding on an arbitrary machine suggests that this should be viewed as an internal attribute.

Thus Halstead has proposed reasonable measures of three internal program attributes which reflect different views of *size*.

However, where the Halstead approach becomes problematic is that the remaining 'measures' are actually nothing more than generally unvalidated (and some would argue intuitively implausible) prediction systems, in which the prediction procedures are not properly articulated. Consider for example the equations for effort E and time T. These are both predicted measures of attributes of the process of *understanding the program* (although it is not made clear at which stage after requirements capture the process is assumed to start). The most serious problem in the case of E, is that it can be shown that this proposed scale of measurement leads to contradictions involving meaningful statements about effort (the attribute being measured) [11].

3.4 A unifying approach to software measurement

'Software metrics' is an all-embracing term given to a wide range of apparently diverse activities. These include:

Cost and effort estimation models and measures
Productivity measures and models
Quality control and assurance
Data collection
Quality models and measures
Reliability models

Performance evaluation and models
Algorithmic/computational complexity
Structural and complexity metrics

When divorced from any conceptual high-level view of software measurement and its objectives, it is easy to continue to view many of these activities as diverse and unrelated. We now hope to show how these fit into our framework. That is, we have to consider which processes, products, and resources are relevant in each case, which attributes (and whether these are internal or external) we are measuring, and whether these are assessments or predictions.

3.4.1 Cost and effort estimation

Here we are generally concerned with predicting the attributes of *cost* or *effort* for the process of *development (from detailed specification through to implementation)*. Typical of the approaches is:

Example 7 Boehm's (simple) COCOMO model [5] asserts that *effort* (measured by E person-months) required for the process of developing a software system, and *size* (measured by S thousands of delivered source statements) are related by

$$E = aS^b \qquad (1)$$

where a, b are parameters which are determined by the type of software system to be developed.

It is intended that the model is used for effort prediction at the requirements capture stage. Thus we need a means first of determining, i.e. predicting, the parameters a, b (Boehm gives three choices for the constants, these being dependent on the type of software system it is classified to be) and of determining, i.e. predicting, the size S of the eventual system.

What we have in this example is not 'the COCOMO model', but rather the COCOMO prediction system. The model is Equation (1). The inference procedures for determining the model parameters are determined by a combination of calibration according to past history, expert judgement, and subjective judgement; the theory provides various means of interpreting the results based on a 'plug-in' rule for the parameters. Thus it is ambiguous to talk about 'the COCOMO' model (or metric) for cost estimation, since any results obtained on the same data will vary according to the particular prediction procedures used. These observations are relevant to most cost/effort estimation models.

In more advanced versions of the COCOMO model, and in other cost estimation approaches, the inference procedures involve considering numerous internal and external attributes of the requirements specification (a product) together with process and resource attributes subjectively provided by users.

The simple COCOMO model, and also Albrecht's function point cost estimation model [2], assert that effort is an indirect measure of a single product attribute. In both cases this attribute is something to do with 'size'. In the case of Albrecht's model 'size' is measured by the number of FPs; as we have seen this is a measure of specifications. Here size is synonymous with a more specific attribute, namely *functionality*. In the case of COCOMO, size is defined as the number of delivered source statements. This is an attribute of the final implemented system. Thus to use the model for effort prediction, one must *predict* this product attribute at the specification phase, i.e. use of the model involves a prediction of an attribute of a future product in order to obtain the prediction of effort. This is rather unsatisfactory since the former prediction problem may be just as hard as the latter. An additional problem is that *number of source statements* captures only one specific view of size, namely length.

3.4.2 Productivity measures and models

Here we are concerned with measuring an attribute of a resource, namely *personnel* (either as teams or individuals) during particular processes. The most commonly used model for productivity measurement is to take productivity as a function of output (value) of the personnel during the process divided by input (cost) of the personnel during the process. In this case the resource attribute of productivity is assumed to be captured as an indirect measure of a product attribute measure and a process attribute measure.

3.4.3 Data collection

Even the simplest models for cost/effort estimation and productivity measurement are dependent on accurate measures of process and resource attributes and to a lesser extent product attributes. While it is conceivable that product measures may be extracted with a minimum of human intervention, this is not the case for process and resource measures. Much of the work on data collection is therefore concerned with how to set in place rigorous procedures for gathering accurate measures of the basic types of process and resource attributes identified earlier [24].

3.4.4 Quality models and measures

The work on quality modelling is largely synonymous with product measurement. The popular quality models, of which Figure 3 is a generic example, break down quality into 'factors', 'criteria'

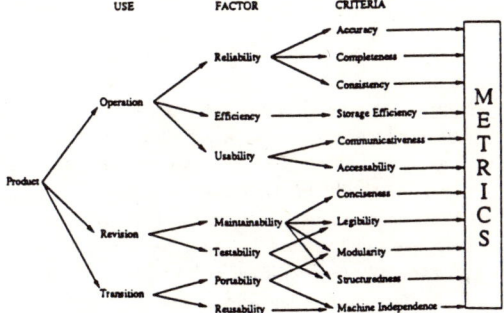

Figure 3: Typical software 'quality model'

and 'metrics'. We now observe that the quality factors generally correspond to *external* product attributes. The criteria generally correspond to *internal* product or process attributes. The metrics generally correspond to proposed measures of the internal attributes. In each case we say 'generally' because there is considerable fuzziness in the quality modelling work.

3.4.5 Reliability models

Reliability is one of the high-level, external product attributes which appears in all quality models. With the accepted view of reliability as synonymous with likelihood of successful operation, the only type of products for which this attribute is relevant is executable code. It is widely viewed as the single-most important quality attribute for code and as such research on measuring and predicting reliability has become a discipline in itself [6]. We have already remarked that the most standard approach used now to measuring reliability is: observe failures (and subsequent fixes) during operation or testing, and then use this information to determine the probability distribution of the next failure (which is a random variable). Measures of reliability are defined in terms of the subsequent distributions (and are thus defined in terms of process attributes). For example we could consider the *mean* or *median* of the distribution or the *rate of occurrence of failures*. In all cases what we have is a *prediction problem*. We are trying to say something about future reliability on the basis of past observations.

Example 8 The Jelinski-Moranda 'model' for software reliability [17] assumes an exponential probability distribution for the time of the ith failure. The mean of this distribution (and hence the Mean Time To i^{th} Failure) is given by

$$MTTF_i = \frac{\alpha}{N-i+1}$$

where N is the number of faults assumed to be initially contained in the program, and ϕ ($= 1/\alpha$) represents the 'size of a fault', i.e. rate at which it causes a failure. (Faults are assumed to be removed on observation of a failure, and each time the rate of occurrence of failures is reduced by ϕ). The unknown parameters of the model, N and α have to be estimated by some means, for example by using Maximum Likelihood Estimation after observing a number of failure times.

Note how in this example it is not enough to simply talk about the 'Jelinski-Moranda', model. We have to specify a *prediction system*, which in this case involves a model together with a statistical inference procedure for determining the model parameters, and a prediction procedure for combining the model and the parameter estimates to make statements about future reliability.

3.4.6 Performance evaluation, and models

Performance evaluation is generally concerned with measurement of the product attribute of *efficiency*. This can be time efficiency (speed of response or computation for given input) or space efficiency (memory required for given input), but is normally the former. Like reliability, *efficiency* is a product attribute which appears at a high-level in most quality models. Classical performance evaluation as described in [13, 19] is concerned with measuring the external attribute of efficiency for executable products. One may be tempted to conclude that efficiency can only be an external attribute in our sense (like reliability), and that no other type of measurement is possible. However, even in the case where little is known about the compiler and target machine, efficiency can generally be predicted quite accurately by considering any representation of the source code. In particular a high-level description of the *underlying algorithm* is normally enough to determine reasonably good predictors of efficiency of the implemented code; in the case of time efficiency, this is done by first determining key inputs and basic machine operations, and then determining the number of basic operations required as a function of input size. This area of work (traditionally the staple diet of computer scientists) is referred to as *algorithmic analysis* or *algorithmic complexity* [16] where complexity is synonymous with efficiency. In terms of our framework efficiency of the algorithm is an internal attribute which can be measured and used to predict the external attribute of efficiency of executable code.

The topic often called *computational complexity* is closely related and also fits in to our software measurement framework. In this case we are interested in measuring the inherent complexity of a *problem* where a problem is considered to be synonymous with the requirements specification (a product in our sense), and complexity is synonymous with the efficiency of the fastest algorithm possible to solve the problem. For example, suppose our requirements specification asserts:

> For an n-node network with known distances between any pair of nodes, it is required to compute the shortest route through the network which visits each node.

This requirements specification (which is seeking a general solution to the so-called *travelling salesman problem*) is considered to be highly complex. This is because the underlying problem is known to be in a complexity class called NP-Complete. There is no known fast algorithm which will solve this problem, and nor is there ever likely to be one.

3.4.7 Structural and complexity measures

Many of the high level 'quality attributes', that is external product attributes, are notoriously difficult to measure. This is why researchers have considered instead measures of *internal* attributes of products. The Halstead measures are examples of these, defined on the source code. There are numerous measures which have been proposed which are defined on graphical models of either the source code or designs. These measure specific internal attributes like control flow structure, information flow, and number of paths of various types.

Unfortunately much work in this area has been blighted by the insistence by some on equating such measures with the external, and poorly understood attribute of 'complexity'. Thus, these measures are expected to have the magical properties of being 'indicators' of such diverse notions as *comprehensibility, correctness, maintainability, reliability, testability*, and *ease of implementation*. A high value for a 'complexity' measure is supposed to be indicative of low comprehensability, low reliability etc. Sometimes (rather ironically) these measures are also called 'quality' measures as they are supposed to relate to quality attributes, i.e. external product attributes like reliability and maintainability. In this case high values of the measure actually indicate low values of the quality attributes.

The danger of attempting to find measures which characterize so many different attributes is that we inevitably find that they have to satisfy *conflicting* aims. Weyuker [27] has listed a number of properties which she believes complexity measures must satisfy if they are to conform to generally accepted expectations. Two of the properties are:

Property A: For any programs P, Q,

$$\text{complexity}(P) \leq \text{complexity}(P; Q)$$

Property B: There exist programs P, Q, and R such that:

$$\text{complexity}(P) = \text{complexity}(Q) \text{ and } \text{complexity}(P; R) \neq \text{complexity}(Q; R)$$

Property A is reasonable for any view of complexity which is related to program *size*, since it asserts that putting two programs together can only increase complexity. However, if complexity 'includes' notions like comprehensibility then this is unreasonable since our general level of comprehension of a program may *increase* as we see more of it. So we conclude from property A that complexity must have something to do with size.

But then Property A is incompatible with Property B. The latter asserts that we can find 2 programs of equal complexity which when separately concatenated to a same third program yield programs of different complexity. This is certainly not satisfied by any size measure, although it should be satisfied by any measure capturing the notion of comprehensibility.

Thus properties A and B are relevant for very different (and incompatible) views of complexity. Hence it is impossible to define a set of consistent axioms for a completely general view of 'complexity'. It is far better to concentrate, as we have proposed, on specific attributes and consider 'axioms' for measures of these. This is the true measurement theory approach.

The valuable lesson to be drawn from Weyuker's properties is that the search for general complexity measures is doomed to failure. However, the general misunderstanding of scientific measurement in software engineering is illustrated in a recent paper [7] which has criticized Weyuker's axioms for the wrong reasons. Cherniavsky and Smith define a code based 'metric' which satisfies all of Weyuker's axioms but, which they rightly claim, is not a sensible measure of complexity. They conclude that axiomatic approaches may not work. There is no justification for their conclusion. On the one hand, as they readily accept, there was no suggestion that Weyuker's axioms were complete. More importantly, what they fail to observe, is that Weyuker did not propose that the axioms were *sufficient*; she only proposed that they were necessary. Since the Cherniavsky/Smith 'metric' is clearly not a measure (in our sense) of any specific attribute, then showing that it satisfies any set of necessary axioms for any measure is of no interest at all.

These problems would have been avoided by a simple lesson from measurement theory. The definition of a numerical mapping does not in itself constitute measurement. It is popular in software engineering to use the word 'metric' for any number extracted from a software entity. Thus while every measure is a 'metric', the converse is certainly not true. The confusion in [7], and also in [27] arises from wrongly equating these two concepts.

3.4.8 'Real' metrics

In Section 2 we asserted that we would not need to use the term *metric* in our exposition of software measurement. There is another more formal reason apart from the reasons described there. In mathematics a *metric* has a very specific meaning, namely it is a function m defined on pairs of objects x, y such that in some sense $m(x, y)$ measures the 'distance' between x, y. Such metrics have to satisfy properties:

1) $m(x, x) = 0$ for all x,
2) $m(x, y) = m(y, x)$ for all x, y, and
3) $m(x, z) \leq m(x, y) + m(y, z)$ for all x, y, z.

There are numerous examples where we might be interested in such 'real' metrics in software:

Example 9 A popular approach taken to increase the reliability of safety-critical systems is to use fault tolerant techniques like *N-version programming*. This would involve, for example, independently developing 5 different versions of the critical software components. The idea is that errors in up to 2 are 'tolerated' because these two erroneous components get 'outvoted' by the 3 correct ones.

Because of problems about getting genuine design independence, we might be interested in knowing the *level of diversity* between two designs, algorithms or programs. We may view this as a metric m, so $m(P_1, P_2)$ is the diversity between two programs P_1 and P_2. In this case the entities are all products. We may also wish to know the level of diversity between two *methods* applied during design. In this case the entities are processes.

Example 10 Program correctness as a measure of the extent to which a program satisfies a specification, may be viewed as a metric $m(S, P)$ where the entities S (specification) and P (program) are both products.

To reconcile these genuine metrics within the framework proposed we have to consider pairs of entities as a single entity. Thus for example in the case of diverse programming, having produced two programs satisfying the same specification, we consider the pair to be a single product 'system' having itself a level of diversity. This is in fact consistent with the systems view of N-version programming anyway. Where we have implemented N versions of the program the diversity of the system consisting of the N versions (plus a voting module) may be viewed as an indirect measure of the pairwise program diversity.

3.4.9 Goal/Question/Metric paradigm

We have argued that software measurement activities must have specific objectives. Once these are known, we can use our framework to identify the entities and attributes that have to be measured. In this sense our framework can be seen as providing structure for a goal-oriented approach to software measurement. The *Goal/Question/Metric* paradigm (GQM) of Basili and Rombach [4] is a well known framework for a wide spectrum of software measurement activities, which is consistent with our approach.

The GQM paradigm provides an informal mechanism for addressing the many kinds of problems which people feel they might be able to help solve through measurement. The idea is that any software measurement activity should be preceded by the identification of a software engineering *goal* (e.g. 'improve programmer productivity') which leads to *questions* (e.g. 'how to increase the amount and quality of code which programmers produce'), which in turn lead to actual *metrics* (e.g. 'number of debugged executable statements per programmer-month'). Just what constitutes a goal or question is left deliberately vague, and several levels of refinement may be required for certain goals and questions – a question may thus be a sub-goal. A goal is normally defined in terms of *purpose, perspective,* and *environment*. Basili and Rombach also provide separate guidelines for defining product-related questions and process-related questions. The questions which have to be addressed are the definition of the process or product, the definition of the relevant attributes, and the feedback relating to the attributes. When it comes to defining the measures, it is accepted that several measures may be required for any one question, and that these may have to include 'subjective' measures, meaning presumably subjective ratings.

We can relate the GQM approach to our own framework. A goal or question can be characterized by one or more entity attribute pairs, each having a choice between assessment or prediction (motivation is a separate issue). Naturally the entity and the attribute have to be properly defined. Thus ultimately we are concerned with quantifiably assessing some attribute of an existing product, process, or resource, or quantifiably predicting some attribute of a future product, process, or resource. The leaves of the hierarchy tree represent directly measurable attributes of entities. So for example, (*maintenance process-cost, estimation*) and (*specification document-quality, assessment*) are two possible goals. Goals which relate to 'controlling quality' or 'minimizing cost' can be seen in terms of assessment and prediction; the crucial additional items of interest are the *models* which attempt to characterize the way in which particular entity-attribute pairs are dependent on others.

GQM is very useful in helping to identify objectives for measurement, and as such it complements our framework. However, it does not help clarify the many problems of measurement which we have highlighted. If not used carefully, it may even help to propagate these.

4 Summary

We have shown that software measurement, like measurement in any other discipline, must adhere to the science of measurement if it is to gain widespread acceptance and validity.

Measurement is the process of assigning numbers or symbols to attributes of entities according to clearly defined rules. All entities of interest in software can be classified as either processes, products, or resources. Anything we may wish to measure is an identifiable attribute of these. Attributes are either internal or external. Although external attributes like reliability of products, stability of processes, or productivity of resources tend to be the ones we are most interested in measuring, we cannot do so directly. We are generally forced to use indirect measures of internal attributes.

Measurement is not just concerned with assessment (of an attribute of some entity which already exists), but also with *prediction* (of an attribute of some future entity). Prediction is very important in software measurement. We want to be able to predict attributes like cost and effort of processes, and reliability and maintainability of products. Effective prediction requires a *prediction system*. This means not just a model but also a set of prediction procedures for determining the model parameters and applying the results. These in turn are dependent on accurate measurements in the assessment sense.

Many misunderstandings and misapplications of software measurement would be avoided if people thought carefully about the above framework. Moreover, this framework highlights the relationships between apparently diverse software measurement activities. By appealing to the representation condition of measurement, it also provides practical help in constructing and validating software measures and prediction systems.

The approach described is also constructive and helpful for practical measurement activities in that it guides the user into determining precisely which entities and attributes have to be considered for measurement. In this sense it supports a goal-oriented approach.

References

[1] Adams E, 'Optimizing preventive service of software products', *IBM J. Research & Development* 28(1), 1984, 2-14.

[2] Albrecht AJ, Measuring application development productivity, Proc. of IBM Applic. Dev. Joint SHARE/GUIDE Symposium, Monterey, CA, 1979, 83-92.

[3] Baker AL, Bieman JM, Fenton NE, Gustafson D, Melton A, Whitty RW, 'A philosophy for software measurement', *JSS*, Vol 12, July 1990, 277-281.

[4] Basili VR, Rombach HD, 'The TAME project: Towards improvement-orientated software environments', *IEEE Trans Soft Eng* 14(6), 1988, 758-773.

[5] Boehm BW, 'Software Engineering Economics', Prentice-Hall, 1981.

[6] Brocklehurst S, Chan PY, Littlewood B, Snell J, 'Recalibrating software reliability models' *IEEE Trans Software Eng*, SE-16(4), 458-470, 1990.

[7] Cheniavsky JC, Smith CH, 'On Weyuker's axioms for software complexity measures', *IEEE Trans Software Eng* SE-17(6), 636-638, 1991.

[8] Conte SD, Shen VY, Dunsmore HE, 'Software Engineering Metrics and Models', Benjamin Cummins Publishing, Inc, 1986.

[9] DeMarco T, 'Controlling Software Projects', Prentice Hall, 1982

[10] Fenton NE, 'The mathematics of complexity in software engineering and computer science', in *The Mathematical Revolution inspired by Computing* (ed. Johnson J. Loomes M), Oxford University Press, 1991, 243-256

[11] Fenton N E, 'Software Metrics: a rigorous approach', Chapman & Hall, 1991

[12] Fenton NE, Melton A, 'Deriving structurally based software measures', *JSS* 12, 1990, 177-187.

[13] Ferrari D, 'Computer system performance evaluation', Prentice Hall, 1978.

[14] Finkelstein L, 'A review of the fundamental concepts of measurement', Measurement Vol 2(1) 1984, 25-34.

[15] Halstead MH, 'Elements of Software Science', Elsevier N-Holland, 1975.

[16] Harel D, 'Algorithmics', Addison Wesley 1987.

[17] Jelinski Z, Moranda PB, 'Software reliability research', in *Statistical Computer Performance Evaluation*, (ed. W. Freiberger), pp 465-484, Academic Press, 1972.

[18] Kitchenham B, Pickard L, Linkman SJ, An evaluation of some design metrics', *Software Eng. J* 5(1), 1990, 50-58.

[19] Kleinrock L, 'Queueing systems: Vol 1 Theory and Vol 2, Computer Applications', J. Wiley and Sons, 1975.

[20] Krantz DH, Luce RD, Suppes P, Tversky A, 'Foundations of Measurement' Vol 1, Academic Press, 1971.

[21] Kyburg HE, 'Theory and Measurement', Cambridge University Press, 1984

[22] Forecasting software reliability', in *Software Reliability, Modelling and Identification*, (Ed S. Bittanti) Lecture Notes in Computer Science 341, 141-209, Springer-Verlag, 1988.

[23] McCabe TJ, 'A complexity measure', *IEEE Trans Soft Eng* SE-2(4), 1976, 308-320.

[24] Mellor P, 'Software reliability data collection: problems and standards', in *Pergammon Infotech State-of-the-art Series* 'Software Reliability', 165-181 and 256-257, 1985.

[25] Roberts FS, 'Measurement Theory with applications to decision making, utility, and the social sciences', Addison Wesley, 1979.

[26] Sydenham PH (Ed.), 'Handbook of Measurement Science', Vol 1, J. Wiley, 1982.

[27] Weyuker EJ, Evaluating software complexity measures, *IEEE Trans Software Eng* SE-14(9), 1357-1365, 1988.

[28] Zuse H, 'Software complexity: measures and methods', de Gruyter, 1990.

Never mind the metrics what about the numbers!

Barbara Kitchenham
National Computing Centre
Oxford Road
Manchester, England

Abstract

Many of the other papers in this volume consider the issues of formality with respect to measurement theory. This paper takes the view that it is equally important to have a formalism for dealing with the values obtained from the measurement process as it is to have a formalism for generating the values. This paper argues that statistics offers the appropriate formalism for dealing with such values because the models we use to interpret measurements are inherently stochastic not deterministic.

In this paper, I examine the mistakes that the software engineering community makes when it ignores the proper formulation and testing of non-deterministic models using examples from the domain of software cost estimation. The empirical work described in this paper is part of the ESPRIT MERMAID project. MERMAID is a collaborative project aimed at developing and automating improved methods of cost estimation.

1 Introduction

In this paper, I argue that practical use of software measurements rests on the discipline of statistics. Constructive use of software measurements not only needs the ability to measure product and process attributes it also needs the ability to describe the relationships and dependencies among attributes as quantitative software models. Statistical methods allow us to formulate our models appropriately by making error terms explicit. Even more importantly, statistical techniques provide the mechanism to test the validity of our models objectively.

I will begin by defining what I believe to be the major problems that software measurement should be attempting to address. I will then attempt to justify my belief that the formalism of measurement theory can only offer a very limited assistance to the major concerns of the software industry whereas the formalism of statistics offers appropriate techniques for developing and testing models required by the industry. The reason for this is that statistics, not logic, is the formalism that supports science and engineering.

As an example, I will look at the problems with cost models from the view point of statistics. My concern as a statistician is that probabilistic models are written and used as if they were deterministic. This means that the assumptions underlying such models are not properly defined and software data relating to cost models is often incorrectly analysed.

I will illustrate these problems by examining the assumptions that have been drawn about cost models in general and the COCOMO model [1] in particular. I will show that many of the assumptions built into cost models are not supported by empirical evidence. In this paper, I provide only a very brief description of results of analysing cost data, for more details see [2].

The purpose of this paper is to argue that as software engineers we must understand the principles of science and the use of statistics if we are going to understand and model the productivity of processes and the quality of our products.

2 Industrial requirements for metrics

In industry, I seldom get asked about the values of a particular software attribute such as structure or size or information flow. The sort of questions I get asked are those that relate to the business concerns of software managers. Typically such questions are concerned with how long it will take to produce a product, how much it will cost to develop and support it, and how a manager can know that a product is "good enough" to release to customers.

With the exception of the last question, it is not hard to assess the attributes that managers are interested in, they are elapsed time and money (where money is often equated to staff hours). It is harder to determine what managers mean by "good enough to ship", but in principle it is often equivalent to "support costs being within my available budget", which in turn is related to the number of bugs/defects users find and report.

The main point I would make about such questions is that they are not questions about measuring an attribute they are questions about predicting a future value of an attribute.

The main reasons software managers are interested in **measuring** software attributes are:

- to provide inputs to predictive models;

- to monitor progress against plans.

Therefore, software metrics workers should be interested in actual values in order to develop and test predictive models.

3 Cost models

Most cost models assume a basic relationship between effort and size characterised by a multiplicative constant "a" and an exponential term "b" of the form:

$$\text{Effort} = a\,(\text{Size})^b * d_1 * d_2 * ... * d_n \qquad (1)$$

The term "a" can be interpreted as "unit productivity" and provides the scale conversion between size and effort and the term "b" identifies level of overhead introduced by product size. "b" is usually close to 1, a value greater than 1 implies that relatively more effort is required to produce large projects than is required to produce small projects which means that there is a diseconomy of scale. A value of "b" less than 1 implies an economy of scale.

Most published models including COCOMO have used a value of b greater than 1, so it has been assumed that software production involves diseconomies of scale.

The basic equation is often further adjusted on the basis of other factors called cost drivers (i.e. d_i, i=1,...,n) which are used to adjust the basic effort-size equation on the basis of specific conditions affecting the particular project. These are factors such "product complexity", "staff capability", "required reliability" that are expected to affect basic productivity. They are normally measured using ordinal-scale metrics with scale points of the sort "very low", "low", "average", "high", and "very high". Each scale point of each cost driver has an associated numerical value that is used to establish the level of the adjustment.

Establishing the values of "a" and "b" has often involved some application of statistics (although the coefficients used in COCOMO were actual derived by expert opinion). People have amassed data on project effort and associated product size, taken the logs of effort and size and used linear regression techniques to obtain estimates of log(a) and b. They have not usually taken the next step in any statistical analysis which is to test the basic model assumptions.

3 A statistical formulation

In statistical terms, the basic cost model (without cost drivers) is similar to the previous formulation but includes an explicit error term:

$$y = a * x^b * (1+e) \qquad (2)$$

The error term "e" has two components:

- a measurement error which is inherent in **all** real measurements;

- an error which is due to the basic model being incomplete or incorrect. This occurs when we do not include all the relevant explanatory variables or when we choose the wrong functional form for our models.

Error terms may be additive or multiplicative. For software cost data it is quite common to observe a multiplicative error and this is what is shown in equation (2).

We expect the error term for models concerning the physical world to be composed of a small measurement error. We should have no such expectation for models concerning software production characteristics. Software production is a human intensive function and it is usually found that models that involve people (whether in medicine, economics, sociology, psychology, or software) are difficult to formulate and usually involve large error terms.

The statistical techniques that are usually used to analyse cost data make a number of assumptions about the nature of error terms particularly for the purpose of hypothesis testing. The usual assumption is that error terms are distributed normally with a zero mean and an unknown variance σ^2. This assumption does not usually hold for software measurements so we often need to use robust techniques and non-parametric tests. However, for the purposes of this paper I will just consider the classical methods. For a discussion of the use of robust and non-parametric methods see [3].

A common method of identifying the best estimates of the coefficients a and b given a data set of effort and size values is called "least squares" regression [4]. This technique assumes that you are able to obtain a data set of n data points where each data point corresponds to the effort (or duration) of a project and the size of the resulting product. This technique assumes that the best values of a and b are those that minimise the sum of the squared residuals (i.e. deviation between each measured y value and the corresponding predicted y value):

$$\text{minimise } \sum_n [\log(y_i) - \log(a_i) - b*\log(x_i)]^2 \qquad (3)$$

The equations used to calculate a and b are determined by taking the partial derivatives of the sum of the squared residuals with respect to a and b respectively, setting each partial derivative equal to 0, and solving the resulting pair of equations.

The first test that should be made as part of a regression analysis is that the independent variable x (i.e. size) does affect the dependent variable y (i.e. effort or duration). This means testing our model (i.e. the alternative hypothesis model) against the default or "null hypothesis model":

$$y = a * (1+e) \qquad (4)$$

It is important to note that statistical hypothesis testing only allows us to make probabilistic statements about models. We might conclude from our analysis that the null hypothesis is rejected at the 0.05 (or 5%) level of significance, but what this means is that 1 in 20 times we will reject the null hypothesis incorrectly. We may also reject the alternative hypothesis when it is actually correct. Thus, statistics emphasises the tentative nature of our assessment of model validity.

4 Empirical results

4.1 Diseconomies of scale

As mentioned in section 3, most published cost models have an exponential term greater than 1. This has led to the general belief that diseconomies of scale are natural in software production. In order to check this assumption, I performed a regression analysis of data from 10 sources that corresponded to 17 data sets. The data sources were a mixture of published data sets and data made available by industry to the MERMAID project.

The results are summarised in Table 1. They showed that most data sets exhibited a relationship between effort and size. However, in only one case was the exponential term significantly different from 1 and in this case the term was significantly less than 1. It should be noted that the COCOMO data was itself included in this analysis.

Thus it appears that the wide-spread belief that software production suffers from diseconomies of scale is not supported by the available evidence.

Table 1. Exponential term in effort-size models

Data set	b	se(b)	b >0	b diff from 1	Projects
Bai-Bas	0.951	0.068	yes	no	19
Bel-Leh	1.062	0.101	yes	no	33
Your	0.716	0.230	yes	no	17
Wing	1.059	0.294	yes	no	15
Kemr	0.856	0.177	yes	no	15
Boehm					
All	1.108	0.085	yes	no	63
Org	0.833	0.184	yes	no	23
Semi	0.976	0.133	yes	no	12
Emb	1.070	0.104	yes	no	28
Kit-Tay					
All	0.814	0.166	yes	no	33
ICL	0.472	0.323	no	-	10
BTSX	1.202	0.300	yes	no	11
BTSW	0.495	0.185	yes	yes	12
DS1					
All	0.944	0.123	yes	no	81
Env 1	1.049	0.125	yes	no	46
Env 2	1.078	0.105	yes	no	25
Env 3	1.086	0.289	yes	no	10
DS2					
All	0.824	0.135	yes	no	30
New	0.178	0.134	no	-	8
Ext	1.025	0.158	yes	no	20
DS3	1.141	0.077	yes	no	15

4.2 Cost drivers

Cost drivers are factors that are assumed to influence software productivity, where productivity is usually assumed to be measured by the ratio of product size to project staff effort:

$$\text{Productivity} = \text{Size/Effort} \tag{5}$$

If we want to assess whether or not a cost driver should be included as an explanatory variable in a productivity model, and the cost driver is an ordinal scale metric (i.e. a metric that takes on a limited number of discrete, ordered values), we can use a technique called analysis of variance [5].

This involves calculating the average value of productivity of a group of projects for each value that the driver can take and assessing whether there are significant differences among the average values. Formally, we test whether including the effect of the different driver levels significantly decreases the variance of the error term:

$$\text{Productivity} = a + d_j + e \tag{6}$$

Analysis of variance compares the model including the cost driver effect with the "null hypothesis" model:

$$\text{Productivity} = a + e \tag{7}$$

The ESPRIT MERMAID project has access to several data sets. Two data sets provided information about potential cost drivers (DS1 and DS2). Both data sets measured size in terms of function points, so productivity was measured in terms of unadjusted function points per hour. DS1 used function point counts based on the sum of the number of transactions and entities, DS2 used conventional Albrecht function points [6].

DS1 included information on 81 projects with data concerning three potential cost drivers: team experience, project manager experience, and environment type (which was a three point nominal scale metric comprising: conventional COBOL, enhanced COBOL, 4GL). DS1 included information on 28 projects and 21 cost drivers: user involvement; user commitment; user experience with application; staff turnover; computer resource availability; system response time; development time constraints; staff constraints; experience of team; requirements stability; system familiarity; problem complexity; complexity of user interface; structured methods usage; familiarity with structured methods; tools/software usage; team experience with tools; programming language level; familiarity with programming language; project management experience of project leader; working environment.

In both data sets, there was only one major effect on productivity and that was the use or not of 4GL's. Thus contrary to popular belief:

- staff experience did not affect productivity;

- small improvements in use of development methods and tools did not increase productivity. In data set 1, there was no difference between a standard COBOL development environment and an enhanced COBOL development environment (which included report generators, IDMS etc). In data set 2, use of structured methods, and use of tools did not affect productivity.

The COCOMO model is one of the reasons that so many people seem to believe staff differences are a major productivity factor. However, analysis of the COCOMO data set itself does not support the assumptions that are built into the model.

Of the 5 personnel factors incorporated into the COCOMO model (analyst ability; application experience, programmer ability, program language experience, virtual machine experience) only two (program language experience and virtual machine experience) have a statistically significant affect on productivity (and even then it is only a difference between the extremes of the driver values). The productivity achieved by projects with "nominal" experienced staff was not significantly different from the productivity achieved by projects with "high" experienced staff. In addition, the effects were not independent because projects for which staff had high experience of the virtual machine were usually the same projects where staff had a high experience of the programming language.

I should emphasise that these results **do not** imply that there are no differences among staff, only that by the time managerial effects on team selection have taken place such differences are not observable at the level of total project productivity.

4.3 Cost driver independence

Cost models such a COCOMO have a large number of cost drivers that are used to make adjustments to the basic model prediction. The models assume that drivers are independent, so that each adjustment can be made independently of the other adjustments. If this assumption is not true, the model will be incomplete (i.e. it will not include significant first order interactions). This will result in an unstable model that will not give accurate predictions. N.B. This problem also affects "size" models like Function Points that include a large number of adjustment factors.

In order to identify whether cost drivers are independent, it is not necessary to test each possible first order interaction, we can use a rather different statistical technique called principal component analysis [7]. This is a method of transforming a set of m variables into a new set of variables such that each variable in the new set is independent. Each new variable (nd_i, i=1,..m) is a linear combination of the old variables (d_i, i=1,..m):

$$nd_1 = a_{11}*d_1 + a_{12}*d_2 + ... a_{1m}*d_m$$

$$nd_2 = a_{21}*d_1 + a_{22}*d_2 + ... a_{2m}*d_m$$

.
.

$$nd_m = a_{m1}*d_1 + a_{m2}*d_2 + ... a_{mm}*d_m$$

It is then possible to determine the total variability of the set of new variables and to apportion that variability among each of the new variables. The variable that accounts for the largest proportion of the variability is called the first principal component, the variable that accounts for the next largest proportion of the variability is called the second principal component, etc. The underlying dimensionality of the original set of m variables corresponds to the number of principal components that account for more than 5% of the variability.

Formally, the vector (a_{i1}, a_{i2},...a_{im}) is the ith Eigen vector (i.e. the ith characteristic vector) of the variance-covariance matrix (or preferably the correlation matrix) of the original variables. The total variability of the transformed variables is the sum of the Eigen values (i.e. characteristic values) of the variance-covariance matrix. The proportion of variability accounted for by the ith principal component is the ratio of the ith Eigen value to the total variability.

Analysis of the DS2 data set which included data on 21 cost drivers showed that the underlying dimensionality of the set of 21 variables was 7. Other researchers have observed similar results when analysing the COCOMO data set [8].

5 Other uses of statistical techniques

I have described the use of statistical methods to formulate and test software cost models, but there are many other areas of software engineering that require statistical methods.

At a fairly basic level, the numbers obtained by applying the measures defined using measurement theory can only be interpreted and used within a statistical framework. If we believe that a measure captures an attribute such as "information flow", we still need to determine what we do with specific values of the measure. This means knowing what the impact of information flow is upon other attributes of interest and establishing procedures such as statistical quality control procedures for dealing with specific measured values [9].

Another important use of statistics is for modelling system and software reliability [10]. It is a matter of personal belief whether or not people accept the software fails in a non-deterministic manner. However, the characteristics of software failures are that they appear to be random events in time and can be modelled as such for the purposes of predicting software support costs [11].

In addition for assessing computer system performance, queuing theory is essential [12]. Deterministic analysis of paths lengths or algorithm times does not produce usable models of system throughput.

6 Discussion

In this paper I have suggested that a number of our basic assumptions about cost models are wrong. This is particularly dangerous when we draw very specific conclusions from invalid models. For example, interpretation of the COCOMO model has resulted in software managers basing productivity improvement strategies on invalid assumptions about diseconomies of scale, staff experience, and the effects of methods and tools.

I believe that the discipline of statistics is essential if we are ever to accumulate a valid body of knowledge about software engineering. It allows us to formulate our models in a way that makes visible the non-deterministic nature of such models. It also allows us to test our models and the conclusions we draw from them in an objective and scientific manner.

The "scientific method" is characterised by drawing unfounded conclusions from inconclusive evidence, but then testing those conclusions rigorously. Scientists regard models (and conclusion) that cannot be falsified as "working hypotheses". They accept that there are no "true" or "correct" models.

The world of mathematics is the world of logic. It is based on deductive reasoning from a set of stated assumptions or axioms. It is agreed to regard axioms as "self-evident truths", so that any conclusion deduced correctly from those axioms must of necessity be true. However, there is no implication that axioms must have any external "truth" in the real world.

It is my view that software engineering is a scientific not a logical discipline and requires the discipline of statistics to ensure we do not wallow in unfounded conclusions but that we proceed rationally via rigorously tested working hypotheses.

References

[1] Boehm, B.W. Software Engineering Economics. Prentice-Hall, 1981.

[2] Kitchenham, B.A. Empirical studies of assumptions underlying software cost estimation models. Information and Software Technology, to be published.

[3] Fenton, N. Software Metrics: A rigorous approach. Chapman & Hall, 1991, pp96-110.

[4] Draper, N.R. and Smith, H. Applied regression analysis. 2nd edn. John Wiley, 1981.

[5] Cochran, W.G. and Cox, G. Experimental design. 2nd edn, John Wiley, 1952.

[6] Albrecht, A.J. and Gaffney, J. Software function, source lines of code, and development effort prediction. 1983, IEEE Trans Software Engineering, SE-9, 6.

[7] Morrison, D.F. Multivariate statistical methods. McGraw-Hill, 1967.

[8] Subramanian, G.H. and Brelawski, S. A case for dimensionality reduction in software development effort estimates. TR-89-02. Dept. Computer and Information Science, Temple University, Philadelphia, 1989.

[9] Kitchenham, B.A., Pickard, L.M., Linkman, S.J. An evaluation of some design metrics. 1990, Software Engineering Journal, 1, pp50-58.

[10]   Littlewood, B. Modelling growth in software reliability. in Software Reliability Handbook, Rook, P (ed.), Elsevier Science Publishers Ltd., 1990 pp137-152.

[11]   Mellor, P. Modelling software support. ICL Technical Journal, 1983, 3 (4), pp407-438.

[12]   Kleinrock, L. Queuing Systems, Volume 1. John Wiley, 1975.

Acknowledgements

The empirical work described in this paper was undertaken for the ESPRIT MERMAID project (Esprit project number P2046). The MERMAID project is a collaborative project part-funded by the Commission for the European Communities.

Moving From Philosophy to Practice in Software Measurement[*]

James Bieman   Norman Fenton[†]   David Gustafson
Austin Melton[‡]   Robin Whitty

July 23, 1991

Abstract

We, the Grubstake Group, are committed to creating an environment in which software metrics can be used confidently, effectively, and in full knowledge of their limitations. We responded to a lack of rigor in software measurement, and concentrated our efforts towards the development of a suitable theory and foundation. We explained our concerns and beliefs for the development of the software metrics field in our paper entitled *A Philosophy for Software Measurement*.

We realize, however, that effective software measurement requires more than a philosophy. Thus, in this paper we continue the work needed so that effective software metrics can be routinely designed, specified and used. The design, specification and use of a good software metric should not be an unusual event.

In addition to discussing some foundational issues, we examine metric specifications, the use of statistics in the designing and defining of a metric, and we further develop an example of how static internal metrics can be useful by showing how such metrics may be used in testing.

1 Introduction

This paper is organized as follows:

---

[*]Research is supported in part by NATO Collaborative Research Grant 034/88.
[†]Research is supported in part by ESPRIT 2 projects PDCS
[‡]Research is supported in part by ONR Grant N00014-88-K-0455.

- Section 1 introduces some of the problems encountered when going from philosophy to practice, and the definitions for document and internal, external, and predictive metrics are also given.

- Section 2 gives guidelines from a mathematical and theoretical prespective on defining software metrics.

- Section 3 describes the importance of rigor in the specification of a software metric. The development of a software metric, much like the development of a program, should include a specification phase. The needed specifications for a metric are given.

- Section 4 delineates, with respect to validation, two distinctly different types of software metrics – internal metrics and predictive metrics. This section also discusses the use of statistics in validating metrics.

- Section 5 gives an example from testing that demonstrates that static software metrics can be very useful; too often we are lead to believe that only external metrics are valuable.

- Section 6 discusses continuing work directed towards moving to the practice of defining useful and well-understood software metrics.

As indicated by the title and mentioned in the abstract, this paper is a sequel to our earlier paper *A Philosophy for Software Measurement*[1]. Some sections in the current paper include reworked and further developed ideas from the *Philosophy* paper; however, in both the furthered developed sections and the new sections we emphasize the transition to practical matters in software development without forgetting the mandates of the foundation we have built.

In many of our earlier papers we used the term "measure" instead of "metric". This terminology was used, in part, to emphasize that a software metric should be defined in accordance with the principles of measurement theory [28]. However, to be consistent with the current common terminology in the discipline, we in this paper use "metric" and "software metric." But, no matter what terms are used, if software metrics involve true measurement, they must be developed within the guidelines of measurement theory.

We use the term "document metric" to refer to metrics based on the products of the development process. We are restricting our discussion to metrics on these products and are not considering metrics on the process of software development.

The main problem or task which we are beginning to address in this paper, moving from philosophy to practice, is both important and difficult. In real-life situations it is (almost) always difficult to move from a mathematical theory to practice because

- the very nature of the work is different,
- the details with which one must pay special attention are much different, and
- in the real world, things do not behave just as they should – according to the underlying theory.

Above we have mentioned internal, external, and predictive software metrics. In this paper we will usually emphasize only the difference between internal-external and predictive metrics, and thus, we will normally not use the terms *internal* and *external*. However, for clarity we give the informal definitions here.

- An *internal software metric* measures a static characteristic or attribute of a software document.
- An *external software metric* measures a characteristic or an attribute which is simultaneously a characteristic of a software document and something external to the document, e.g., a machine on which the document must run or a person who must work with the document.
- A *predictive software metric* estimates a characteristic or attribute of a software document which does not (at the time of predicting) exist or which for some other reason is not available at the time of the measuring (predicting).

In Section 4 we discuss (internal-external) metrics and predictive metrics. Although we often group internal and external metrics together, many of our comments would in a very exact setting only be valid for internal metrics; the external factor in external metrics necessitates some extra precautions for these metrics. For a more detailed discussion of the three types of metrics, see [29].

2 Developing Software Metrics

The following gives the basic steps in defining a software metric.

1. Specify the domain set for the metric, i.e., specify the set of software documents on which the metric is to be defined. This set should consist of similar software documents, e.g., specification documents, high-level design documents, or source code documents.

2. Specify the attribute of the documents which the metric is to measure.

3. Specify a model for the software documents; this model must highlight the attribute. In other words the model gives us an abstraction of the documents, and the abstraction is based on the attribute.

4. Define a mapping from the document set to the set of model instances. This mapping usually defines itself. It is really just the "model" map from the documents to the model instances. (We use the term "model" or "model type" for the general model such as flowgraphs, and we use the term "model instance" for an individual instance of a model (type) such as an individual flowgraph.)

5. Define an order on the set of models instances. In many cases this order is naturally imposed by the model itself. (See the example following these basic steps.) This order must reflect the relative "amount" of the attribute present in the documents.

6. Define an answer set which has a partial order defined on it. This order must at least be able to reflect the ordering on the model instances.

7. Define a function from the set of model instances to the answer set. This function should be at least "order-preserving" which means that $a \leq_F b \Rightarrow m(a) \leq m(b)$. It would be better if the function were "relation-preserving" in the measurement theory sense which means that $m(a) \leq m(b) \Leftrightarrow a \leq_F b$.

The actual metric is the composition of the model map and the order-preserving map. This composition map is naturally order-preserving because the document set "inherits" via the model mapping the order from the set of model instances thus making the model map order-preserving and the composition of order-preserving maps is order-preserving.

Some of the above steps are illustrated in the following example. Consider flowgraphs as an model of source programs, and to define an order on flowgraph instances consider the following two transformations:

Definition 2.1 Given a flowgraph $G = (N, E, s, t)$, then a flowgraph $G' = (N \cup \{x\}, E', s, t)$ is obtained from G by a *node addition transformation* (T_1) if:

1. $x \notin N$,

2. $\exists (y, z)[(y, z) \in E \wedge E' = (E - \{(y, z)\}) \cup \{(y, x), (x, z)\}]$, and

3. the only differences between G and G' are given in 1. and 2.

This first transformation allows a new flowgraph to be generated by adding a node along an existing edge of a given flowgraph.

Definition 2.2 Given a flowgraph $G = (N, E, s, t)$, then a flowgraph $G' = (N, E \cup \{e\}, s, t)$ is obtained from G by an *edge addition transformation* (T_2) if $e \notin E$ and $e = (x, y)$, where $x \in N - \{s\}$ and $y \in N - \{t\}$.

This second transformation allows a new flowgraph to be generated by adding a new edge between existing nodes in a given flowgraph.

Now define $\leq_F$ for flowgraphs G_1 and G_2 so that $G_1 \leq_F G_2$ iff G_2 can be obtained from G_1 by a finite (including an empty) sequence of applications of T_1 and T_2. The set of transformations and the associated partial order provide one perspective on the structural complexity of flowgraphs. In fact, the authors have shown that McCabe's cyclomatic complexity measure preserves this partial order $\leq_F$ [2].

The partial order $\leq_F$ formalizes a notion of *containment* for flowgraphs. A flowgraph G is contained in a flowgraph G' if and only if $G \leq_F G'$. Similar notions of containment may be defined on many different document sets given a finite set of transformations. The transformations must define a partial order on the document set, and the set of transformations must be constructively complete. The transformations are constructively complete if they are sufficient to construct the entire document set from a given finite set of "initial" documents. The trivial flowgraph with just a start node, a terminal node, and one edge from the start node to the terminal node is the only initial document needed to construct all flowgraphs using the two given transformations.

Preserving a partial order (as for McCabe) is a weaker notion than the idea of preserving relations in the representational theory of measurement. McCabe's measure does NOT preserve the partial flowgraph order in the representational sense.

Consider the flowgraph ordering $\leq_F$. There is an assumption that the answer set is the set of real numbers and that the relation $\leq_F$ corresponds under the cyclomatic complexity measure to the usual ordering $\leq$ on the real numbers. What we have shown is that

$$A \leq_F B \Rightarrow M(A) \leq M(B)$$

This is what was meant when we said that the cyclomatic complexity 'preserves' the partial order. However, this does not "preserves the relation" in the measurement theory sense because the reverse implication is not true.

The problem is that the 'answer set' is not the right one for the representation condition. An 'answer set' that would work is the set of natural numbers together with the partial order DIVIDES.

Example 2.3 A metric M which preserves $\leq_F$ in the representational sense could be defined as follows:

Let P1 be the trivial one-arc flowgraph. Then $M(P1) = 1$.

Let P2 be the flowgraph formed from P1 by adding a node. Then $M(P2) = 2$.

Let D2 be the flowgraph formed from P1 by adding an edge (loop) to top node. Then $M(D2) = 3$.

Let D0 be the flowgraph formed from P1 by adding an edge from top node to bottom node. Then $M(D0) = 5$.

These are the only flowgraphs which can be formed in one step from P1. Note how M(P1) divides each of M(P2), M(D2), and M(D0) but the latter numbers are all relatively prime and so don't divide each other. So far the relation is preserved completely (i.e. in both directions).

We can now recursively extend the measure to all flowgraphs as follows: Suppose that F1, F2, ..., Fn is the set of flowgraphs generated at stage k (i.e. by k transformations), and suppose we have assigned values M(F1), M(F2),..., M(Fn). Now for each Fi list all of the flowgraphs that can be generated from Fi by a single transformation.

A problem is that different Fi's can give rise to the same flowgraph, in which case we have to make sure that the value we assign is divisible by each such Fi. Suppose for example that F1, F2 and F3 all give rise to the flowgraph G. Then define M(G) = M(F1)M(F2)M(F3).

To deal with all the other new flowgraphs G1,...,Gm is easy. Let p1,...,pm be distinct prime numbers not already used. Just define M(Gi)=pi.

Thus, we have an answer set (integers) with an ordering (divides) that matches the ordering on the model (flow graphs).

In summary, for an answer set to suitable for preserving the relations in the model, the ordering on the answer set must match the order on the model. If the answer set is the reals with the usual order (which is a total order), then the order on the model must also be a total order.

3 Specifying Software Metrics

Specifying software metrics is an important area of research. For software engineering to be successful at applying software metrics it is necessary to be able to specify precisely the metrics of important attributes of software.

We also feel that it is important to be able to analyze metrics as to what properties they possess [16]. This analysis will require a formal notation for the specification of the metric.

Our approach to work on specifying software (document) metrics has been based on the approach of the previous section. This approach dictates the following parts of a specification.

Description This is an informal description of the metric. Care must be taken so it does not supersede the formal description that follows. However, the formal description is not intended as a tutorial introduction to the metric but as a formal specification. This section is intended to serve as the tutorial introduction for a reader who has never heard of the metric.

Model A model or abstraction that emphasizes the attribute of interest is important and needs to be specified.

Mapping to the Model How the document and instances of the model are related must be specified. This is usually done by specifying a mapping of the document to the model.

Partial Ordering How the instances in the model are related to each other is important. This is usually specified by a partial ordering on the model.

Answer Set This is a specification of the codomain of the metric.

Mapping from the Model to Answer Set Finally, a mapping from the model to the answer set is specified. This gives the value of the metric.

In the following sections we will give two examples of metrics using a possible specification method. This method will be refined or replaced as we research the problems of analyzing metrics.

3.1 McCabe's Measure

The cyclomatic complexity metric [27] is one of the most commonly used metrics.

Description The cyclomatic complexity metric concerns the control flow of the program. Although the metric is usually counted in terms of decisions in the source code, it is formally defined in terms of nodes and arcs in the control flow graph.

This metric is based on modules(or functions). That is, the metric is calculated on each function.

Model The model used is the control flow graph(CFG). The CFG consists of a set of Nodes N and edges E. It also has a single start node S and a terminal node T. Every node is reachable from S and T is reachable from every node.

Mapping to the Model The following maps source code to the control flow graph. It assumes initially that N = {S,n,T} and E = {(S,n),(n,T)}. The description is built by assuming that each statement has a node s in the node set and there are arcs (b,s) and (s,a) in E.

The table shows what is added for each structure. It assumes that the node s is removed and similarly that the arcs of the form (b,s) and (s,a) are also removed.

statement	additions to N	additions to E
If exp **Then** smt1 **Else** smt2 ;	$s_{exp}, s_{smt1}, s_{smt2}$	$(b, s_{exp}), (s_{exp}, s_{smt1}),$ $(s_{smt1}, a), (s_{exp}, s_{smt2}),$ (s_{smt2}, a)
While exp smt ;	s_{exp}, s_{smt}	$(b, s_{exp}), (s_{exp}, a)$ $(s_{exp}, s_{smt}), (s_{smt}, s_{exp})$
For (exp)smt	s_{exp}, s_{smt}	$(b, s_{exp}), (s_{exp}, s_{smt})$ $(s_{smt}, s_{exp}), (s_{exp}, a)$
smt1 ; smt2	s_{smt1}, s_{smt2}	$(a, s_{smt1}), (s_{smt1}, s_{smt2}),$ (s_{smt2}, b)

Partial Order The partial order on the CFG is defined by the transformations defined in section 2. That is, $G_1 \leq_F G_2$ iff G_2 can be obtained from G_1 by a finite sequence of applications of T_1 and T_2.

Answer Set The answer set is the Natural Numbers.

Mapping from the Model to the Answer Set

$$C_{mccabe} = |E| - |N| + 2$$

where $|E|$ represents the size of that set, that is, the number of elements in that set.

Example As an example, consider the following program:

```
main()
{
int i;

i=12;
while (i>10)
{
i=i-2;
}
printf("the result is %d",i);
}
```

The initial set of nodes would be {S,n,T} where n stood for the whole program. Applying the last rule twice would give us N={S, n1, n2, n3, T} where n1 stands for the assignment to i, n2 for the while loop and n3 for the print statement. Applying the while rule would give the set of nodes {S, n1, n2a, n2b, n3, T } where n2a stands for the while condition and n2b stands for the loop body. The set of arcs consists of { (S,n1), (n1,n2a), (n2a,n3), (n2a,n2b), (n2b,n2a), (n3,T) }.

Thus, the value of the cyclomatic complexity on this example is $C = 6 - 6 + 2$.

3.2 Halstead's Measures

Description Halstead [8] did empirical work in the early 70's looking for the intrinsic attributes in software that should be measured. He decided that the most fundamental objects in code were operands and operators. The operands were tokens that had values, e.g. constants, variables, etc. Every other token was considered to be an operator.

A syntax approach considers all the language specific notation to be operators and all the user-defined tokens to be operands.

Model The model used is sequences of tokens from two sets of tokens. One sequence, S_1, is the sequence of operator tokens in the program from ηset_1, the set of operator tokens. Simliarly, S_2 is the sequence of tokens from the set, ηset_2, of operand tokens. Note that sequences can have duplicates but sets do not.

Mapping to the Model The mapping from source code to the model depends on finding the tokens in the source code and deciding whether they are operators or operands. Operands have value and are usually user-defined. Operators do not have value and are usually part of the language.

statement	additions to $S_1, \eta set_1$	additions to $S_2, \eta set_2$
function-name (var-list)	$t_{()}$	
If exp Then smt1 Else smt2 ;	$t_{ite}, t_;$	
While exp smt ;	$t_w, t_;$	
For (exp) smt ;	$t_f, t_{()}, t_;$	
var = exp ;	$t_=, t_;$	t_{var}
{ exp }	$t_{\{\}}$	
(exp)	$t_{()}$	
exp op exp	t_{op}	
var , var-list	$t_,$	t_{var}
var		t_{var}
constant		t_{cons}
"any string"		t_{string}

Partial Order Let T be a transformation that concatenates a token onto the end of the sequence. $H_1 \leq_h H_2$ iff H_2 can be obtained from H_1 by a finite sequence of applications of T.

Answer Set The Answer set is the real numbers.

Mapping from the Model to Answer Set

$$\eta_1 = \mid \eta set_1 \mid$$

where $|\eta set_1|$ represents the size of that set, that is, the number of elements in that set.

$$\eta_2 = |\eta set_2|$$

$$N = |S_1| + |S_2|$$

$$\hat{N} = \eta_1 log_2 \eta_1 + \eta_2 log_2 \eta_2$$

$$V = (\eta_1 + \eta_2) log_2 (\eta_1 + \eta_2)$$

Example For the example used in the cyclomatic complexity metric subsection:

$$\eta set_1 = \{t_{()}, t_{\{\}}, t_{int}, t_;, t_=, t_w, t_-, t_{printf}, t_,\}$$

$$\eta set_2 = \{t_i, t_{12}, t_{10}, t_2, t_{string}\}$$

$$S_2 = (t_i t_i t_{12} t_i t_{10} t_i t_i t_2 t_{string} t_i)$$

4 Validation[1]

4.1 Two Types of Validation

Many software metrics are described in the literature. Not only do these metrics aim to measure a wide range of attributes but also there are often many irreconcilable metrics all claiming to measure or predict the same attribute such as cost, size or complexity. The reason for this state of affairs is commonly attributed to a general lack of *validation* of software metrics. While accepting this reason, we propose more fundamentally that there is a lack of understanding of the meaning of validation of software metrics.

In the literature references to software metrics can in fact refer to two separate concepts:

---

[1] Much of the material in this section also appears in *Software Metrics* [12].

1. *Measures* which are defined on certain objects and characterise numerically some specific attribute of these objects. (This is how we have defined software metrics)

2. *Prediction systems* involving a mathematical model and prediction procedures for it.

The fact that the software metrics community has generally not differentiated between these two concepts is a major reason for the confusion surrounding the notions of, and obligations for, validation.

The two concepts require different types of validation. In the case of metrics we turn to measurement theory for the notion of validation:

Definition 4.1 *Validation* of a software metric is the process of ensuring that the metric is a proper numerical characterisation of the claimed attribute.

Example 4.2 A valid measure of the attribute of coupling of designs must not contradict our intuitive notions about coupling. Specifically it requires a formal model for designs (to enable objectivity and repeatability) and a numerical mapping which preserves any relations over the set of designs which are intuitively imposed by the attribute of coupling. Thus the proposed measure of coupling should indeed measure precisely that; in particular if it is generally agreed that design D_1 has a greater level of coupling than design D_2 then any measure m of coupling must satisfy $m(D_1) > m(D_2)$. An example of a specific metric for coupling which satisfies these (measurement theory) criteria is given in *Deriving software measures throughout the develpment process* [11].

This type of validation is central in our use of measurement theory. Practitioners may prefer to regard this as ensuring the well-definedness and consistency of the metric. To stress this where necessary we may also refer to it as *internal validation*, since it may require consideration of the underlying models used to capture the objects and attributes.

We use Littlewood's definition [26] of *prediction systems* to encompass the notion of the underlying "model" and the prediction procedures:

Definition 4.3 A *prediction system* consists of a mathematical model together with a set of prediction procedures for determining unknown variables and parameters.

For prediction systems we have:

Definition 4.4 *Validation* of a prediction system is the usual empirical process of establishing the accuracy of the prediction system in a given environment by empirical means, i.e., by comparing model performance with known data points in a given environment.

This type of validation is well accepted by the software metrics community. When people talk about an attempt to validate, for example, the COCOMO model or a particular software reliability model, they would certainly be attempting the kind of validation described in the definition although they may not know that these are actually prediction systems.

So why is there confusion between these two separate concepts?

It is because of a basic (and poorly articulated) misconception that a software metric must always be part of a prediction system.

The misconception is normally presented in something like the following manner:

> "A software measure is only *valid* if it can be shown to be an accurate predictor of some software attribute of general interest, like cost or reliability".

Suppose that we have some good metric of internal product attributes, like size, structuredness, modularity, functionality, coupling, and cohesion. Then it is apparently not enough that these metrics accurately characterise the stated attributes because these are not considered to be of 'general' interest. Since there is generally no specific hypothesis about the predictive capabilities of such metrics they are shown to be 'valid' by correlation against any 'interesting' metrics which happen to be available as data. For example a measure of coupling might be claimed to be valid or invalid on the basis of a comparison with known *development costs* if the latter is the only 'data' available. This would be done even though no claims were ever made about a relationship between coupling and development costs!

It is conceivable that a metric could be shown to be valid in the sense of it being a component of a valid prediction system even though no hypothesis existed. For this to happen the 'data' which happens to be available would have to be shown to be consistently related via a formula determined initially by regression analysis. If such validation does occur let us call it *external validation* of the metric to distinguish it from the (internal) validation which should initially take place to show that it actually measures some attribute:

Definition 4.5 *External validation* of a metric m is the process of establishing a consistent relationship between m and some available empirical data puporting to measure some useful attribute.

Given our poor understanding of the relationships between various software products and processes, external validation seems highly unreliable. **And yet we are expected to accept that this as the major approach to validation!**

It may be of some comfort to the many software researchers who have taken the above approach to validation for software metrics, to note that they have not been alone in making the same mistakes. See [10]. And speaking quite generally about measurement validation, Krantz [22], asserts:

> "A recurrent temptation when we need to measure an attribute of interest is to try to avoid the difficult theoretical and empirical issues posed by fundamental measurement by substituting some easily measured physical quantity that is believed to be strongly correlated with the attribute in question: hours of deprivation in lieu of hunger; skin resistance in lieu of anxiety; milliamperes of current in lieu of aversiveness, etc. Doubtless this is a sensible thing to do when no deep analysis is available, and in all likelihood some such indirect measures will one day serve very effectively when the basic attributes are well understood, but to treat them now as objective definitions of unanalysed concepts is a form of misplaced operationalism.
>
> Little seems possible in the way of careful analysis of an attribute until means are devised to say which of two objects or events exhibits more of the attribute. Once we are able to order the objects in an acceptable way, we need to examine them for additional structure. Then begins the search for qualitative laws satisfied by the ordering and the additional structure."

It must be stressed that we (and we are sure Krantz) are not claiming that measurement and prediction are completely separate issues. On the contrary we fully support the observation of Kyburg [23]:

> "If you have no viable theory (prediction system) into which X enters, you have very little motivation to generate a measure of X"

The reason we are interested in measuring internal attributes like size, structuredness, modularity, control flow complexity, data flow complexity, cohesion, and coupling, is because we believe that not only are these important concepts in their own right but also because they will necessarily play a role in many types of prediction systems. Indeed in the case of size, we already note that it is a component of almost all cost and productivity models and prediction systems; at the very least we should already have ensured that the proposed measures of size capture our intuitive understanding of size!

5 Useful Structural metrics

Simple structural metrics when carefully applied can be extremely useful. Successful measures of structural properties can be developed when important structural properties can be unambiguously identified, modeled, and understood.

The software attribute that we examine is the "difficulty" of applying a particular testing strategy to software. We demonstrate that for a valid software metric to be useful it is not necessary

- that it be part of a predictive system,
- that it be a measure of "understandability" or "psychological complexity", or
- that it be complex in itself.

In fact the work reported on in this section shows that simple structural metrics when carefully applied can be extremely useful. Rather than try to develop measures of such elusive program attributes, we suggest a less grandious strategy. Successful metrics of structural properties can be developed when important structural properties can be unambiguously identified, modeled, and understood.

The software attribute that we examine is the "difficulty" of applying a particular testing strategy to software. There are several components of this "difficulty" attribute. These components include:

1. the amount of "effort" necessary to determine whether testing criteria are satisfied,

2. the "difficulty" of generating the necessary test data, and

3. the number of test cases needed for a particular strategy.

The third component is measurable and we will focus our discussion on measures that estimate how many test cases are needed for particular testing strategies. We will show that this component of "testing difficulty" is measurable and that such measures are useful. A metric that accurately estimates the number of required tests obviously satisfies all reasonable intuition concerning the difficulty of using a testing strategy.

Structural metrics are most applicable to structural testing strategies. Structural testing prescibes that particular sets of program paths with certain structural properties be tested. *Testing criteria* are used to determine whether particular levels of test coverage are met. Much effort has been spent deriving criteria that aid in selecting the smallest set of test data that will uncover as many errors as possible.

Common criteria based on the flow of control include the *all statements*, *all branches*, and *all paths* criteria. Branch testing is considered a minimum control flow coverage requirement and is described in [15, 19, 21]. Other criteria are based on the flow of data through a program [17, 25, 32, 34]. These data flow criteria suggest the testing of specific sets of paths that follow the flow of data from expressions through assignments to other expressions.

Testing criteria which are more capable of uncovering errors tend to require a greater number of test cases. Tai, Weyuker, Ntafos, and Laski use a worst case analysis as a metric of of the required number of test cases needed to meet criteria [36, 37, 33, 24]. One can also directly measure the required number of test cases on a program. Such estimation techniques can be used to determine how practical a criterion is on specific software.

Ntafos suggests the use of strategies that require at most $O(n^2)$ test paths [33]. Such strategies are most likely to require a reasonable and practical number of test cases. A testing strategy that requires an exponential number of test cases is not realistic. However, the actual number of test cases can be much less than the worst case. Ntafos also notes that these worst case bounds may not reflect the actual number of required test cases.

The strongest testing strategies that have the highest worst case bounds may actually be feasible on real programs. Structural metrics may be used to estimate the number of test cases required to satisfy testing criteria. Such measures can simply count the number of complete paths through a program necessary to meet a criterion.

The forgoing path counting metrics are estimates of the required number of test cases because some of the counted paths may be infeasible — no test data exists which will cause the path to execute. Since determining whether a path is feasible is undecidable [38, 15, 20], metrics based on the number of feasible paths cannot be developed [14]. Another limitation of these testing metrics is that they measure the size of a minimal set of paths rather than the minimum set. The problem of finding the **minimum** number of complete paths to cover specified sets of node pairs is intractible [30, 31]. Despite these limitations, metrics that estimate the required number of test cases necessary to satisfy testing criteria are useful.

Using such a measurement tool, Bieman and Schultz conducted an investigation to determine how many test cases are actually needed to satisfy the all-du-paths testing criterion [5, 7, 4]. The tools developed by Bieman and Schultz identify minimal sets of complete program paths that satisfy the all-du-paths and all-uses testing criterion. The cardinality of these minimal sets measures the estimated number of test cases needed to satisfy the criteria. The metrics were used in an empirical study with results that indicate that the criterion is much more practical than previous analytical results suggest.

The all-du-paths criterion is one of a family of criteria defined by Rapps and Weyuker and based on data flow relationships [34]. These criteria focus on the program paths that connect the definitions and uses of variables (du-paths). Of these criteria, the all definition/use criterion (all-du-paths) is the "strongest". This criterion includes all of the other data flow criteria and requires testing the greatest number of program paths. Thus, the all-du-paths criterion should be the most effective of the data flow criteria in discovering errors.

Although the all-du-paths criterion is comparatively effective in revealing errors, it may require a large number of test cases. In the worst case, it can take an enormous number of test cases. Weyuker shows that the all-du-paths criterion requires 2^t test cases in the worst case, where t is the number of conditional transfers [37].

The all-du-paths criterion can potentially require an exponential number of test cases. However, results using the measurement tools designed by Bieman and Schultz indicate that the worst case scenario is rare. In a case study of a commercial software system, they found that the all-du-paths criterion can usually be satisfied by testing fewer than ten complete paths, and units requiring an exponential number of tests are rare. The results demonstrate that the all-du-paths criterion may be more practical than previously believed.

This example shows that researchers and practitioners can gain valuable insights when they focus on the direct implication of a structural metric. A metric that determines the size of a minimal set of paths necessary to satisfy a structural criterion is quite useful. The number of test cases needed for a particular testing strategy is clearly a component of the difficulty of using the strategy. Such a metric can be used to determine the practicability of the criterion. We can also use such a measure to estimate the required number of test cases and identify hard to test program units. Such a measure need not predict the elusive "understandability" property to be useful.

This example shows that researchers and practitioners can gain valuable insights when they focus on the direct implication of a structural measure. A measure that determines the size of a minimal set of paths necessary to satisfy a structural criterion is quite useful. The number of test cases needed for a particular testing strategy is clearly a component of the difficulty of using the strategy. Such a measure can be used to determine the practicability of the criterion. We can also use such a measure to estimate the required number of test cases and identify hard to test program units. Such a measure need not predict the elusive "understandability" property to be useful.

This example shows that researchers and practitioners can gain valuable insights when they focus on the direct implication of a structural measure. A measure that determines the size of a minimal set of paths necessary to satisfy a structural criterion is quite useful. The number of test cases needed for a particular testing strategy is clearly a component of the difficulty of using the strategy. Such a measure can be used to determine the practicability of the criterion. We can also use such a measure to estimate the required number of test cases and identify hard to test program units. Such a measure need not predict the elusive "understandability" property to be useful.

6 Conclusion

In this paper we are reporting on the efforts of the Grubstake Group in making the transition from establishing a foundation upon which software measurement can be rigorously developed to establishing guidelines and criteria for designing useful metrics. In this paper we

- introduce the notion of specifying a metric (We should point out that this idea is being simultaneously introduced in [16].),

- give guidelines for defining a software metric,
- give guidelines for validating a software metric, and
- by example show that a static software metric can be extremely useful in software development and management.

There is of course still much to do in the understanding of how to routinely develop reliable and understandable software metrics. We hope that work in this paper will help convince some researchers that software measurement *theory* can exist and theorical and foundations issues are in fact helpful in actually defining software metrics.

We would like to end with a comment on theory and our current work. As we mentioned in the Introduction, the real-world never seems to work exactly as it should according to theory. In light of this axiom, one of the perhaps unexpected benefits of moving from philosophy to practice is that it forces us to understand the philosophy and theory more clearly. When our theory says that a certain phenomenon should (or should not) happen but it doesn't (or does) happen, then we must re-evaluate our theory. Thus, one of the future tasks in this process of moving to practice is the continual testing and fine tuning of the theory.

References

[1] A. Baker, J. Bieman, N. Fenton, D. Gustafson, A. Melton, and R. Whitty. A philosophy for software measurement. *Journal of Systems and Softare*, 12:277–281, 1990.

[2] A. Baker, J. Bieman, D. Gustafson, and A. Melton. Modeling and measuring the software development process. *Proc. 20th Hawaii International Conference on Systems Sciences (HICSS-20)*, II:23–30, January 1987.

[3] Baker AL, Bieman JM, Gustafson DA, Melton AC, 'Modelling and measuring the software development process', HICCS-20 (2) 1987, 23-30

[4] J. Bieman. A Tool for Estimating Software Testing Requirements. *Microcomputer Applications* 9(3):72–79, 1990.

[5] J. Bieman and J. Schultz. Estimating the number of test cases required to satisfy the all-du-paths testing criterion. *Proc. Software Testing, Analysis and Verification Symposium (TAV3-SIGSOFT89)*, pages 179–186, December 1989.

[6] J. Bieman and J. Schultz. An empirical evaluation of the all-du-paths testing criterion. submitted to *Software Practice & Experience*, 1989.

[7] J. Bieman and J. Schultz. An empirical evaluation (and specification) of the all-du-paths testing criterion. submitted to *Software Engineering Journal*, 1991.

[8] Conte SD, Shen VY, Dunsmore HE, Software Engineering Metrics and Models, Benjamin Cummins Publishing, Inc, 1986

[9] Fenton NE, 'Software measurement: educational report', METKIT (ESPRIT II project 2384), 1990.

[10] Fenton NE, 'Software measurement: theory, tools and validation', *Software Eng J*, 1990

[11] N. Fenton and A. Melton. Deriving software measures throughout the development process. *Journal of Systems and Software*, 12:177–187, 1990.

[12] Fenton NE. *Software Metrics*, Chapman & Hall, 1991.

[13] Finkelstein L, 'Representation by symbol systems as an extension of the concept of measurement', Kybernetes, Vol 4 215-223, 1975

[14] P. G. Frankl and E. J. Weyuker. An applicable family of data flow testing criteria. *IEEE Trans. Software Engineering*, 14(10):1483–1498, 1988.

[15] J. B. Goodenough and S. L. Gerhart. Toward a theory of test data selection. *IEEE Trans. Software Engineering*, SE-1:156–173, June 1975.

[16] D. Gustafson and B. Prasad. Properties of Software Measures *Proceedings of FACS Workshop on Software Metrics*

[17] P. M. Herman. A data flow analysis approach to program testing. *The Australian Computer Journal*, 8(3):92–96, November 1976.

[18] J. Howatt and A. Baker. Rigorous definition and analysis of program complexity measures: an example using nesting. *The Journal of Systems and Software*, 10(2): 139–150.

[19] W. E. Howden. Methodology for the generation of program test data. *IEEE Trans. Computers*, C-24(5):554–559, May 1975.

[20] W. E. Howden. Reliability of the path analysis testing strategy. *IEEE Trans. Software Engineering*, SE-2(3):208–215, 1976.

[21] W. E. Howden. Functional program testing. *IEEE Trans. Software Engineering*, SE-6(2):162–169, March 1980.

[22] Krantz DH, Luce RD, Suppes P, Tversky A, 'Foundations of Measurement' Vol 1, Academic Press, 1971

[23] Kyburg HE, 'Theory and Measurement', Cambridge University Press, 1984

[24] J. W. Laski. On the comparative analysis of some data flow testing strategies. Technical Report 87-05, School of Engineering & Computer Science, Oakland University, Rochester, MI, 1987.

[25] J. Laski and B. Korel. A data flow oriented program testing strategy. *IEEE Trans. Software Engineering*, SE-9(3):347–354, May 1983.

[26] Littlewood B, 'Predicting software reliability', Phil. Trans. R. Soc. Lond. A 327, 513-527, 1989

[27] T. McCabe. A Complexity Measure. *IEEE Transactions on Software Engineering*, SE-2, 4 (Dec76) pp308-320.

[28] A. Melton, D. Gustafson, A. Baker, and J. Bieman. A mathematical perspective for software measures research. *IEE Softare Engineering Journal*, 5(5):246–254, 1990.

[29] A. Melton. Specifying Internal, External and Predictive Software Metrics. *Proceedings of FACS workshop on Software Metrics*

[30] S. C. Ntafos and S. L. Hakimi. On path cover problems in digraphs and applications to program testing. *IEEE Trans Software Engineering*, SE-5(5):520–529, September 1979.

[31] S. C. Ntafos and S. L. Hakimi. On structured digraphs and program testing. *IEEE Trans. Computers*, C-30(1):67–77, January 1981.

[32] S. C. Ntafos. On required element testing. *IEEE Trans. Software Engingeering*, SE-10(6):795–803, November 1984.

[33] S. C. Ntafos. A comparison of some structural testing strategies. *IEEE Trans. Software Engineering*, 14:868–874, June 1988.

[34] S. Rapps and E. J. Weyuker. Selecting software test data using data flow information. *IEEE Trans. Software Engineering*, SE-11(4):367–375, April 1985.

[35] Roberts FS, 'Measurement Theory with applications to decision making, utility, and the social sciences', Addison Wesley, 1979

[36] K. C. Tai. Program testing complexity and test criteria. *IEEE Trans. Software Engineering*, SE-6(6):531–538, November 1980.

[37] E. J. Weyuker. The complexity of data flow criteria for test data selection. *Information Processing Letters*, 19:103–109, August 1984.

[38] L. J. White. Basic mathematical definitions and results in testing. In B. Chandrasekaran and S. Radicchi, editors, *Computer Program Testing*, pages 13–24. North-Holland, 1981.

2. Formal Measurement in Practice

Deriving Measures of Software Reuse in Object Oriented Systems[*]

James M. Bieman
Department of Computer Science
Colorado State University
Fort Collins, Colorado 80523 USA
(303) 491-7096
bieman@cs.colostate.edu

Abstract

The analysis and measurement of current levels of software reuse are necessary to monitor improvements. This paper provides a framework for the derivation of measures of software reuse and introduces several definitions, attributes, and abstractions of potentially measurable reuse properties. The framework is applied to the problem of measuring reuse in object oriented systems which support "leveraged" reuse through inheritance. I describe the importance of the perspective of the observer when analyzing, measuring, and profiling reuse. Three perspectives are examined: the server perspective, the client perspective, and the system perspective. Candidate reuse metrics are proposed from each perspective.

Copyright ©1991 by James M. Bieman

---

[*]This research is partially supported by the NATO Collaborative Research Grants Program under RG. 0343/88

1 Introduction

Research on formal aspects of software measurement tends to focus on properties of measures, measurement theory, measurement scales, and requirements for predictive measures. This paper reports on the practical application of techniques developed in formal studies of software measurement. The overall aim is to derive and measure intrinsic properties of software documents and processes.

Measurement theory is the foundation for practical software measurement. A measure allows us to numerically characterize intuitive attributes of software objects and events. We need a clear definition and understanding of a software attribute before we can define measures. We must be able to determine that one software entity has more or less of some attribute before we can use measurement to assign a numerical quantity of the attribute to the entity. And the orderings of the software entities implied by the measurement must be consistent [BBF+90, MGBB90, FM90].

Software reuse is one important measurable property. Software quality, reliability, and productivity should improve when we reuse our programs, designs, specifications, etc. Software reuse reduces the quantity of software that must be developed from scratch and thus allows a greater focus on quality. The reuse of well-tested software should result in greater reliability. And the high cost of verification of a reused module can be spread out over many products. With reuse, software development becomes a capital investment. The development effort for each product is used to build a software infrastructure which can be utilized in subsequent products [Weg84].

The rigorous measurement of reuse will help developers monitor current levels of reuse and help provide insight into the problem of developing software that is easily reused. Conte [CDS86], Boehm [Boe81], Bailey [BB81], and Fenton [Fen91] describe reuse measures that are based on comparisons between the length or size of reused code and the size of newly written code in particular software products. Modifications to the reused code are not considered by these researchers. The purpose of Conte's reuse measure is estimating coding effort. Reuse reduces coding effort, and this reduction affects effort estimation techniques. In a similar light, Boehm and Bailey use the size of reused code to adjust cost predictors. Fenton also develops a measure of reuse based on the dependencies in an associated call graph. Selby [Sel89] classifies modules into categories based on the percentage of new versus reused code in a module. The categories are (1) completely new modules, (2) reused modules with major revisions ($\geq 25\%$ changed),

(3) reused modules with slight revisions (< 25% changed), and (4) modules that are reused without change. The foregoing reuse measurement techniques look at reuse in a one-dimensional fashion. Except for Fenton's measure of private reuse described in Section 3.1, all of the foregoing reuse measurements are based on one attribute, program size (or program length). Only Selby addresses the measurement of reuse with modifications.

Proponents assert that a major benefit of object oriented design and programming is the generation of reusable software components [Mey87]. Components can be reused as is, or modified using subclassing facilities. Class libraries promote the reuse of well tested components of general or special interest. Object oriented systems promote reuse through language features such as data abstraction and inheritance constructs, and through system support such as browsers.

To support or refute claims that object oriented software is easier to reuse, we must be able to measure reuse in these systems. Measuring reuse in object oriented systems requires that we define attributes, abstractions, and measures appropriately for these support mechanisms. Only with meaningful measures can we determine whether object oriented systems really promote reuse.

Ultimately we want to determine whether there are structural properties that make software more likely to be reused. If there are such properties, we want to identify them. We believe that there are – software engineering practices have long supported the notion that certain internal structure such as structured programming, data abstraction, information hiding, etc result in higher quality software products.

The existence of structural properties which improve the level of reuse can only be determined empirically. To investigate this issue, we need to be able to characterize reuse in actual systems. Determining whether object oriented techniques promote greater reuse requires that we be able to measure the quantity of reuse.

Measurement of the current state of industrial practice is of great concern to the software engineering community [GC87]. Only with accurate measures of the "level" of actual reuse can projects be monitored and "improvement" measured.

I want to be able to measure reuse related to object oriented class libraries. Reuse occurs within a class library; library classes may used by other library classes. Library classes may also be reused by a new system. Data from industry can be examined to learn how reuse naturally occurs in object oriented systems. Experiments can help us relate the "level" of reuse to other software properties. But first, the important reuse attributes must be identified.

My goal is to derive a set of measurable, intuitively meaningful reuse attributes, and then use the derived measures in empirical research. This paper describes the process of deriving measurable reuse attributes and is a prerequisite to future empirical investigations. The focus here is on code reuse. In the future, I plan to investigate the derivation of measures of specification and design reuse.

This paper is organized as follows. Section 2 describes the process, borrowed from measurement theory, for deriving new measures of software reuse. Section 3 introduces a number of definitions related to reuse, reuse attributes, and describes prospective abstractions which capture the reuse attributes. In Section 4, the definitions, attributes, and abstractions described in Section 3 are applied to reuse in object oriented systems. An additional abstraction is proposed and a set of candidate reuse measures is introduced. A summary of the results presented in the paper and conclusions are given in Section 5.

2 A Method for Deriving Reuse Measures

Measurement theory provides guidance for deriving reuse measures. Aspects of the "quantity of reuse" are internal product attributes related to properties of particular software documents [Fen91]. Measurement theory suggest the following process [BBF+90]:

1. Identify and define intuitive and well-understood attributes of software reuse. We must qualitatively understand what we want to measure.

2. Specify precisely the documents and the attributes to be measured. We must be able to describe precisely the object that we measure, and the property of the object that the measurement is to indicate.

3. Determine formal models or abstractions which capture these attributes. Formal models are required to unambiguously produce numerical measurement values.

4. Derive mappings from the models of attributes to a number system. The mappings must be consistent with the orderings implied by the model attributes.

The first three steps are critical. Good definitions of reuse attributes, the documents, and abstractions are needed before the attributes can be meaningfully measured.

A long term goal is to be able to use reuse measures to make predictions on external software process attributes such as the development time, maintainability, defects, etc. Industry's need for predictors is often the overriding issue when new measures are introduced and validated. For a measure to be effective in making predictions we need theories relating different measures, and empirical support. Otherwise the use of a measure for prediction is only based on speculation. The requirement that an internal measure effectively predict external process attributes has had a negative impact on software metrics research, especially affecting research directed towards developing measures of structural "complexity" [Fen91]. However, a measure can be useful even if it is not an effective predictor. To be useful, a measure must give a numerical value to a software attribute that is of genuine interest. I defer worrying about the added requirements for using measures for predictions, and simply seek valid and useful reuse measures.

To derive reuse measures we need clear definitions of software reuse attributes, precise definitions of the documents to be measured, formal models of the reuse attributes, and a method for generating consistent numerical values from the documents and attributes.

3 Reuse Definitions, Attributes, and Abstractions

Our derivation of reuse measures concentrates on clear definitions of reuse properties and abstractions which capture these properties.

3.1 Public and Private Reuse

Fenton defines *public reuse* as "the proportion of a product which was constructed externally" [Fen91]. He determines this proportion in terms of program lengths. The following is a modified version of a definition of public reuse from [Fen91]:

$$\text{public reuse} = \frac{\text{length}(E)}{\text{length}(P)}$$

where E is the code developed externally and P is the new system including E. This definition of public reuse makes use of any acceptable abstraction of program length, which may be lines of code or the number of characters.

To use such a measure, one must be able to clearly distinguish between the components (lines or characters) that are from the external source and the components that are completely new. Abstractions based on more generic components are also appropriate.

Assume the existence of a library of previously developed software components. Useful components are imported from library when a new system is developed. Components may be modified when imported. The import mechanism may be designed into the environment, or ad hoc. Reuse is determined by the relation between the new system and the library.

In the ensuing discussion in this section, let L = "reuse library" and N = "new system", assuming L and N are sets of software "components." A component may be a source line of code, a statement, a procedure, a module, or an entire sub-system. I can define *reuse* as the use of $e \in L$ in N. (use is not formally defined).

The software entity from the library that is being reused is called the *server* and the software entity that makes use of the the library component is the *client*.

Fenton defines *private reuse* (or perhaps more appropriately *internal reuse*) as the "extent to which modules within a product are reused within the same product" [Fen91]. He uses the call graph as an abstraction which captures the "essence" of private reuse. A call graph is a (directed) graph which represents the control flow connections between modules. Call graph nodes represent modules, and nodes are connected with an edge if a module represented by one of the nodes invokes the the module represented by the other node. Figure 1 is an example call graph. Here M0 directly uses M1, M2, and M3. M1 uses M4, M2 uses M3 and M4, and M3 uses M4 and M5. Since M4 is used by M1, M2, and M3, and M3 is used by M0 and M2, M3 and M4 are used by more than one other module. Using Fenton's interpretation [Fen91], M3 and M4 are the only modules used more than once or reused. Fenton's measure of private reuse is:

$$r(G) = e - n + 1$$

where e is the number of edges and n is the number of nodes in the call graph. This measure is exactly the number of modules which are invoked by more than one other module. Thus, the private reuse in the program represented by Figure 1 is $r(G) = 3$. This measure matches an intuitive notion of reuse; M4 is *reused* twice since it is used by three other modules (M1, M2, and M3) and M3 is *reused* once since it is used by two other modules (M0 and M2). In this case, a reuse occurs on the second or subsequent uses.

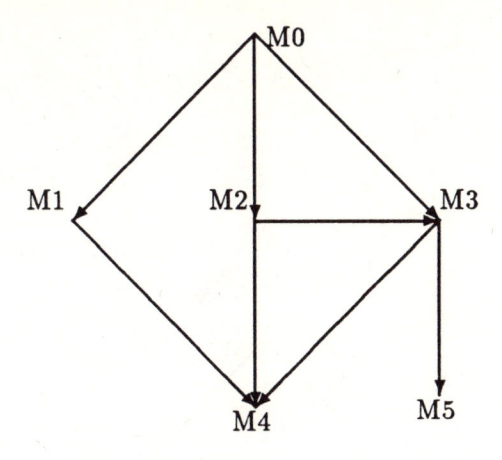

Figure 1: A call graph abstraction

One limitation of the measure is that it is not sensitive to more than one invocation of module A by module B, and is not sensitive to the size of the system. In fact, the call graph abstraction is not an adequate abstraction for developing reuse measures that are sensitive to the number of times that module B invokes module A. An alternative abstraction is a *call multigraph*. A call multigraph has an edge for each invocation of A by B, thus two nodes may be connected by several edges. Figure 2 contains a call multigraph. The figure has two edges connecting M1 and M4, and connecting M3 and M5. These edges represent duplicate calls of M4 by M1 and M5 by M3. Fenton's measure of this graph gives us an $r(G) = 5$ accounting for the two additional reuses.

Both the call graph and call multigraph are not adequate for measuring the relative size or length of the reused software units. If relative size of reused code is important when measuring public reuse, it should be important when measuring private reuse. Perhaps an annotated call multigraph is appropriate.

We can quickly realize that there are many reuse attributes; no one abstraction is appropriate for measuring all of the attributes.

3.2 Verbatim and Leveraged Reuse

Verbatim reuse is reuse without modifications. Importing code from the

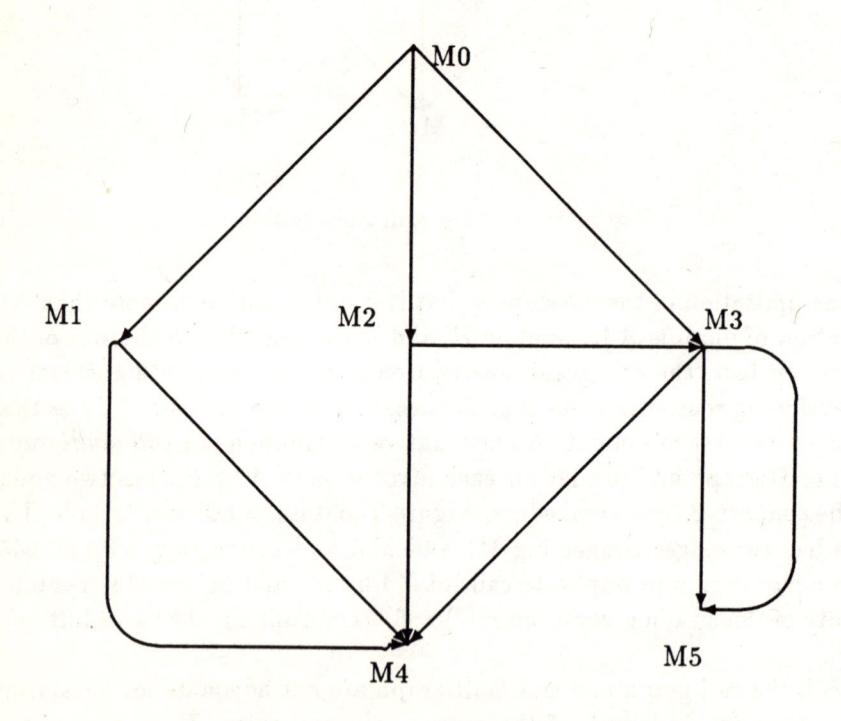

Figure 2: A call multigraph abstraction

library without change is verbatim public reuse. Verbatim public reuse is traditionally accomplished with a subroutine activation of program libraries, instantiation of predefined public types, importation of public modules, etc. Using sets of modules as abstractions, we can define verbatim reuse.

$$\forall e [e \in L \land e \in N \Rightarrow \text{``}e\text{ is reused verbatim''}]$$

We can define measures of reuse in terms of modules (rather than lengths) with the above abstraction. But sets are not adequate abstractions for measuring multiple uses of a library module in the new system. Bags (sets with duplicate entries) may be a better choice.

Verbatim private reuse is essentially the same as verbatim public reuse, except that the reused software entity is not from a library that existed prior to the new product development. Rather, the reused software was developed earlier in the developing the current product. Appropriate abstractions for deriving measures of private verbatim reuse include the call graph and call multigraph as described in Section 3.1.

Leveraged reuse is reuse with modifications. In *leveraged public reuse*, code from L is tailored to a new use. An example of leveraged reuse is when

$$\exists e, f [e \in L \land f \in N \land f \text{ ``is derived from'' } e].$$

Leveraged reuse applies to taking an old piece of code and "hacking away at it" until it does what the new requirements demand. We refer to this undisciplined reuse as *ad hoc leveraged reuse*. Leveraged reuse also applies to reuse with more disciplined modifications, and modifications with some language support. In order to measure leveraged reuse we need abstractions which capture the "is derived from" relationship. Again, sets are not adequate. We need to relate components of a new module to components from the library. Thus, we must be able to break modules into smaller units. Here, code statements may be the correct level of abstraction, and reuse can be measured through statement comparisons. However this will not capture modifications to individual statements or expressions. Perhaps only process information — transcripts recording program behavior is effective for measuring ad hoc leveraged reuse. We will see in Section 4 that there are abstractions that can effectively capture leveraged reuse, when leveraged reuse is supported by the language or programming environment.

3.3 Direct and Indirect Reuse

Direct reuse is reuse without going through an intermediate entity. Subroutine calls, instantiations of a type, or importations of modules are direct reuses (or uses). "Direct reuse" is used to distinguish from "indirect reuse." The previous discussion in this section really refers to direct reuse.

Indirect reuse is reuse through an intermediate entity. When module A invokes module B, and B invokes module C. Then A indirectly reuses C, and C was indirectly reused by A. For *private indirect reuse* a call graph or call multigraph are appropriate abstractions for deriving measures.

The *Distance (or level) of indirection* is the number of intermediate entities between user (client) and used (server) For example assume that A uses B, B uses C, and C uses D. Then for the pair (A, D) there is a *1-level* indirection, or the distance of indirection is 2. It follows that when M_0 uses $M_1, \ldots, M_n$ uses M_{n+1} then (M_0, M_{n+1}) has an *n-level* indirect reuse. The concept of "distance" or "level" of indirection can also be applied to both verbatim and leveraged reuse. There may be different possible paths connecting two call graph nodes. Thus, there may not be a unique distance of indirect reuse between two modules in a system. For example, in Figure 1, M0 indirectly uses M5 with two distinct reuse paths. The indirect reuse of M5 via the **direct** use of M3 is a *1-level* indirect use, while the reuse of M5 through M2 and M3 is a *2-level* indirect use.

3.4 Reuse Perspectives

Different reuse attributes are visible when reuse is examined from different perspectives. Consider a system where individual modules access some set of existing software entities. When module M uses program unit S, M is a client and S is the server. Thus we consider the program unit being reused as the server, and the unit accessing the unit as the client. One can observe reuse from the perspective of the server, the client, and the system. Each of these perspectives is relevant for the analysis and measurement of reuse in a system. We can derive a set of potentially measurable attributes based on profiles of reuse from each perspective. Rather than one measure of one component of a reuse attribute, we end of with measurements of many reuse attributes.

Server Perspective

The *server perspective* is the perspective of the library or a particular library component. Given a particular program entity, the analysis focuses on how this entity is being reused by all of the clients.

A set of reuse measurements can be taken from the server perspective. Such a profile of server reuse describes how the library is reused by clients. The *server reuse profile* can help determine which library components are being reused and in what manner (verbatim, leveraged, directly, indirectly). Potential measures of server reuse attributes include the number of times a library component is reused, average for library, etc

Client Perspective

The *client perspective* takes the point of view of the new system or a new system component. Here we are interested in how a particular program entity reuses other program entities.

Reuse measurements can also be taken from the perspective of the client entity. The *client reusing profile* describes how a new system uses entities in the library.

We can determine the extent that a software entity takes advantage of the reuse library. The reusing profile is focused on the previously implemented code that A takes advantage of. The client reusing profile can include an analysis of the verbatim reuse in A, and profiles the instantiation and references of externally defined program entities. Potential measures include the number of reuse occurrences in new system, the percentage of the new system that is reused code, kinds of reuse, etc.

System Perspective

The *system perspective* is a view of reuse in the overall system, both servers and clients. The analysis is of the reuse throughout an entire system. This may include a synthesis of the reuse in individual clients and servers in the system.

A *system reuse profile* includes both system-wide private reuse, and system-wide public reuse. It includes measurement of indirection, direct, and verbatim reuse. We are interested in both the absolute number of occurrences of various kinds of reuse, and the reuse related to the size of the system (reuse density).

3.5 Language Support & Leveraged Reuse Measurement

Given a library L and new system N, How do we measure the quantity or percentage of ad hoc leveraged reuse? If the language or programming environment does not support reuse, then reuse can be examined either through automatic text comparisons, or records of programmer behavior. Both techniques are not dependable.

With support mechanisms, reuse attributes can be analyzed and measured accurately. Object oriented languages and environments provide such support. In the following section we examine the effect of the object oriented paradigm on reuse attributes, abstractions, and measurement.

4 Object Oriented Reuse

Object oriented languages support reuse through the class system, as well as through the instantiation and use of previously defined entities. Leveraged reuse is supported through inheritance. In object oriented systems it is difficult to distinguish between public and private reuse; a new system is built as an extension to an existing class library. Thus, the ensuing discussion does not distinguish between public and private reuse, and the term "reuse" refers to either one.

4.1 Object Oriented Terminology

Object oriented programming and object oriented languages make use of terminology which is somewhat unique. Here, I introduce some object oriented terminology especially as it relates to software reuse. For a more comprehensive introduction to object oriented software see the excellent texts by Meyer and by Booch [Mey88, Boo91].

Essentially, an object oriented software system is a collection of abstract data types called classes. A *class* is an encapsulated specification of both the persistent state of an abstract data type and its operations. An instantiation or *instance* of a class is an *object*. There may be several concurrently active objects of one class; each instantiation is a different object. Suppose a class defines a stack abstract data type. We can instantiate several stack objects, and each object may contain different values in their stack frames.

Objects perform actions in response to *messages*. These messages are essentially procedure calls. Upon receiving a message an object responds by sending other messages, changing state, and/or returning a message to the object which sent the message. The only way to affect an object is by sending a message. To change the internal state of an object, a message with a specified state changing effect must be sent to the object. Responses to messages are specified via *methods* which are components of classes. Methods are essentially procedures which are local to a class. They may have parameters, assignments to local variables and persistent class variables, and may send other messages. A stack class will contain methods for common stack operations such as *push, pop, top, isempty,* etc.

To reuse an unmodified (verbatim reuse) object oriented software entity, rather than invoke a procedure several times, one sends several messages to the same object. Instantiating a class several times is also a form of verbatim reuse. Verbatim reuse of object oriented software entities is very similar to verbatim reuse of more traditional software. Both the call graph and call multigraph abstractions are appropriate for deriving measures of reuse in object oriented software. Object oriented support of leveraged reuse provides an enhanced ability to analyze and, hopefully, to measure leveraged reuse. I will not address ad hoc leveraged reuse in object oriented systems. Inheritance is a powerful support tool for leveraged reuse and I assume that this mechanism is used.

4.2 Leveraged Reuse via Inheritance

Inheritance provides language support for specifying "I want something just like that except ... ." A developer can modify a particular class to create a new class which behaves somewhat differently than the parent class. The original class is the *superclass* and the new leveraged class is the *subclass*. The subclass can be modified in several basic ways:

- adding new state variables.
- adding new methods.
- changing existing methods.

The first two modifications extend the specification of the superclass, and can be called *extension modifications*. The third modification changes the behavior of a superclass method and can be dubbed an *overload modification*. When creating a subclass, a developer need only specify the differences from the superclass. Clearly, the inheritance mechanism supports reuse of previously written classes.

The class, superclass, subclass hierarchy can be represented by a class hierarchy graph. Figure 3 shows an example class hierarchy graph from a object oriented data base of university records. The figure shows that both "faculty" and "student" inherit certain common data fields (perhaps information such as name, identification number, age, etc.) and operations (such as add/delete person) from the parent or superclass "person." The

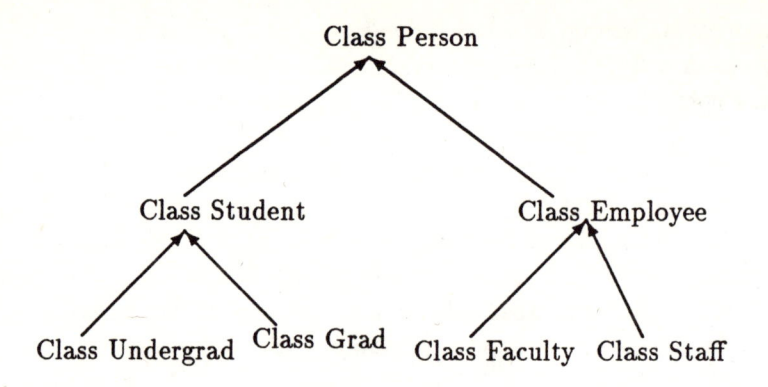

```
                    Class Person
                    ↗         ↖
          Class Student       Class Employee
          ↗        ↖          ↗         ↖
Class Undergrad  Class Grad  Class Faculty  Class Staff
```

Figure 3: Inheritance hierarchy graph abstraction

subclasses "undergrad" and "grad" inherit information and operations from their superclass "student." The subclasses reuse these operations and data through inheritance. However, the reuse is leveraged since (language supported) changes are made to the earlier functionality and data structures. For example, fields for course grades and an operation to create a transcript may be added to Class Person when creating Class Student. The inheritance graph abstraction can be used to describe potential reuse attributes and derive their measures. (Note that many object oriented languages, such as $C++$ support *multiple inheritance*, and so one class may have several superclasses.)

Unfortunately, the class hierarchy graph cannot be used to distinguish between extension and overload modifications. We need to look inside the classes to distinguish between the classes of modifications. The abstraction used to model overload and extension reuse must include the distinction, perhaps through colored edges, in order to derive measures reflecting these leverage categories. For now, I defer the extension of the inheritance graph abstraction to model the classes of modification. In this paper, the inheritance graph serves as the abstraction for the derivation of object oriented leveraged reuse attributes and measures.

As in more traditional software, we can analyze object oriented reuse from the server, client, and system perspective. In each case, we suggest measurable attributes.

4.3 OO Server Reuse Profile

The server reuse profile of a particular class (say class A) will characterize how the class is being reused by the client classes in the system.

The *verbatim server reuse* in an object oriented system is essentially the same as in non object oriented systems. However, we use object oriented terminology. We can measure number of instance creations of objects of class A in a new system and the number of instance references of class A objects in a new system. These attributes can be determined either statically or dynamically.

Leveraged server reuse is supported through inheritance, and is characterized by an analysis of the subclass hierarchy using the inheritance hierarchy graph as the abstraction. We can count the number of subclasses of A, analyze the size and shape of the inheritance hierarchy graph. We can examine the *indirect leveraged server reuse* through an measurements of the inheritance graph; we can find the number of indirect clients and calculate the average distance of indirect leveraged reuses. A count of the number of paths in the inheritance graph between a particular server and its clients is a measure of the instances of indirect reuse. With an extended inheritance graph abstraction we can examine and categorize each instance or reuse. A client can reuse the server either by *extension*, adding methods to the server, or by *overload*, redefining methods.

4.4 OO Client Reusing Profile

The client reusing profile characterizes how a new class A reuses existing library classes. This reuse can be verbatim reuse within A, and measures include the number of instance creations of library objects, the number of instance references of library objects, and the percentage of objects created or referenced by A which are from the library. These verbatim reuses can also be modeled and measured using the call multigraph abstraction. Potential indirect client reuse measures include the number of servers which are indirectly reused, the number of paths to indirect servers, and the lengths of these paths.

The client can leverage its reuse of library class(es) via inheritance. Again, the inheritance hierarchy graph is an appropriate abstraction. We can count the number of servers, the number of indirect servers, the number of paths to indirect servers, and the average lengths of such paths.

Some potential client reuse attributes require an extended inheritance hierarchy graph to distinguish between the classes of reuse. Measures of such attributes include the percentage of server methods changed or unchanged, measures of the the kinds of modifications made (whether extension or overloading).

4.5 OO System Reuse Profile

The system profile characterizes overall reuse of library classes in the new system.

Measurable system reuse attributes include

- Percentage of the new system source text imported from the library. This requires information not contained in the call multigraph, information related to class lengths.

- Percentage of new system classes imported verbatim from library.

- Percentage of the new system classes derived (leveraged reuse) from library classes, and the average percentage of these leveraged classes that are imported.

- The average number of verbatim and leveraged clients for servers, and, conversely, the average number of servers for clients.

- The average number of verbatim and leveraged indirect clients for servers, and the average number of indirect servers for clients.

- The average length and number of paths between indirect servers and clients for both verbatim and leveraged reuse.

I am interested in both the reuse of library classes and reuse within the new system. That is, classes developed for the new system that may be completely new or derived from library classes may be reused within the new system. The may be reused verbatim or leveraged. The "shape" of the class/superclass hierarchy is an attribute of the system reuse profile.

Connections between verbatim and leveraged reuse are also part of the system reuse profile. Leveraged server B of client C may have made verbatim use of module A. Thus, there is a reuse chain connecting module A to module C. This chain can be analyzed by examining the two abstractions. Any appropriate measures will make use of both graphs.

4.6 Observations

The process of identifying meaningful and measurable attributes of reuse in object oriented software has not provided just one or two appropriate measures. Rather, I find that there are many reuse properties to examine and to potentially measure. The specific questions that one is trying to answer will help determine which reuse properties to measure. Reuse attributes also depend on the particular perspective of the observer. One can use the point of view of the server, client, or system.

Two abstractions seem especially appropriate for deriving object oriented reuse measures: the call multigraph and the inheritance hierarchy graph. The call multigraph is used to derive measures of verbatim reuse, while the inheritance hierarchy graph is used to derive measures of leveraged reuse. Table 1 shows several measures derived from the two abstractions and three perspectives. Additional abstractions will be necessary to derive reuse measures that are sensitive to the kind of modifications made in leveraged reuse.

The analysis (and measurement) of leveraged reuse is clearly eased by the support of inheritance in object oriented software. With reuse supported by inheritance, we can identify exactly the library source(s) of leveraged reuse and the kind of modifications made to the server(s). This analysis can be made by examining the software documents directly. With ad hoc leveraged reuse, either the programmers must supply the information or we need an elaborate system to track access to the library and editing changes made to library components.

We can still speculate about the relationship between the quantity of reuse and "reusability," assuming that reusability is an internal property of a software document. The level of reuse may be related to internal software properties such as

- Class size: A large class may be harder to understand, and thus more difficult to reuse. Leveraged reuse of a larger sized class may be especially difficult.

- Nature and "complexity" of control flow: A class with a complicated decision structure in the implementation of a class method may also be more difficult to reuse, especially if modifications are necessary.

- Nature and "complexity" of data flow: Many data dependencies may also make reuse more difficult.

reuse class	abstraction	perspective	candidate measures
verbatim	call multigraph (CMG)	server	# direct clients # client invocations of server # indirect clients # paths to indirect clients lengths of indirect paths
		client	# direct servers # server instance creations # distinct server instance creations # indirect servers # paths to indirect servers lengths of indirect paths
		system	"size" & "shape" of CMG: $r(CMG) = e - n + 1$ # nodes/edges in CMG # paths in CMG # connected node pairs average indirect distance
leveraged	inheritance hierarchy graph (IHG)	server	# direct clients # direct client uses # indirect clients # paths to indirect clients lengths of indirect paths
		client	# direct servers # server uses # indirect servers # paths to indirect servers lengths of indirect paths
		system	"size" & "shape" of IHG: $r(IHG) = e - n + 1$ # edges in IHG # paths in IHG # connected node pairs average indirect distance

Table 1: Object oriented reuse measures from two abstractions

- Size and "complexity of interfaces: Many speculate that a large and complicated interface makes reuse more difficult. I suspect that interface complexity will affect direct reuse of a server entity more than the above internal attributes.

The foregoing are all attributes from the server perspective, the perspective of the entity being reused.

The amount of reuse of a particular class is also related to external properties such as the "usefulness" of a class in particular application domains. If the particular functionality of a class is often needed, then the class is more likely to be reused often. Another external attribute is related to the nature of the software development process. If reuse is encouraged by management and/or if reuse is supported by good browsers and information retrieval systems, then reuse is more likely. Thus, the quantity of reuse is not a direct function of the internal properties or internal "reusability" of a class. Because of the numerous external factors, "reusability" is not an attribute of a software document.

Measuring external attributes is generally more difficult than measuring internal attributes. Often needed are measures related to the "ability" of the personnel, the "quality" of the environment, and the "usefulness" of a particular potentially reusable software entity. Yet these are generally subjective attributes, and are not amenable to scientific measurement.

5 Conclusions

In this paper, I introduce the problem of deriving measures of software reuse from a measurement theory perspective. I define several reuse terms including verbatim, leveraged, direct, and indirect reuse. I describe three important perspectives of reuse: the server perspective, the client perspective, and the system perspective. One needs to use well defined perspectives to ensure that reuse measures are taken of the desired attribute.

Using the measurement theory approach, I derive reuse metrics applicable to object oriented systems. Two abstractions are used: a call multigraph and an inheritance hierarchy graph. The call multigraph can be used to define measures of verbatim reuse in both traditional and object oriented systems. The inheritance hierarchy graph is appropriate for defining measures of leveraged reuse when leverage is supported by inheritance. Several candidate measures of object oriented software reuse are proposed. The inheritance hierarch graph abstraction can be extended to allow the definitions of measures of leveraged reuse that take into account the nature of the modifications.

A long term goal of this research is to determine what makes software reusable. Before we can satisfy this ambitious goal, we need to be able to measure both the quantity of reuse and many "independent" variables. These variables include structural attributes of the software entities, and external attributes of the software process. The internal attributes can be readily defined and measured, while measuring the external attributes is problematic. Assuming that we can measure the independent variables, we must derive theories relating the quantity of reuse to the independent variables, and then conduct empirical investigations to support or refute the theories.

This work directed towards measuring the quantity of reuse allows us to monitor reuse levels and is a first step towards our ultimate aim. Determining what makes software reusable remains a long term goal. Measures of the quantity of reuse have immediate, practical applications. Current levels of reuse can be measured and improvements can be monitored.

References

[BB81]   J.W. Bailey and V.R. Basili. A meta-model for software development resource expenditures. *Proc. Fifth Int. Conf. Software Engineering*, pages 107–116, 1981.

[BBF+90]   A.L. Baker, J.M. Bieman, N. E. Fenton, A. C. Melton, and R.W. Whitty. A philosophy for software measurement. *Journal of Systems and Software*, 12(3):277–281, July 1990.

[Boe81]   B. W. Boehm. *Software Engineering Economics*. Prenntice-Hall, Englewood Cliffs, NJ, 1981.

[Boo91]   G. Booch. *Object Oriented Design with Applications*. Benjamin/Cummings, 1991.

[CDS86]   S.D. Conte, H.E. Dunsmore, and V.Y. Shen. *Software Engineering Metrics and Models*. Benjamin/Cummings, Menlo Park, California, 1986.

[Fen91]   Norman Fenton. *Software Metrics A Rigorous Approach*. Chapman & Hall, London, 1991.

[FM90]   N. Fenton and A. Melton. Deriving structurally based software measures. *Journal of Systems and Software*, 12(3):177–187, July 1990.

[GC87]   R.B. Grady and D.L. Caswell. *Software Metrics: Establishing a Company-wide Program.* Prentice Hall, NJ, 1987.

[Mey87]   B. Meyer. Reusability: The case for object-oriented design. *IEEE Software*, 4(2):50–64, March 1987.

[Mey88]   B. Meyer. *Object-oriented Software Construction.* Prentice Hall, Englewood Cliffs, NJ, 1988.

[MGBB90] A.C. Melton, D.A. Gustafson, J.M. Bieman, and A.L. Baker. A mathematical perspective for software measures research. *IEE Software Engineering Journal*, 5(5):246–254, 1990.

[Sel89]   Richard W. Selby. Quantitative studies of software reuse. In Ted J. Biggerstaff and Alan J. Perlis, editors, *Software Reusability Vol. II Applications and Experiences*, pages 213–233. Addison-Wesley, 1989.

[Weg84]   P. Wegner. Capital-intensive software technology. *IEEE Software*, 1(3):7–45, July 1984.

Language Independent Definition of Axiomatic Metrics

Norbert Fuchs, Sieglinde Stainer

Alcatel Austria-ELIN Research Centre
Ruthnergasse 1-7
A-1210 Wien
Austria

Abstract

The aim of this paper is to present a way of getting a more objective measurement of different attributes concerning both implementations as well as specifications of software systems. In order to gain this goal we are using a general basis on which all the information is stored, which is necessary and useful, when analyzing the corresponding implementation or specification by applying different metrics. As a starting point for this general basis the usage of flowgraphs was taken, as flowgraphs are a well-known and frequently used method for presenting the control flow and the structure of a program.

In fact, using flowgraphs as white-box description was only reasonable in so far as the analyzed documents has clear notions of control flow. We were forced to modifications in order to handle specification languages like LOTOS (Language Of Temporal Ordering Specification, standardized by CCITT) where we have different constructs which only can be mapped onto the same flowgraph structure. So, we clearly came to a more syntax oriented theory than flowgraphs. This development resulted in the so-called descriptor theory which is much more general and flowgraphs can be seen as a special case.

The work was carried out as part of the ESPRIT II project COSMOS[1,2] (Cost Management with Metrics of Specification).

1 Introduction

The theory developed by Fenton and Whitty is based on flowgraphs and can be seen as a means, with which we are able to generate a general basis of information presentation onto which we can apply metrics. Using a general presentation irrespective of the corresponding language should provide the possibility of having a more objective measurement. Moreover, the definition of the different metrics is much easier, when using the theory of Fenton and Whitty. With the help of this theory, the way of presenting the information, which is measured afterwards, is done in the same structured manner.

When using the flowgraph theory in practice some disadvantages and even inaccuracies do appear. Two main aspects will be discussed in this paper. The first disadvantage concerns the unique mapping of the control flow onto flowgraphs. In practice one can find a lot of examples where it is impossible to map the real control flow onto flowgraphs without losing valuable information. Some examples will be given in the paper. Second, as this theory is based on the structuredness defined by Dijkstra problems occur whenever mapping a language onto the general basis, which is - seen from the point of view of

---
[1] COSMOS is supported by the CEC under ESPRIT II project 2686 and by the Austrian "Innovations- und Technologiefond".

[2] Partners of the project are TechForce, Alcatel Austria-ELIN Research Centre, British Telecom Research Labs, Goldsmiths' College London, The Netherland School of Business and Telefonica Sistemas.

Dijkstra's structuredness - not structured. But the attribute of being non structured in this way occurs in nearly every implementation or specification language. Whenever we try to map e.g. recursion onto flowgraphs we produce a non structured behaviour. Decomposing this flowgraphs results in the generation of decomposition trees with a lot of new big primes. This doesn't seem to be a problem, when seen from the theoretical point of view. Whenever this situation occurs in practice problems occur in the evaluation of these new primes.

So, as a consequence we tried to modify the flowgraph theory of Fenton and Whitty in a way which prevents producing situations we can't handle in an adequate and correct way. We therefore introduced so-called 'descriptors'. A descriptor is a data structure which contains all the information necessary and useful for the metrics evaluation. Within this descriptor we store all the information concerning the control flow or information strongly related to the control flow of the corresponding program. As a consequence, the intermediate step of producing flowgraphs and decomposing them afterwards is no longer necessary. The basis on which we can apply all the different metrics is no longer the decomposition tree used in the Fenton and Whitty theory but a so-called 'descriptor tree'. This descriptor tree is quite similar to the former decomposition tree but doesn't contain primes at all, only descriptors. Nevertheless, we still can apply the simple way of defining the metrics as proposed by Fenton and Whitty.

In the following chapters this descriptor theory is motivated and explained in more detail. At the end detailed information about the way how to classify language constructs and how to define classes and subclasses is given.

2 Decomposition Theory

As it is already well-know and extensively discussed in literature the control flow of a program can be presented with the help of flowgraphs. Fenton and Whitty have used the flowgraphs as a basis on which they have built their theories. They aimed to define a sound theoretical basis on which the evaluation of structural metrics can be done in a more objective and better defined way.

2.1 Flowgraphs and its Decomposition

Flowgraphs can be used for modeling control flow. In [4] a flowgraph is defined as consisting of a directed graph (that is a set of objects called *vertices* and a set of arrows called *arcs* each of which points from any vertex to itself or to any other vertex) together with two distinguished vertices of the graph, a and z, satisfying

1. Every vertex can be reached from a by following a sequence of arcs in a direction consistent with the directions on these arcs.

2. Every vertex can reach z in a similar manner.

3. Moreover, no arcs are directed out of z.

We refer to a as the *startnode* and to z as the *stopnode* of F respectively. Apart from this definition of the two special and always existing vertices of a flowgraph, we differ between two types of nodes occurring in a flowgraph, namely the *process* vertices and the *control* vertices. A process vertex is a node with an outdegree of 1 and all other vertices are called control vertices. Notice that the start vertex a may be either but the stop vertex z must be a control vertex, by virtue of condition (2).[3]

Mapping a well-structured program onto a flowgraph means composing a flowgraph with the help of well-known and defined flowgraph substructures which are called *prime flowgraphs* or just *primes*. As Dijkstra has demonstrated, a Pascal program (without goto-statements) can be mapped onto a flowgraph using only a small set of primes called the *D-primes* representing the constructs of structured programming. The restriction Dijkstra has defined on his theory is that only well-structured programs are mappable on flowgraphs using this small set of basic primes, so a mapping of a program which consists of commands like a goto is not applicable. The set of the primes used is shown in figure 1 where the start and stop vertices of the primes are distinguished diagrammatically from the other nodes by encircling.

Composing a flowgraph out of basic structures requires not only the corresponding basic structures – the *primes* – but also some operators for combining the structures. Essentially, there are two ways to construct 'new' flowgraphs from old ones, namely combining in sequence or nesting[12]. As already noted in [8] the two operators for the combination of primes, are defined as :

1. *Sequencing ($F_1 \bullet F_2$)*: Given two flowgraphs F_1 and F_2. The sequencing of these two flowgraphs is obtained by concatenating F_1 and F_2 by identifying the stop vertex of F_1 with the start vertex of F_2.

2. *Nesting ($F_1 \leftarrow F_2$)*: Given a flowgraph F_1 with some process vertex x, a second flowgraph F_2 is nested on x by deleting the unique arc leading out of x, identifying the stop vertex of F_2 with the vertex this arc led to in F_1 and identifying the start vertex of F_2 with x.

The process of *sequencing* is shown in figure 2 where two flowgraphs, F_1 and F_2, are sequenced and resulting in the new flowgraph F. The *nesting* operation can be seen in figure 3. The nesting grants the possibility to nest directly into another structure and is therefore the more general one of these two operators. The operator *sequencing* can be viewed as a special case of *nesting* onto the flowgraph P_n, where n is the number of primes (or flowgraphs) which are concatenated.

The reason why the composition is explained in such a detail is the fact that the decomposition of flowgraphs is just the inverse operation to the composition. Decomposing a flowgraph into basic substructures, namely *primes*, is the inverse usage of the above defined operators *sequencing* and *nesting*.

In figure 4 a program written in a language similar to PASCAL and the corresponding flowgraph composed of the respective primes is shown. (Other examples are presented in the Appendix). In order to derive objective measurement of the software the theory decomposes a program into its basic components by defining the respective inverse operations of *nesting* and *sequencing*. The output of the theory is a tree structure called a decomposition tree. The tree nodes either indicate a prime, in which case it is a leaf, or

---

[3]In the literature we can find another naming convention for these vertices as well: Vertices with an outdegree of 1 are called procedure nodes and vertices with an outdegree of more than one are called predicate nodes[8]. The disadvantage of this terminology is that the stop node z cannot be classified according to this scheme. As a consequence we would have to speak about three different types of nodes which can occur in the flowgraph, namely process nodes, procedure nodes and the stop node.

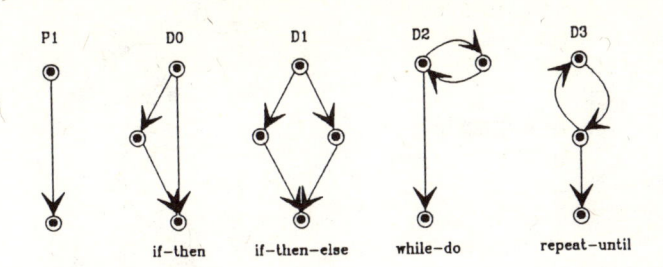

Figure 1: The basic set of Primes including the well-known Dijkstra Primes.

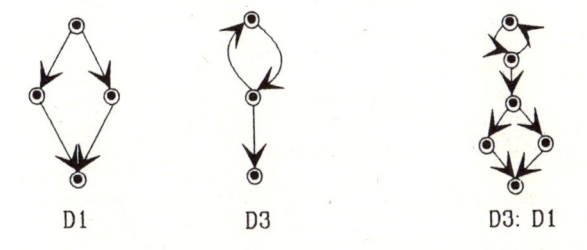

Figure 2: Sequencing of two flowgraphs F_1 and F_2.

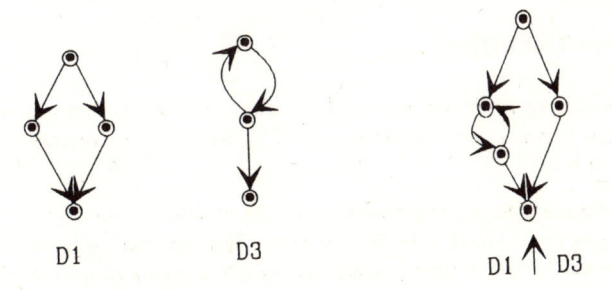

Figure 3: Nesting of the flowgraph F_2 into F_1.

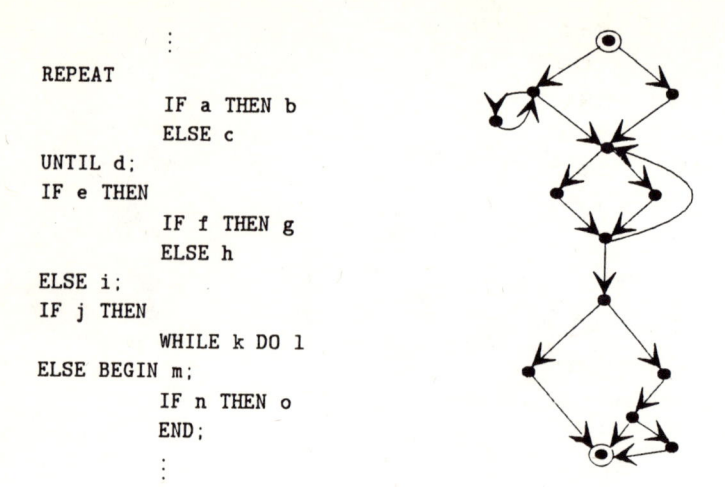

```
        ⋮
REPEAT
        IF a THEN b
        ELSE c
UNTIL d;
IF e THEN
        IF f THEN g
        ELSE h
ELSE i;
IF j THEN
        WHILE k DO l
ELSE BEGIN m;
        IF n THEN o
        END;
        ⋮
```

Figure 4: left side: Program fragment, right side: Corresponding flowgraph.

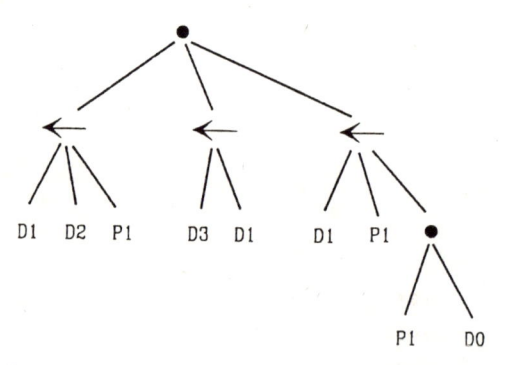

Figure 5: Decomposition tree belonging to the flowgraph of figure 4.

one of the sequencing/nesting operators (indicated by • and ←). The decomposition tree belonging to the flowgraph of figure 4 is shown in figure 5.

2.2 Metrics Definition

The flowgraph theory described in chapter 2 allows to define objective size and complexity metrics. These metrics are evaluated with the help of the information 'stored' in the decomposition tree.[4]

The metric is defined by the determination of the evaluation strategy for the used primes and the two operators sequencing and nesting. The approach adopted for handling the metrics in the way we do, is based on an axiomatic formulation of measurement due to [5]

---

[4]The decomposition tree itself is generated by decomposing the flowgraphs of the programs which should be evaluated.

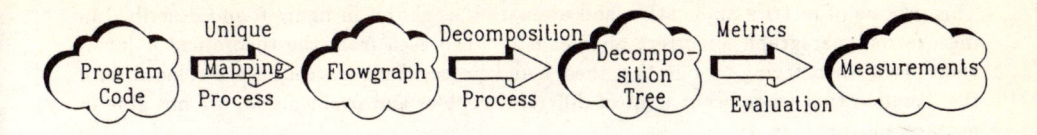

Figure 6: The process necessary when evaluating structural metrics in the flowgraph theory.

and [6]. So a metric ν can be expressed in three axioms:

- **M1** The function *M1* specifies the value $\nu(P)$ for to each prime flowgraph.
- **M2** The function *M2* defines how the metric values have to be combined whenever a sequencing occurs in the decomposition tree, i.e. defining $\nu(F_1 \bullet F_2 \bullet \ldots \bullet F_n)$ in terms of $\{\nu(F_j)\}_{j=1,2,\ldots,n}$.
- **M3** The function *M3* explains how the values have to be combined whenever a nesting occurs, i.e. defining $\nu(P \leftarrow F_1, F_2, \ldots, F_n)$ in terms of $\{\nu(F_j)\}_{j=1,2,\ldots,n}$ and $\nu(P)$.

As an example the definition for the McCabe [7] metric is given:

The flowgraph we want to decompose and afterwards evaluate is the one presented in figure 4, the corresponding decomposition tree is shown in figure 5.

M1: $\quad \nu(P) = \sum_{x \epsilon PN}(OD(x) - 1)$
where PN is the set of predicate nodes

M2: $\quad \nu(F_1 \bullet F_2 \ldots \bullet F_n) = [\sum_{j=1}^{n} \nu(F_j)] + (1 - n)$

M3: $\quad \nu(P \leftarrow F_1, F_2, \ldots, F_n) = [\nu(P) + \sum_{j=1}^{n} \nu(F_j)] - n$

Using the McCabe metric to evaluate the flowgraph of figure 4 decomposed in figure 5 the metric results in $\nu(P) = 7$.

3 Descriptor Theory

Using flowgraphs for storing control flow information and decomposition trees for the metric evaluation of a program written in any language (programming as well as specification language) in an objective way, as proposed in chapter 2, has some weak points and restrictions. In order to make the following points of discussions clearer, the process necessary for evaluating metrics when using the flowgraph theory is shown in figure 6.

The input for this metric evaluation is the source code of a program which can be written in both a formal specification language as well as a programming language. The structural information of this source code is mapped in a unique way onto the flowgraph structure. These flowgraphs are decomposed afterwards and this decomposition process results in the decomposition trees representing all the control flow information of the program which is necessary and useful for the evaluation of metrics. The metrics evaluation results in the measurements of the different applied metrics.

This process of metrics application and evaluation as shown in figure 6 and described in the previous paragraph is correct and realistic when seen from the theoretical point of view. But when trying to put this theory and process into practice we are faced with the situation that there occur a lot of different troubles and problems we are not able to manage and/or solve.

In principle, there are two steps where problems are occurring when using this evaluation process in practice. These are the unique mapping process and the decomposition process. But exactly within those two steps the influence on the resulting measurements are the most troublesome and important one. Within those steps the information necessary for the evaluation is handled in some way. Every problem occurring during this handling of the information can result in a loss of information. This loss of information can be a problem within the following metrics evaluation.[5]

When looking closer to the process of mapping the control flow information of a program onto the flowgraph structure we are faced with the situation that there are a lot of different possibilities within a certain language where this mapping process is not unique any longer. In principle, there are two reasons for the loss of uniqueness of the mapping process.

The information stored in the flowgraph is limited when considering that some constructs of certain languages cannot be mapped onto a prime in the way that the real control flow is represented in the corresponding flowgraph.[6] As a consequence, we must accept the impossibility of finding a unique mapping of *every* existing syntactical structure onto flowgraph structures without using artificial new primes.[2] E.g. for the mapping of a choice operator in LOTOS (which is similar to an if-statement) and a parallel operator we intuitively use the same flowgraph namely a D1.

The second process where problems may occur when using the flowgraph theory in practice is the process of decomposing the flowgraphs into their basic structures, i.e. the primes. When using the Fenton-Whitty theory described in chapter 2 and in [8] for mapping the control flow onto the flowgraphs we have to cope with the situation that new primes[7] are introduced. In figure 7 a small example demonstrating this situation is given. On the left side of this figure a code part written in a pseudo-code is given. The main point here is the usage of a direct recursion which is modelled in the flowgraph by a backwards arc to the startnode of the procedure. This very simple example of a source code was chosen on purpose to show that the generation of new primes is a process which happens quite often and not only when having special languages and/or tricky algorithms. The corresponding flowgraph for this source code is shown on the right side of figure 7.

Comparing the control flow of the source code and the control flow represented by the flowgraph we see that the mapping process itself is not to blame for any loss of information. But when decomposing this flowgraph into its basic structures we result in the existence of a large new primes, eliminating a large amount of valuable information (e.g. depth of nesting metric or structuredness metric). The result of the decomposition, namely the decomposition tree is shown in figure 8. The control flow of the code segment of figure 7 is now reduced and presented with the help of two different primes, where one of them being a large new prime. Evaluating this new prime according to a certain metric definition is

---

[5] Whenever information necessary for the evaluation of a certain metric is lost during the information handling process the resulting measurement will be, due to the not existent information, incorrect or totally wrong.

[6] In [2] p. 374 an example concerning the control flow of the LOTOS (Language Of Temporal Ordering) construct ≫ (enabling) is given. A mapping actually representing the control flow of this construct is not feasible.

[7] We call all primes which are not member of the set of Dijkstra primes as new primes.

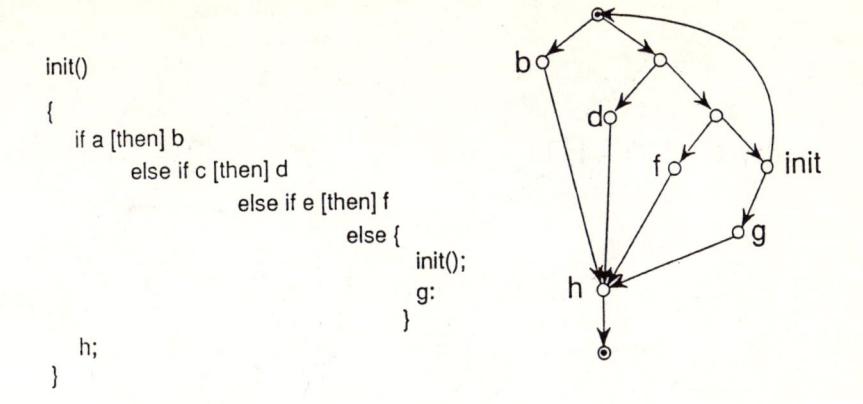

```
init()
{
    if a [then] b
    else if c [then] d
        else if e [then] f
            else {
                init();
                g:
            }
    h;
}
```

Figure 7: A source code segment and its corresponding flowgraph.

a process which is closely connected with the loss of accuracy. E.g. the depth of nesting metrics results in 2.

Taking these disadvantages into consideration we have to rethink the process of evaluating metrics based on the information provided by flowgraphs and decomposition trees, respectively. This process shown in figure 6 has in fact to be replaced by the process presented in figure 9. We are faced with the situation that a unique mapping of the control flow of any construct is not possible. Beside this inconsistencies, the decomposition process results in a decomposition tree which contains in most of the cases a high amount of new primes, which are quite difficult to evaluate in a correct way. As a consequence, we have at the very end of this evaluation process no measurements but estimations which are more or less precise.

As these disadvantages exist we have to abandon all hope using a flowgraph structure representing the logical control flow of a source code segment. If we omit the idea of using flowgraphs for mapping, some fairly important benefits will result. Just think of the inevitable decomposition of the generated flowgraphs. Decomposing a flowgraph has the complexity $O(n^3)$ (where n is the number of nodes) and is a quite complex and complicated algorithm especially if the flowgraph is allowed to have new primes, which is certainly the fact if using the Fenton-Whitty theory described in chapter 2 and in [8] for the mapping process. Another problem, occurring especially when using some very tricky metrics is the evaluation of primes not belonging to the well-defined set of Dijkstra-primes. So every new prime – primes can be generated very frequently especially when mapping specification languages onto flowgraphs – is rather troublesome to evaluate. The evaluation of new primes turns out to be a difficult job when considering the metric definition troubles of new primes. We know what the metric should evaluate, but it may happen that we can't get the essential and necessary information out of this prime. So measuring new primes seems to be rather an estimating exercise – in the sense of assigning approximate values.

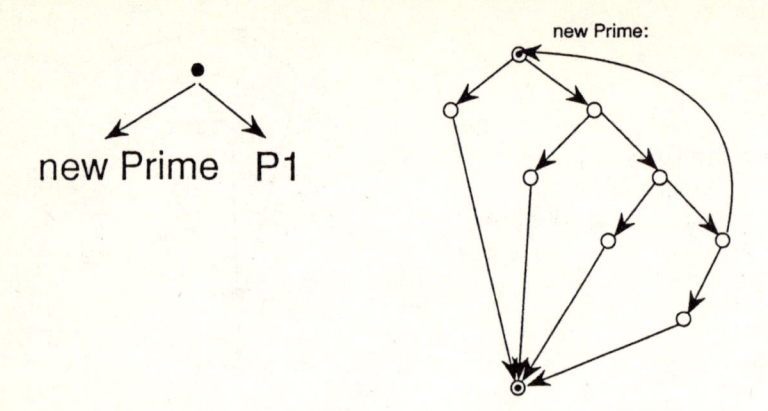

Figure 8: The decomposition tree which is produced when decomposing the flowgraph of figure 7.

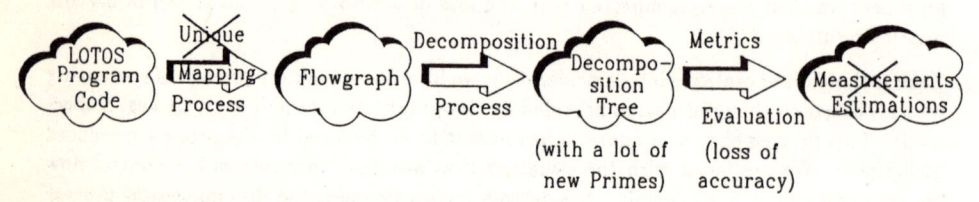

Figure 9: The process of metrics evaluation as existent when using the flowgraph theory in practice.

3.1 Definition of Descriptors

The attempt to improve the theory and eliminate the disadvantages, results in the idea to grant an additional possibility for storing information and data. Let us call this additional facility *descriptor*. At this stage of development it doesn't seem to be important to determine the exact syntax of these descriptors. First of all, we have to decide *what* kind of information we want to store. Only after this decision, we are able to develop the corresponding syntax needed for storing the type of information defined at the very beginning of this approach.

In order to reach language independent metric definitions the original idea of having a general model (the flowgraph) must be applied to the descriptor theory as well. This means that we have to start thinking about a way how to classify language constructs in the sense of finding out functionalities common to the languages. The first thought after introducing descriptors is the storage of all the information not represented by the flowgraph structure within this new data structure. But the more you realize how important – in the sense of representing information – these descriptors can be the more you think of storing *all* the information – structural, semantic and even syntactical – needed for metric evaluation in this structure. As a consequence the information (especially the control flow) represented by the flowgraphs of the Fenton and Whitty theory can be stored in descriptors when using our approach. So, in fact the flowgraph as an internal representation has been replaced by descriptors totally.

The main advantage of using descriptors is that they are much more exact and therefore more usable as metrics based on the flowgraph only. The main reason is that with the use

Figure 10: The process of metrics evaluation by using descriptors.

of descriptor much more information – not only about the structure of a program – can be used for the definition and evaluation of metrics.

In figure 10 we see how the introduction of descriptors has changed the process of metrics evaluation to come back to a unique mapping without generating new primes.

To be able to get most benefits out of the use of descriptors we have to use them as language independent as possible. This means we need a distinct classification, dividing similar programming language constructs into classes and subclasses. The classes are coarsely divided by semantic meaning, while the subclasses are a refinement corresponding to specific languages. Whenever the gain in important information is large enough, the descriptor is extended by an integer incorporating additional details useful for complexity measures.

The classes defined so far are shown in table 1 where the column C gives the ASCII letter used for the class. In the following text and the corresponding tables, S denotes the letter used for the corresponding subclass, and *arg* stands for the integer argument, explained in more detail in chapter 3.1.1. The tables 1 – 5 are only contained in this paper for offering more detailed information to the interested reader; for more details please refer to [9].

3.1.1 Descriptor Arguments

As mentioned we need to have even more information to use for more detailed metric definition. For each subclass there is the additional possibility for storing one integer argument together with the class and subclass information. As you can see in the table 2 – 5, not every descriptor has a number attached to it. Wherever the gain in important information is large enough, the corresponding descriptor is extended by an integer incorporating additional details useful for complexity measures.

In general a descriptor argument may be a positive integer. Only in one case a negative integer is used. The rule is that negative numbers are used only for constructs including an ELSE branch. So if the program contains an IF-THEN statement, the descriptor would be CC 1, but an IF-THEN-ELSE would generate CC −2, because this statement contains *two* paths, one of which is an ELSE. Even for descriptors requiring an argument, the number may legally be omitted, in which case *it defaults to 0*.

The following is a detailed description of the arguments as stated in table 2 – 5:

- assertions The number of assertions applied to the database record.
- excepts The number of exceptions generated or handled.
- exits The number of exits from the middle of the loop.
- fields The number of fields of the affected database record.
- keys The number of keys of the affected database record.
- params The number of parameters in this procedure/function call.
- passes The number of passes through a FOR loop, if that number is determinable at compile time. If that number is not fixed, a value of 0 seems appropriate.
- paths The number of paths in the corresponding syntactical program unit.
- processes The number of processes involved in this syntactical program unit.
- records The number of database records affected.
- signals The number of signals (messages, semaphores, i.e. information transport units) involved in this construct.

3.1.2 Class Control Transfer

This class covers all types of control transfer statements like GOTO, IF, WHILE, procedure calls, and recursion (for the interested reader its subclasses are shown in table 2).

- The "conditional" subclass contains all types of conditional control transfers, i.e. IF-THEN, IF-THEN-ELSE and CASE.
- The "unconditional" subclass covers all types of unconditional control transfers like GOTO, BREAK, EXIT, RETURN, CONTINUE, etc.
- The "loops" subclass covers endless as well as 'exit from the middle' loops.
- The "complex sequencing" subclass is used for sequencing with an additional complexity, like the enabling operator ($\gg$) in LOTOS. Plain sequencing on the contrary doesn't have a descriptor at all.
- We additionally mark a procedure call as direct or indirect recursion, if the call is to the procedure itself or to a procedure that in turn calls the current procedure respectively[8].
- Sequencing is a special type of sequential control transfer found for example in the LOTOS operator $\gg$ (enabling).
- A subclass which seems not to fit into the scheme of this class is the assignment. After all, we decided to regard it as a certain kind of sequencing.

---

[8] While direct recursion is simple to handle, indirect recursion is rather tricky and involves collection of huge amounts of semantic information. As it is impossible to find out indirect recursive calls in a single pass, we could make the descriptor CI optional.

C	class
C	Control Transfer
D	Database Operations
E	Exception Handling
P	Parallel Processes

Table 1: Descriptor classes (section 3.1)

S	arg	subclass
A	–	Assignment
C	±paths	Conditional control transfer
D	–	Direct recursion
F	passes	FOR loops
I	–	Indirect recursion
L	exits	Loops
P	params	Procedure call
R	–	REPEAT
S	–	complex Sequencing
U	–	Unconditional control transfer
W	–	WHILE

Table 2: Subclasses for the Control Transfer descriptor class (section 3.1.2)

S	arg	prime(s)	subclass
A	assertions	P_1	Assert
D	records	P_1	Delete
F	keys	P_1	Find
L	records	P_1	Lock
M	records	P_1	Modify
R	records	P_1	Read
S	fields	P_1	Sort
U	records	P_1	Unlock
W	records	P_1	Write

Table 3: Subclasses for the Database Operations descriptor class (section 3.1.3)

S	arg	subclass
G	excepts	Generation
H	excepts	Handling

Table 4: Subclasses for the Exception Handling descriptor class (section 3.1.4)

S	arg	subclass
B	±signals	Conditional Receive
C	processes	Choice
N	processes	start New processes
P	processes	Parallel
R	±signals	Receive
S	signals	Send
T	processes	Terminate processes
W	±signals	Wait for synchronization

Table 5: Subclasses for the Parallel Processes descriptor class (section 3.1.5)

3.1.3 Class Database Operations

This class covers different aspects of database operations; its subclasses are shown in table 3. The subclass Write should be seen as an insertion operation, i.e. creation of a new record, whereas the Modify subclass is meant to signify an update operation.

3.1.4 Class Exception Handling

This class covers any kind of exception handling; its subclasses are shown in table 4.

Generation covers all the forms of exception generation, like ASSERT and CAUSE in CHILL, whereas handling covers the different forms of exception handling constructs of programming languages, like the operator [> (disabling) in LOTOS.

3.1.5 Class Parallel Processes

This class covers all the different aspects of concurrency, parallel process execution, and interprocess communication; for detailed information please refer to table 5 where its subclasses are shown.

Start new processes and terminate process indicate birth and death of new processes. Send and receive capture all the means of interprocess communication like signals, messages and semaphores, while wait covers any other form of process synchronization.

Conditional receive denotes any receive action guarded by additional conditions, like the enabling signal in SDL.

3.2 Descriptor Tree

Because of the fact that we don't generate new primes the process of decomposing a flowgraph implicitly into a decomposition tree is not necessary any longer. So, instead of mapping onto flowgraphs one just has to generate directly the descriptor trees for the corresponding source code segments which also reduced the performance time.

In chapter 2.2 the metrics evaluation on the basis of decomposition trees was defined. As this process of defining metrics onto the information provided by decomposition trees has proved to be a very simple but powerful one we aim to reuse this definition theory

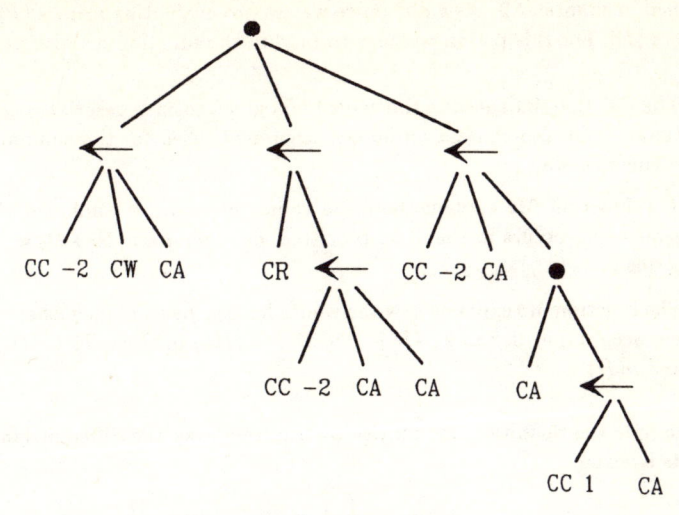

Figure 11: Descriptor Tree

again. Granting this possibility of defining different metrics in a simple way, we defined the syntax of the descriptor tree very similar to the syntax of the decomposition trees. This is possible only because of the fact that a descriptor tree is quite the same as a decomposition tree without primes.

Besides this facility of metric definitions, there are no longer troubles about the objectivity of the corresponding measurements. Up to now, there was a strong connection between the implementation of a metric and the language in which the programs which should be evaluated are written[9]. By introducing this additional level of abstraction we loosen this connection making it possible to define metrics in a language independent way.

Globally seen, we can state that the information contained in the descriptors of our descriptor trees is a superset of that held in the flowgraphs and the decomposition trees. Moreover, the descriptor theory is defined in a general way that enhancing the information which should be stored within descriptors is easy to do.

To make the usage of descriptor trees clear and obvious an example is given in figure 11. The descriptor tree shown in figure 11 is generated on the basis of the program in figure 4 and is therefore the counterpart to the decomposition tree in figure 5.

3.3 Metrics Definition for Evaluating the Descriptors

Of course we want to keep the possibility to define size and complexity metrics in an objective way when using the metrics definition strategy proposed in chapter 2.2. It is not obvious that the same axioms can be used for descriptor trees as for decomposition trees. But fortunately only slight modifications have been necessary. The structure of the decomposition tree being the basis of the measuring, still remains the same as well as the operators sequencing and nesting. As a consequence we still can keep on the strategy of defining the metrics in three axioms. The functionality of the functions $M1$, $M2$ and $M3$

---

[9] As a result two metric implementations done for one metric by different programmers resulted very often in having two different measurement results.

is explained in chapter 2.2. As a difference we are not evaluating primes (P) anymore, but descriptors (D). For this reason we have to modify the function definitions slightly.

- *M1* The function *M1* specifies the value $\nu(D)$ given to each descriptor. Please note that D can also contain an integer argument, used for the computation in a predefined way.

- *M2* The function *M2* explains how the values have to be combined whenever a sequencing occurs in the descriptor tree, i.e. defining $\nu(D_1 \bullet D_2 \bullet \ldots \bullet D_n)$ in terms of $\{\nu(D_j)\}_{j=1,2,\ldots,n}$.

- *M3* The function *M3* explains how the values have to be combined whenever a nesting occurs, i.e. defining $\nu(D \leftarrow D_1, D_2, \ldots, D_n)$ in terms of $\{\nu(D_j)\}_{j=1,2,\ldots,n}$ and $\nu(D)$.

As an example the definition complexity metric weighting the different kind of language constructs is given:

M1 :
$$\nu(D) = \begin{cases} 1 & D = CA \\ 2 & D = CL, CU \\ 3 & D = CR, CW \\ 1 + abs(arg(D)) & D = CP, CC \end{cases}$$

M2 : $\quad \nu(D_1 \bullet D_2 \ldots \bullet D_n) \;=\; \sum_{j=1}^{n} \nu(D_j)$

M3 : $\quad \nu(D \leftarrow D_1, D_2, \ldots, D_n) \;=\; \nu(D) + \sum_{j=1}^{n} 1.5 * \nu(D_j)$

The descriptor tree we use to analyze is shown in figure 11 the corresponding flowgraph and decomposition tree are shown in figure 4 and figure 5.

Applying this metric definition results in the complexity figure 32.25 .

To demonstrate the advantage and improvement of the situation we show in figure 12 the decomposition tree for the example used in figure 7 and 8. The direct recursion is reflected in the descriptor CD only and not responsible for generating a new prime any longer. So, e.g. the depth of nesting metric results is – as supposed – three.

In the following the depth of nesting metric is defined in full detail.

M1 : $\qquad\qquad \nu(D) \;=\; 0$

M2 : $\quad \nu(D_1 \bullet D_2 \ldots \bullet D_n) \;=\; \max_{j=1\ldots n}(\nu(D_j))$

M3 : $\quad \nu(D \leftarrow D_1, D_2, \ldots, D_n) \;=\; \max_{j=1\ldots n}(\nu(D_j)) + 1$

4 Conclusion and Future Work

One of the hypotheses of the COSMOS project was that it is possible to handle design and specification languages in the same way as it was demonstrated in the Fenton and Whitty theory resulting from an Alvey project for programming languages. It was by no means obvious that the theory was extentable outside the class of structured programming languages. In this paper it was shown how this extension could be done. As a result we got a much more general theory which can be apllied to languages like C, Pascal, Fortran but also to specification notations like LOTOS, SDL or Z.

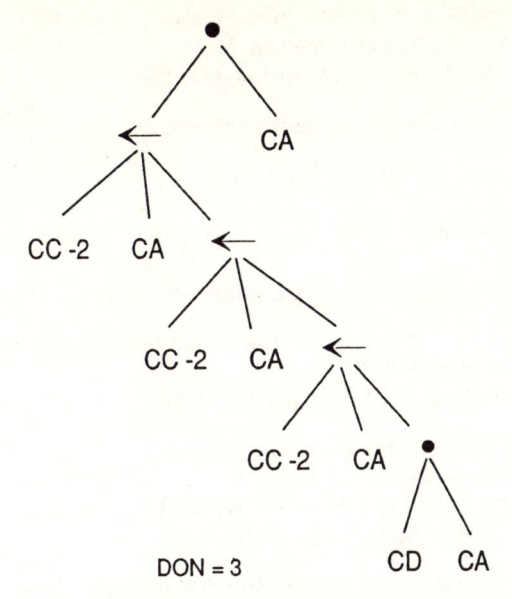

Figure 12: The descriptor tree for example figure 7.

It should be pointed out that applying measurements on formal representations was not state of the art at the beginning of this project. The work described here can be seen as a first step towards a new field of applications for measurements based on earlier software life cycle phases.

For the future this theory opens a new field for hypotheses how metrics can be used much earlier in the software life cycle. A class of questions covering the relations between different life cycle phases can be attacked in a much more structures and formal way.

References

[1] Structural Metrics and Cost Management – the COSMOS project
Whitty, R.W. and Lockhart, R.
Goldsmiths' College London SE14 6NW, 1990

[2] General Strategy for Mapping different Languages onto a Flowgraph Structure
Stainer, S. and Fuchs, N.
AQuIS'91 Proceedings, International Conference on Achieving Quality in Software, Pisa, pp. 369–389, 1991

[3] Introduction to Graph Theory, 3rd Edition
Wilson, R.J.
Longman Scientific and Technical, 1985

[4] The Flowgraph Model of Sequential Processes
Whitty, R.
Alvey Project, Alvey-SE69/GCL/004/01, ????

[5] A generalized mathematical theory of structured programming
Fenton, N.E., Whitty, R. and Kaposi, A.A.
Theoretical Computer Science 36, pp 145-171, 1985

[6] An axiomatic theory of software complexity measure
Prather, R.E.
The Computer Journal, vol 29, pp 340-347, 1984

[7] A complexity measure
McCabe, T.A.
IEEE Transactions on Software Engineering, vol SE-2, pp 308-320, 1976

[8] Axiomatic approach to software metrication through Program Decomposition
Fenton, N.E. and Whitty, R.W.
The Computer Journal, vol 29, pp 340-347, 1984

[9] Specification of the flowgraph modelling policy
Stainer, S., Michalopulos, N. and Fuchs, N.
COSMOS Project Report COSMOS/Al/WP1/TEC/9.3
TechForce BV, Leiden, Netherlands, 1990

[10] Assessing feasibility of formal specification language and model – Extension of the flowgraph-model
Fuchs, N. and Stainer, S.
COSMOS Project Report COSMOS/Al/WP1/TEC89011.4
TechForce BV, Leiden, Netherlands, 1989

[11] A Standard Representation of Imperative Language Programs for Data Collection and Software Measures Specification
Bieman, J.M., Baker, A.L., Clites, P.N., Gustafson, D.A. and Melton, A.C.
The Journal of Systems and Software, vol 8, pp 13-37, 1988

[12] Metrics and Software Structure
Fenton, N. and Kaposi, A.
Information and Software Technology, vol 29, no 6, pp 301-320, 1987

A   C-Program

```
{
msg_type = *(a + 3) & 0x0f ;
b() ;
switch (msg\_type)
{
    case A :
        send_err_msg(4, msg_type) ;
        break ;
    case B :
        if (c->d != h NULL)
            c->wread != PAD_RD_WCLR ;
        else
          {
            snd_clr() ;
            prf_clear(CLR_INV) ;
          }
        c->wclose != PAD_INV_CLR ;
        c->lu_state = PST_CLEAR ;
        if (c->param[PAR_4] && !(c->param[PAR_15]))
            e(TO_DATA) ;
        break ;
    case C :
        if (pad_size > 4)
          {
            if ((f = hb_padalloc(3)) == NULL)
              {
                pad_error() ;
                return ;
              }
            g = &f->buf_data[f->offset];
            if ((*(a + 4) == 0x08) && (*(a + 5) == 0x01))
              {
                *g++ = SET_MSG ;
                *g++ = 0x08 ;
                *g++ = 0 ;
              }
            else
              {
                *g++ = ERR_MSG ;
                *g++ = 0x02 ;
                *g++ = BRK_MSG ;
              }
            snd_padpk(f, Q_ON) ;
          }
        prf_break() ;
        break ;
    case D :
        pad_error() ;
```

```
            break ;
        case E :
            c->recall = i ;
            i = h;
            if (c->d != h)
                c->wread != PAD_RD_WCLR ;
            else
                snd_clr() ;
            c->lu_state = PST_CLEAR ;
            c->wclose != j;
            if (c->param[PAR_4] && !(c->param[PAR_15]))
                e(TO_DATA) ;
            break ;
        case F :
            c->recall = i ;
            i = h;
            if (c->d != h)
                c->wread != PAD_RD_WCLR ;
            else
                snd_clr() ;
            c->lu_state = PST_CLEAR ;
            c->wclose != j;
            if (c->param[PAR_4] && !(c->param[PAR_15]))
                e(TO_DATA) ;
            break ;
        case G :
            par_rw_msg(msg_type) ;
            break ;
        default :
            send_err_msg(1, msg_type) ;
            break ;
    }
```

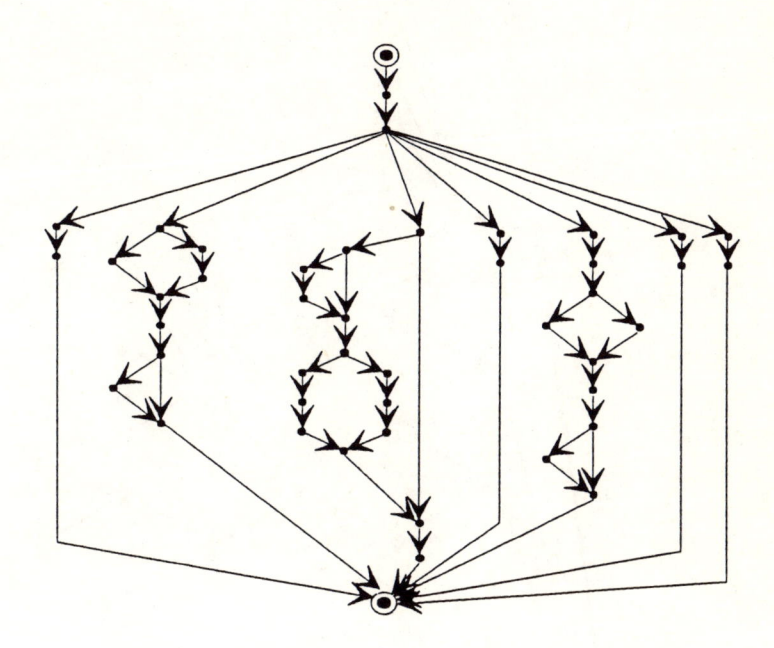

Figure 13: The corresponding Flowgraph.

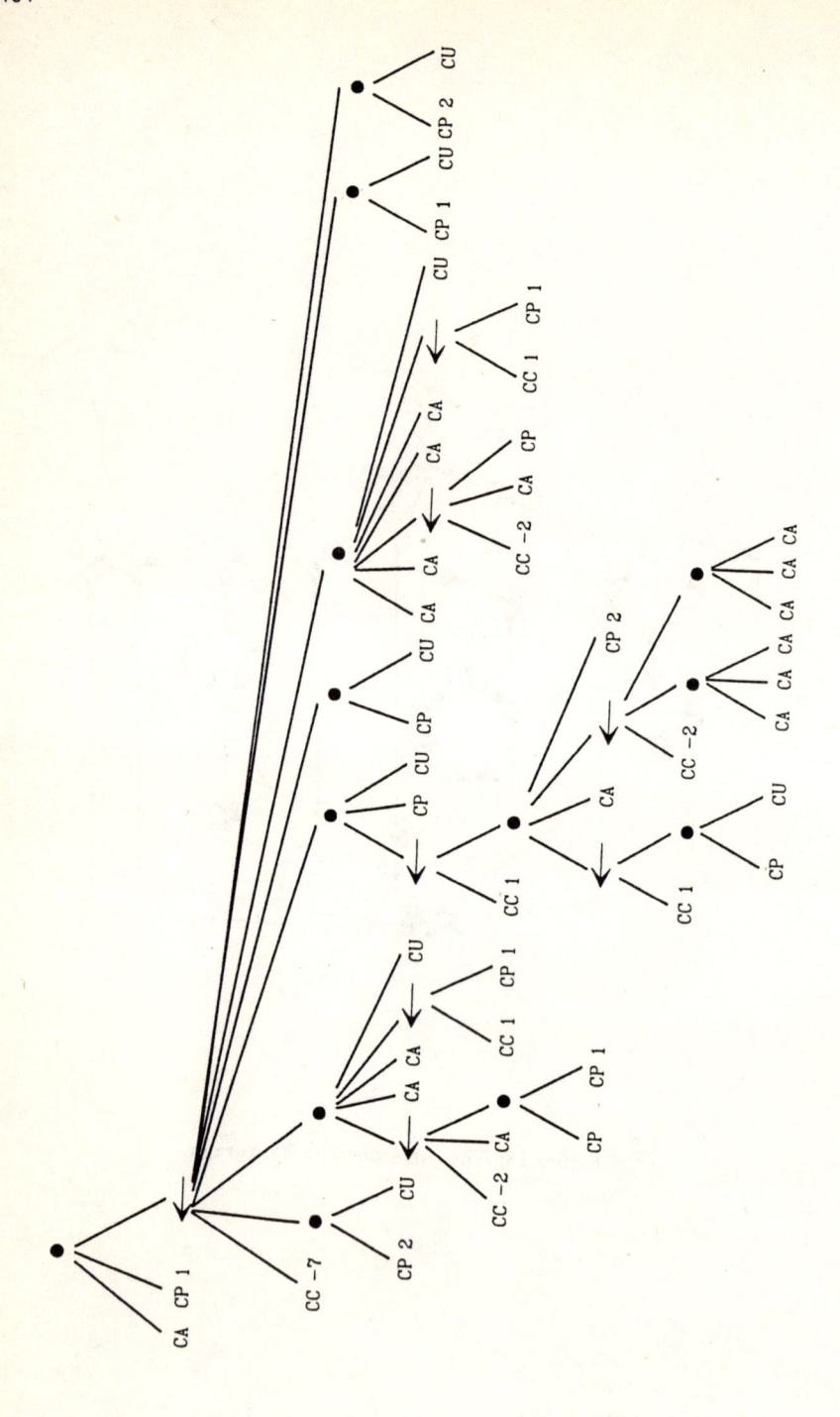

Figure 14: The corresponding Descriptor Tree.

B LOTOS-Program

```
process H[action,access](a : number) : noexit
:=
  action ! b ! a;
  access ! c ! a;
  access ! d ! a;
  access ! e ? z : bool;
  (
    [not(z)] ->
     access ! f ! a;
     access ! g ! a;
     access ! e ? z : bool;
     (
       [not(z)] ->
        action ! h ! a;
        access ! i ! a;
        (
          A[action,access](a)
            []
          B[action,access](a)
            []
          C[action,access](a)
            []
          D[action,access](a)
            []
          E[action,access](a)
            []
          F[action,access](a)
        )
        []
       [z] ->
        access ! j ! a;
        access ! e ? k ; number;
        action ! l ! a ! k;
        access ! i ! a;
        (
          F[action,access](a)
            []
          H[action,access](a,k)
            []
          G[action,access](k,a)
        )
     )
    []
    [z] ->
     action ! m ! a;
     access ! f ! a;
     access ! g ! a;
     access ! e ? z : bool;
```

```
        (
          [not(z)] ->
           action ! h ! a;
           access ! i ! a;
           (
             A[action,access](a)
               []
             B[action,access](a)
               []
             C[action,access](a)
               []
             D[action,access](a)
               []
             E[action,access](a)
               []
             F[action,access](a)
           )
           []
           [z] ->
            access ! j ! a;
            access ! e ? k : number;
            action ! l ! a ! k;
            access ! i ! a;
            (
              F[action,access](a)
                []
              G[action,access](a,k)
                []
              G[action,access](k,a)
            )
          )
        )
endproc
```

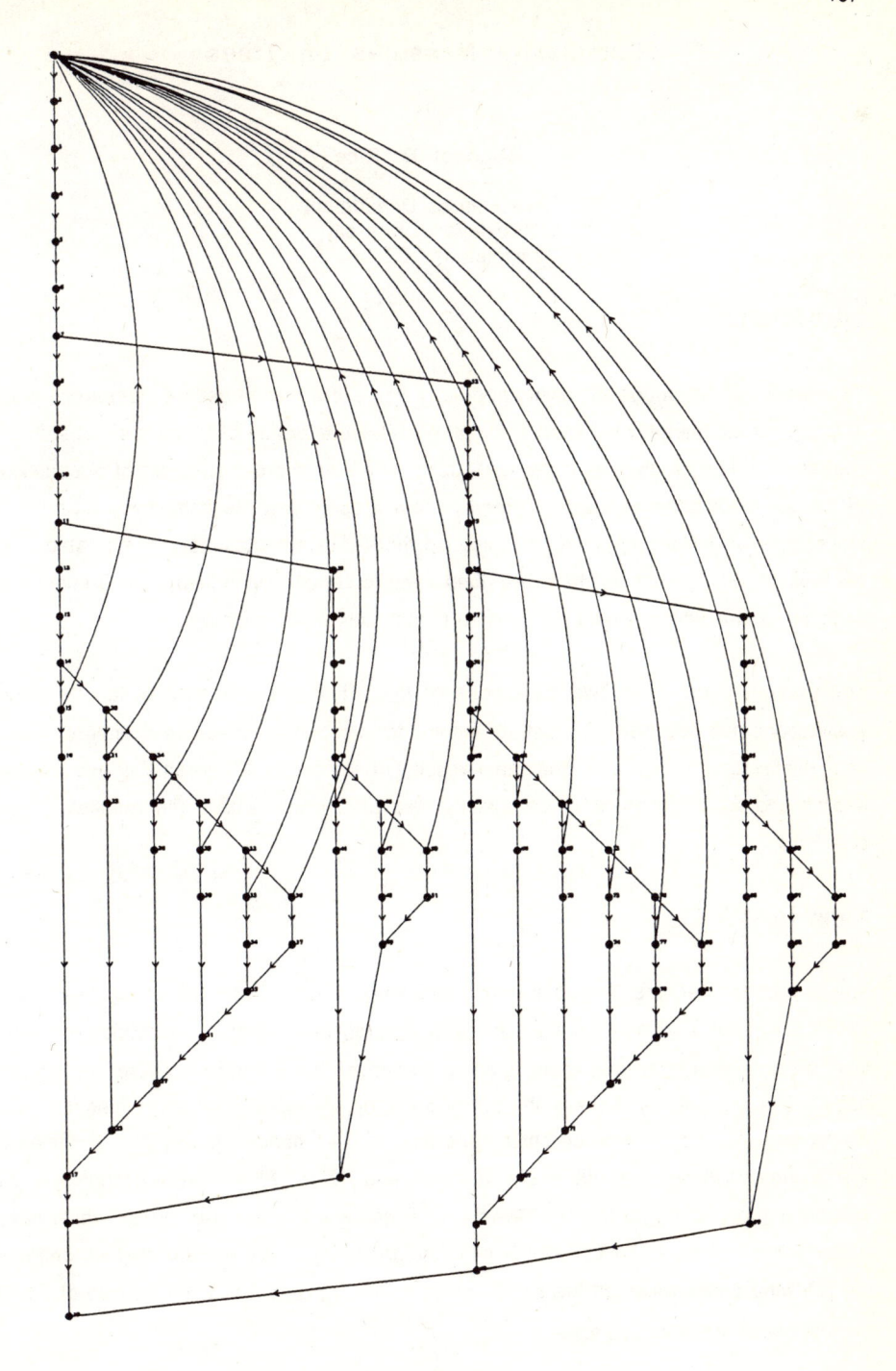

Figure 15: The corresponding Flowgraph.

Complexity Measures on Trees

by

Michael D. Rice

Mathematics Department
Wesleyan University
Middletown, CT 06459

Introduction

The work in [5] suggests a methodology for software measures research which emphasizes the interplay between a complexity measure and an order on a set of software documents. Frequently, this order is induced by a partial order on a set of abstractions of the set of documents, such as trees or flow graphs, and the complexity measure is induced by an order-preserving mapping on the set of abstractions. In a related vein, the work in [3], [4], and [6] has described specific complexity measures and suggested possible axioms which should be satisfied by any complexity measure.

The present paper uses two collections of <u>trees</u> T and T_b as models for the set of abstractions and describes two sets of axioms for complexity measures defined on these sets (Definitions 1 and 2). The main results of the paper (Theorems 1 and 2) give explicit characterizations of all complexity measures which satisfy the respective sets of axioms.

Notation

The symbol R^+ denotes the set of non-negative real numbers with the usual linear order $\leq_R$. The symbol T denotes the set of <u>finite ordered</u> trees, that is, the nodes on every level are totally ordered and there is no restriction of the number of children of a given node. The symbol T_b denotes the set of <u>finite binary</u> trees. For each integer $n \geq 0$, A_n denotes the linearly ordered chain consisting of $n+1$ nodes. Given $T \in T$, for each $x \in T$, $height(x)$ denotes the height of x in T and $height(T) = \max\{height(x) : x \in T\}$ assuming that $height(root) = 0$. Given $T \in T$ and $k \geq 0$, the set of nodes which have $height = k$ are denoted by $L(T,k) = \{x \in T : height(x) = k\}$. We assume that $\leq_T$ denotes the following partial order on the set T: given $S, T \in T$, $S \leq_T T$ if S is a subtree of T and the root nodes of S and T coincide.

For each pair S, T ∈ T and x ∈ S, S#$_x$T denotes the tree constructed as follows: the root node of T is identified with the node x and every descendent of x in the tree S <u>precedes</u> each descendent of the root in the tree T. In particular, if x is the root node of S, then S#$_x$T represents a natural "merging" of the trees S and T.

In general, @ will denote a <u>binary operation</u> on the set R^+. For later reference, we list the following properties which might be satisfied by @:

(0) 0 @ 0 = 0
(1) @ is <u>associative</u> : x @ (y @ z) = (x @ y) @ z for every x, y, z ≥ 0
(2) @ is <u>continuous</u> : lim(x_n @ y_n) = lim(x_n) @ lim(y_n) as n → +∞
(3) @ is <u>strictly monotonic</u> : (0 ≤ a < b) ∧ (x ≥ 0) ⇒ (a@x < b@x) ∧ (x@a < x@b)

Complexity Measures

The type of measures that will be discussed in this paper are special instances of the notion of a complexity measure defined in [5]. The basic idea is the following. Given a set D consisting of "similar" software documents with a preorder ≤$_D$, a <u>structural complexity measure</u> is an order-preserving mapping $m : (D, ≤_D) → (R^+, ≤_R)$. As a special instance of this idea, [5] discusses the situation where the document set D is represented by a a partially ordered set of "abstractions" $(A, ≤_A)$ and an abstraction mapping $abs : D → A$. Then any order-preserving mapping $m^* : (A, ≤_A) → (R^+, ≤_R)$ induces a <u>structural complexity measure</u> $m = m^* \circ abs$ on D.

For our purposes, the set A of abstractions will be represented by either T or T$_b$ and the mapping m^* will be denoted by **comp**. We will be interested in the following two definitions of order-preserving mappings **comp** defined on T and T$_b$, respectively.

<u>Definition 1</u>: A mapping **comp** : T → R^+ is <u>@-additive</u> if it satisfies the following conditions:

(a) **comp**(A_0) = 0

(b) Given S, T ∈ T, S ≤$_T$ T ⇒ **comp**(S) ≤$_R$ **comp**(T)

(c) Given S, T ∈ T and x ∈ L(S,n),
    comp(S#$_x$T) @ **comp**(A_n) = **comp**(S) @ **comp**(B)

(where B is the tree constructed by identifying the root of T with the leaf node of A_n)

Condition (b) states that **comp** is an order-preserving mapping on T. Condition (c) stipulates a type of combination formula. In particular, if 0 is an identity element for @ (x @ 0 = x), then for every pair S, T ∈ T, **comp**(S#$_r$T) = **comp**(S)@ **comp**(T), where r = root(S).

Condition (c) can be reformulated in a more direct manner if @ has a natural inverse operation. For example, if @ is the usual operation '+', then (c) can be restated as

$$\textbf{comp}(S\#_xT) = \textbf{comp}(S) + \textbf{comp}(B) - \textbf{comp}(A_n).$$

(The preceding equation was the original motivation for the definition of a @-additive mapping.)

<u>Definition 2</u>: A mapping **comp** : T_b → $\mathbb{R}^+$ is <u>@-recursive</u> if it satisfies the following condition: for every T ∈ T_b,

$$\textbf{comp}(T) = \textbf{comp}(T_L) \text{ @ } \textbf{comp}(T_R)$$

where T_L (resp. T_R) denotes the left (resp. right) subtree of T.

The definition of a @-recursive mapping is natural based on the familiar recursive structure of binary trees. However, it is not immediately clear if every @-recursive mapping is order-preserving. With additional assumptions on @, this fact follows from the characterization of @-recursive mappings provided by Theorem 2.

Main Results

The first result characterizes the @-additive mappings when the binary operation @ satisfies the additional conditions (0)-(3).

<u>Theorem 1</u>: Assume that @ satisfies conditions (0)-(3). If **comp** : T → $\mathbb{R}^+$ is a @-additive mapping, there exists a continuous strictly increasing function F : $\mathbb{R}^+$ → $\mathbb{R}^+$ satisfying F(0) = 0 such that for every T ∈ T,

$$(\%) \quad \textbf{comp}(T) = F^{-1}\left(\sum \{ w_k\ |L(T,k)| : 1 \leq k \leq \text{height}(T) \} \right),$$

where $w_k = F(\textbf{comp}(A_k)) - F(\textbf{comp}(A_{k-1})) \geq 0$, k ≥ 1.

Conversely, if **comp** is defined by (%), where $w_k \geq 0$, then **comp** is a @-additive mapping, where @ is defined by x@y = $F^{-1}[F(x) + F(y)]$.

Proof: By the main theorem in [1], if a binary operation @ on R^+ satisfies properties (1)-(3), there exists a continuous strictly increasing function $F : R^+ \to R^+$ such that for every $x, y \geq 0$, $x @ y = F^{-1}[F(x) + F(y)]$. Since 0@0 = 0, it follows that $F(0) = 0$. By properties (a) and (b), $0 = \text{comp}(A_0) \leq \text{comp}(A_1) \leq ...$, so $0 = F(\text{comp}(A_0)) \leq F(\text{comp}(A_1)) \leq ..$; hence $w_k = F(\text{comp}(A_k)) - F(\text{comp}(A_{k-1})) \geq 0$ for $k \geq 1$.

Define
$$\text{meas}(T) = F^{-1}(\Sigma \{ w_k |L(T,k)| : 1 \leq k \leq \text{height}(T) \}).$$

We will show that **comp**(T) = **meas**(T) for every $T \in \mathcal{T}$ by using induction on the number of nodes in the tree. If $|T| = 1$, then $T = A_0$, so by definition **meas**(T) = $F^{-1}(0)$ = 0; hence by property (a), **comp**(T) = **meas**(T).

Assume that **comp**(S) = **meas**(S) holds for every $S \in \mathcal{T}$ satisfying $|S| \leq n$. Suppose $T \in \mathcal{T}$ and $|T| = n + 1$. Choose a leaf node p in T such that $h = \text{height}(p) = \text{height}(T)$ and p is greater than q for every other sibling q of p. Let x = parent(p) in T and let S be the tree obtained from T by deleting p.

By the definition of #, $T = S \#_x A_1$, so by property (c),
$$\text{comp}(T) @ \text{comp}(A_{h-1}) = \text{comp}(S) @ \text{comp}(B),$$
where B is the tree obtained by attaching the root of A_1 to the leaf node of A_{h-1}. Hence $B = A_h$, so it follows that **comp**(T) @ **comp**(A_{h-1}) = **comp**(S) @ **comp**(A_h). Since $a @ b = F^{-1}[F(a) + F(b)]$, the previous equality can be written in the form

($) $\quad F(\text{comp}(T)) = F(\text{comp}(S)) + F(a_h) - F(a_{h-1}) = F(\text{comp}(S)) + w_h$

where $a_n = \text{comp}(A_n)$. By the induction hypothesis, **comp**(S) = **meas**(S), so

($$) $\quad F(\text{comp}(S)) = \Sigma \{ w_k |L(S,k)| : 1 \leq k \leq \text{height}(S) \}$

By construction, $|L(S,k)| = |L(T,k)|$ for $1 \leq k \leq h - 1$ and $|L(T,h)| = |L(S,h)| + 1$.

If height(S) = h -1, then $|L(T,h)| = 1$, so it follows from ($) and ($$) that

$$F(\text{comp}(T)) = \Sigma \{ w_k |L(T,k)| : 1 \leq k \leq h-1 \} + w_h$$
$$= \Sigma \{ w_k |L(T,k)| : 1 \leq k \leq \text{height}(T) \}.$$

If height(S) = h, then it follows from ($) and ($$) that

$$F(\mathbf{comp}(T)) = \Sigma \{ w_k |L(T,k)| : 1 \leq k \leq h - 1 \} + w_h |L(S,h)| + w_h$$
$$= \Sigma \{ w_k |L(T,k)| : 1 \leq k \leq \text{height}(T) \}.$$

Therefore, in either case, **comp**(T) = **meas**(T), which concludes the proof of the first part of the theorem. [ ]

To establish the converse, assume $\mathbf{comp}(T) = F^{-1}(\Sigma \{w_k |L(T,k)|: 1 \leq k \leq \text{height}(T)\})$, where $w_k \geq 0$ and $F : \mathbb{R}^+ \to \mathbb{R}^+$ is a continuous strictly increasing function satisfying $F(0) = 0$. We will verify properties (a)-(c).

(a): By definition, $\mathbf{comp}(A_0) = F^{-1}(0) = 0$, so (a) holds.

(b): If $S, T \in \mathbf{T}$ and $S \leq_T T$, then height(S) $\leq$ height(T) and $|L(S,k)| \leq |L(T,K)|$ for every $k \geq 0$. Since $w_k \geq 0$ and F is strictly increasing, $\mathbf{comp}(S) \leq_R \mathbf{comp}(T)$, so (b) holds.

(c): By definition, $a_n = \mathbf{comp}(A_n) = F^{-1}(\Sigma \{ w_k : 1 \leq k \leq n \})$, so

($) $\quad F(a_n) = \Sigma \{ w_k : 1 \leq k \leq n \}, n \geq 0.$

Suppose $S, T \in \mathbf{T}$, $x \in L(S,n)$, and h = height(T). Let B be the tree constructed by identifying the root of T with the leaf node of A_n. Then $|L(B,j)| = 1$ for $1 \leq j \leq n$ and $|L(B,j)| = |L(T, j - n)|$ for $n + 1 \leq j \leq n + h$. Therefore,

$$\mathbf{comp}(B) = F^{-1}(\Sigma \{ w_j |L(B,j)| : 1 \leq j \leq n \} + \Sigma \{ w_{k+n} |L(B,k+n)| : 1 \leq k \leq h \})$$
$$= F^{-1}(\Sigma \{ w_j : 1 \leq j \leq n \} + \Sigma \{ w_{k+n} |L(T,k)| : 1 \leq k \leq h \}),$$

so it follows from ($) that

$$\mathbf{comp}(B) = F^{-1}(F(a_n) + \Sigma \{ w_{k+n} |L(T,k)| : 1 \leq k \leq h \}).$$

By definition, $\mathbf{comp}(S) = F^{-1}(\Sigma \{ w_k |L(S,k)| : 1 \leq k \leq \text{height}(S) \})$; hence

($$) $\quad \mathbf{comp}(S) @ \mathbf{comp}(B) = F^{-1}(F(a_n) + \Sigma \{ w_k |L(S,k)| : 1 \leq k \leq \text{height}(S) \}$
$\qquad\qquad\qquad\qquad\qquad + \Sigma \{ w_{k+n} |L(T,k)| : 1 \leq k \leq h \}).$

By definition, **comp**$(S\#_xT) = F^{-1}(\Sigma \{ w_k|L(S\#_xT,k)| : 1 \leq k \leq \text{height}(S\#_xT)\})$. If $1 \leq k \leq h$, then $|L(S\#_xT,k+n)| = |L(S,k+n)| + |L(T,k)|$. If either $1 \leq k \leq n$ or $n+h+1 \leq k \leq \text{height}(S)$, then $|L(S\#_xT,k)| = |L(S,k)|$. Therefore,

($\$\$\$$)

$$\begin{aligned}\textbf{comp}(S\#_xT) &= F^{-1}(\Sigma \{w_k|L(S,k)|: (1 \leq k \leq n) \vee (n + h + 1 \leq k \leq \text{height}(S))\} \\ &\quad + \Sigma \{w_{k+n}|L(S,k+n)|: 1 \leq k \leq h\} + \Sigma \{w_{k+n}|L(T,k)|: 1 \leq k \leq h\}) \\ &= F^{-1}(\Sigma \{w_k|L(S,k)|: 1 \leq k \leq \text{height}(S)\} + \Sigma \{w_{k+n}|L(T,k)|: 1 \leq k \leq h\}).\end{aligned}$$

Hence, **comp**$(S\#_xT)@\ a_n = F^{-1}(F(\textbf{comp}(S\#_xT)) + F(a_n)) = \textbf{comp}(S)@\ \textbf{comp}(B)$ follows from ($\$\$$) and ($\$\$\$$), which establishes (c).

[ ]

Examples:

1. Define $F(x) = x$ and let $w_k = r^k$ for every $k \geq 1$, where r is a fixed positive real number. Therefore $x@y = x + y$ and @ satisfies properties (0)-(3), so by Theorem 1, a measure **comp** is @-additive if and only if

$$\textbf{comp}(T) = \Sigma \{ r^k|L(T,k)| : k \geq 1\}.$$

In particular, if $r = 1$, then **comp**$(T) = |T|-1$ and if $r = 1/2$, then **comp**$(T_n) = n$ and **comp**$(A_n) = 1 - (1/2)^n$, where T_n denotes the complete binary tree of height n.

2. Define $F(x) = 2^x - 1$. Then $x@y = \log_2(2^x + 2^y - 1)$ and @ satisfies properties (0)-(3), so a measure **comp** is @-additive if and only if

$$\textbf{comp}(T) = \log_2(\Sigma \{w_k|L(S,k)|: k \geq 1\} + 1).$$

3. One can prove that the mapping which assigns each tree T its height(T) is not @-additive for any binary operation @ which satisfies (0)-(3). However, the binary operation @' defined by $x@'y = \max\{x, y\}$ satisfies (0)-(2) and the following weaker form of (3): $(0 \leq a < b) \wedge (x \geq 0) \Rightarrow (a@'x \leq b@'x) \wedge (x@'a \leq x@'b)$. Furthermore, assuming that a measure **comp** satisfies **comp**$(A_n) = n$, $n \geq 0$, one can prove that **comp** is @'-additive if and only if **comp**$(T) = \text{height}(T)$.

The second result characterizes the @-recursive mappings when @ satisfies the additional conditions (1)-(3).

Theorem 2: Assume that @ satisfies conditions (1)-(3). If **comp** : $T_b \to R^+$ is a @-recursive mapping such that **comp**(nil) = 0, where **nil** is the empty tree, there exists a continuous strictly increasing function $F : R^+ \to R^+$ such that for every $T \in T_b$,

$$(\%) \quad \text{comp}(T) = F^{-1}[F(0)(|T| + 1)],$$

Conversely, if **comp** is defined by (%), then **comp** is a @-recursive mapping, where @ is defined by $x@y = F^{-1}[F(x) + F(y)]$.

Proof: By the main theorem in [1], there exists a continuous strictly increasing function $F : R^+ \to R^+$ such that $x@y = F^{-1}[F(x) + F(y)]$ for every $x, y \geq 0$. We will show that (%) holds for every $T \in T_b$ by using induction on the number of nodes in a binary tree. If $|T| = 1$, then since **comp** is @-recursive,

$$\text{comp}(T) = \text{comp}(\text{nil}) @ \text{comp}(\text{nil}) = 0 @ 0$$
$$= F^{-1}[F(0) + F(0)] = F^{-1}[F(0)(|T| + 1)],$$

so (%) holds.

Assume that (%) holds for every $S \in T_b$ satisfying $|S| \leq n$. Suppose $T \in T_b$ and $|T| = n + 1$.

Since **comp** is @-recursive,

$$\text{comp}(T) = \text{comp}(T_L) @ \text{comp}(T_R)$$
$$= F^{-1}[F(\text{comp}(T_L)) + F(\text{comp}(T_R))],$$

so applying the induction hypothesis to the subtrees T_L and T_R, one obtains

$$\text{comp}(T) = F^{-1}[F(0)(|T_L| + 1) + F(0)(|T_R| + 1)]$$
$$= F^{-1}[F(0)(|T_L| + |T_R| + 2)]$$
$$= F^{-1}[F(0)(|T| + 1)],$$

which concludes the proof of the first part of the theorem. The proof of the converse assertion that every complexity mapping **comp** defined by the formula (%) is @-recursive is left to the reader.

[ ]

Examples:

1. Define $F(x) = x + 1$. Then $x@y = x + y + 1$ and @ satisfies properties (1)-(3), so by Theorem 2, a measure **comp** satisfying **comp**(nil) = 0 is @-recursive if and only if

$$\mathbf{comp}(T) = |T|.$$

2. Define a binary operation @ by $x@y = \max\{x, y\} + 1$. Then @ is non-associative [for example, $(2@3)@4 \neq 2@(3@4)$], so Theorem 2 cannot be applied. However, one can show directly that a measure **comp** satisfying **comp**(nil) = 0 is @-recursive if and only if

$$\mathbf{comp}(T) = \text{height}(T) + 1.$$

3. Define a binary operation @ by $x@y = r(x + y + 2)$, where $r > 0$. Then @ is non-associative, so Theorem 2 cannot be applied. However, one can show directly that a measure **comp** satisfying **comp**(nil) = -1 is @-recursive if and only if

$$\mathbf{comp}(T) = \sum \{ r^k |L(T,k)| : k \geq 1 \}.$$

This is essentially the same additive complexity measure presented in the earlier examples based on the function $F(x) = x$ and the coefficients $w_k = r^k$.

Acknowledgement : I would like to thank Dr. Austin Melton and Dr. Thomas Gerasch for useful references and conversations about the contents of this paper.

References

1. Aczel, J., Sur les operations definies pour nombres reels, Bull. Math. Soc. France, v. 76 (1949), 59-64.

2. Fenton, N.E., <u>Software Metrics - a rigorous approach</u>, Van Nostrand & Reinhold, 1991.

3. Fenton, N.E. and Whitty, R.W., Axiomatic approach to software metrication through program decomposition, Comput. J. 1986, 29, (4), 329-339.

4. McCabe, T.J., A complexity measure, IEEE Trans. SE-2, 1976, (4), 308-320.

5. Melton, A.C., Gustafson, D.A., Bieman, J.M., and Baker, A.L., A mathematical perspective for software measures research, Software Engineering Journal, September, 1990, 246-254.

6. Prather, R.E., An axiomatic theory of software complexity measure, Comput. J., 27, (4), 340-347.

Multi-dimensional Software Metrics [1]

Robin Whitty
CSSE
School of Computing, Information Systems and Mathematics
South Bank Polytechnic, Borough Road, London SE1 0AA, UK

Abstract

Most of the program complexity metrics in the literature can be defined in terms of a parse tree of program structure. This is achieved by treating a metric as an 'attribute' calculated during the parsing process. In other words the metric can be calculated by passing data values up the parse tree towards the root. We propose that the complexity of the data type required for this purpose gives a measure of how complex the metric is. We give several examples and argue that the complexity of a metric relates to how the metric should be used in practice.

1 Introduction

Let us start by making a distinction between two kinds of software metrics: there are metrics which try to measure complexity in some structural sense; and there are those which merely count and classify things. Because we are in the domain of computing science we have recourse to the well-understood concepts of parsing and lexical analysis. Halstead's Software Science is based on lexical analysis metrics: counts of the quantity and variety of two classes of tokens. These counts can be called non-structural in distinction to measures that require program code to be parsed according to a BNF syntax. The 'fog-index' metrics of writing style are non-structural. A measure such as sentence length perhaps implies some kind of textual structure; but sentence length is in clear distinction to measures derived from a parsing of sentence structure according to the grammatical rules of natural language.

Starting with the basic distinction between structural and non-structural, our plan is to take things further by proposing a way to distinguish between different types of structural metrics. The goal of these distinctions is to help us decide when and how metrics should be used. There are times when a non-structural metric does not seem to provide enough information for us to understand what is going on. Conversely, our very lack of understanding may sometimes seem to undermine attempts to use sophisticated structural metrics. Our hypothesis is that there are degrees of sophistication within the domain of structural metrics and that it is useful

---

[1] Research supported in part by the Commission of the European Communities under ESPRIT project 2686 COSMOS and by NATO under Collaborative Research Grant 0343/88.

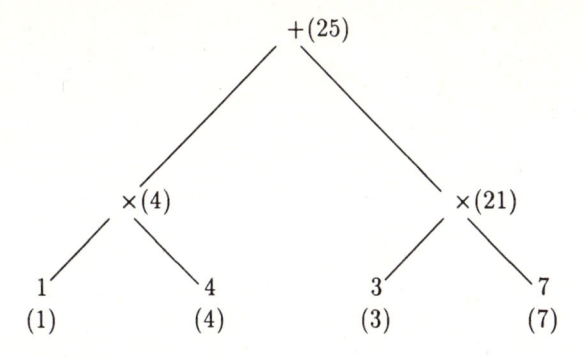

Figure 1: syntax tree for 1 × 4 + 3 × 7 with attribute values.

to be aware of these different degrees when choosing what to measure and for what purpose.

We shall rely on the concept of parsing to put our plan into practice. This seems a justifiable approach because parsing is fundamentally related to structure within computing science. Moreover, parsing is already equipped with its own measurement apparatus, through the use of *attribute grammars*. We shall impose a simple and natural classification on attribute grammars, and additionally show how structural metrics can be defined in terms of attribute grammars. The result is a classification of structural metrics which is also simple and natural; this gives us grounds for hoping that it may be of use in practice.

A quick example will illustrate the whole plan. Suppose we want to calculate the value of the arithmetic expression 1 × 4 + 3 × 7. Given the syntax tree of the expression (Fig. 1), this 'structural metric' is calculated bottom up: first obtain a value at the '×' nodes by calculating the products 1 × 4 and 3 × 7; then obtain a value at the root by taking the sum of the '×' values (4 and 21). The values being obtained are an 'attribute' of the parsing process. The attribute value at the root (25) is the value that we require.

Now suppose we want to calculate a different structural metric, the complexity of evaluating the arithmetic expression, that is, how many computational steps the evaluation requires. We will assume that naive arithmetic algorithms are used in which addition and multiplication of two n-bit numbers require $\mathcal{O}(n)$ steps and $\mathcal{O}(n^2)$ steps respectively. The calculation of our metric proceeds as before: the values at the leaves of the syntax tree and are used to obtain values at all the nodes up to the root. But the attribute involved is now more complex: to obtain the number of computational steps at the root we have to total the number of steps for the left and right subexpressions and then increment this total by the steps required for the final addition. To be able to do this requires a pair of attribute values: (value of expression, number of computational steps). The syntax tree with these attribute values is shown in Fig. 2.

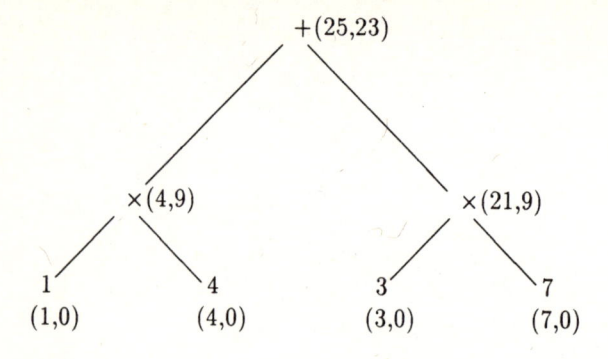

Figure 2: syntax tree for 1 × 4 + 3 × 7 with attribute pair values.

Our simple classification of structural metrics now becomes clear: the 'number of computational steps' metric is more complex than the 'expression value' metric in the sense that it requires a two-dimensional attribute instead of a one-dimensional attribute. The remainder of the paper will explore the implications of this idea for structural software metrics.

The idea of defining structural software metrics using attribute grammars is by no means new, although it has remained only implicit in the literature[2] [3,4,7,15,16,18]. Research into this area has been confined to metrics of control flow based on parsing *control flowgraphs*. We will stay within these confines because that is where the examples are to be found and it will help to keep the discussion coherent and concrete. We believe that a similar analysis could be applied to other areas of metrics research, for instance information flow metrics, once the translation to parsing theory has been worked out.

2 Flowgraph theory

The theory of control flow metrics is conveniently formulated using graph theory. Reference [19] provides a standard and accessible reference to such graph theory as we need, but we hope that our account is reasonably self-contained.

A *flowgraph* is a directed graph in which two nodes, the *start node*, and the *stop node*, obey special properties: the stop node has outdegree zero; and every node lies on some directed walk from the start node to the stop node.

The *indegree* and *outdegree* of a node are the number of edges which arrive at and leave the node respectively. Note that we use the term *walk*, as in [19], to mean a sequence of consecutive directed edges, some of which may occur more than once during the sequence. This corresponds to the usage of the term *path* often found in

---

[2]The NPATH measure of Nejmeh [14] is an exception, see Section 4.4.

Figure 3: D structures.

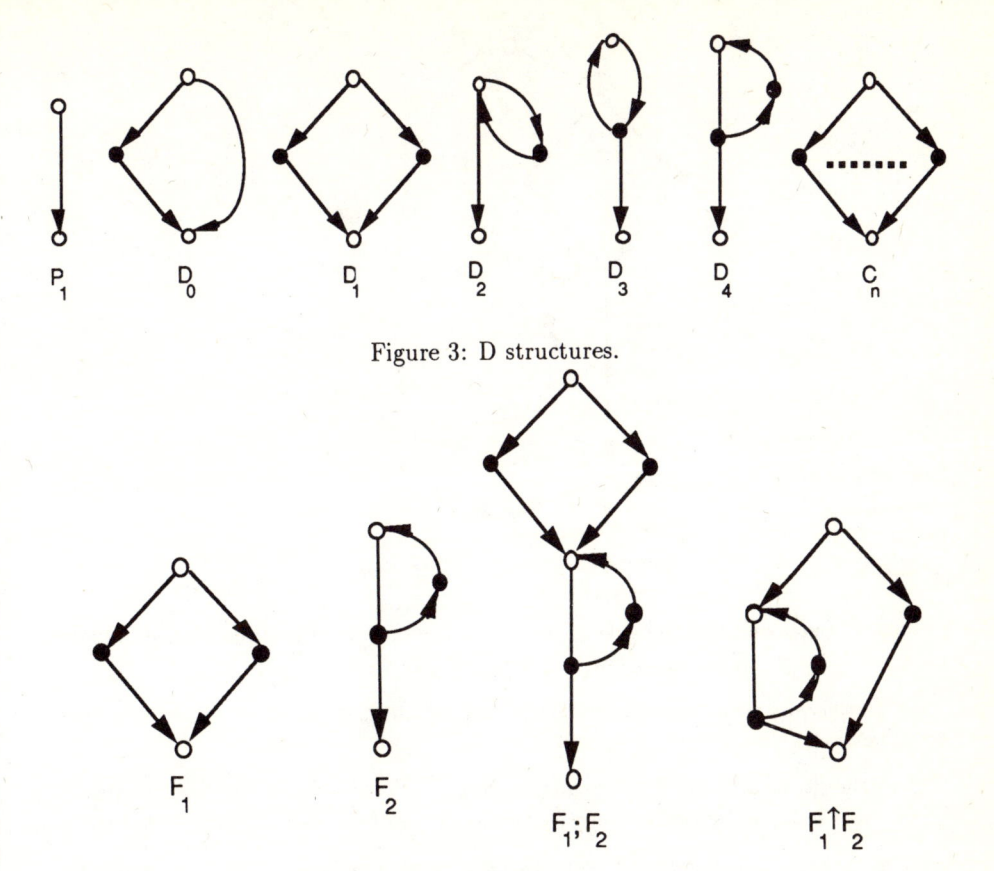

Figure 4: sequencing and nesting.

the context of control flow analysis.

We refer to flowgraph nodes with outdegree equal to 1 as *process nodes*; all other nodes are termed *control nodes*.

Fig. 3 depicts some flowgraphs commonly associated with the idea of D-structured programming [17]. They model some of the common control structures of high level programming languages.

Given two flowgraphs, F_1 and F_2, one can produce a new flowgraph $(F_1 \, ; \, F_2)$ by simply regarding the stop node of F_1 as identical with the start node of F_2. This is the process of *sequencing* flowgraphs (Fig. 4(a)).

Again, given F_1 and F_2, it may happen that F_1 has a process node v. In that case, we may produce a new flowgraph $(F_1 \uparrow_v F_2)$ by replacing the single edge leading from v by the whole flowgraph F_2. Thus, the start node of F_2 is identified with v and the stop node of F_2 is identified with the successor node of v in F_1. This is the process of *nesting* flowgraphs (Fig. 4(b)).

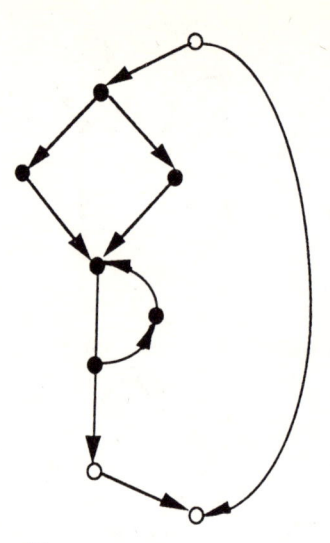

Figure 5: non-prime flowgraph.

In many of our examples the actual node v nested onto is of no importance. Where there is no danger of confusion we use notation like $F_1 \uparrow F_2$.

Prime flowgraphs are flowgraphs which cannot be built up non-trivially by sequencing or nesting.

Each of the flowgraphs in Fig. 3 is prime, but the flowgraph in Fig. 5 is not prime because it is built up by nesting into D_0 the sequence of D_1 and D_4: $(D_0 \uparrow (D_1; D_4))$.

Associated with any flowgraph is a *decomposition tree* which describes how the flowgraph is built by sequencing and nesting primes. Decomposition trees are just syntax trees which arise in the 'arithmetic' of flowgraphs in which the two operations are sequencing and nesting and the 'numbers' are prime flowgraphs. This will be made more explicit in Section 3. The decomposition tree for the flowgraph in Fig. 5 is shown in Fig. 6.

3 Defining metrics using attribute grammars

For our purposes a grammar G will consists of a number of *production rules* of the form $P \to \sigma$. The rule replaces a 'non-terminal' symbol P with a string of symbols σ some of which may be 'terminal'. Any non-terminal symbols in σ may be again replaced using a production rule. In this way G generates 'sentences' of terminal symbols. A standard example is a grammar whose sentences are arithmetic expressions[3]:

   1. $E \to E + E$
   2. $E \to E \times E$
   3. $E \to$ **number**

---

[3]the grammar is ambiguous but this is not important to our discussion.

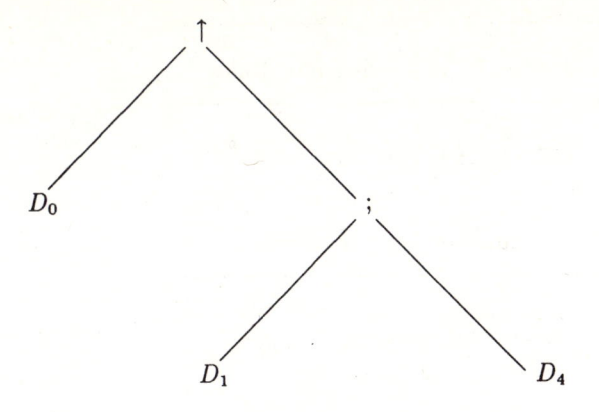

Figure 6: decomposition tree.

An example is

$E \to E \times E \to 1 \times E \to 1 \times E + E \to 1 \times E + E \times E \to 1 \times E + E \times 7 \to 1 \times E + 3 \times 7 \to 1 \times 4 + 3 \times 7$.

Given a sentence σ generated by grammar G we may parse σ to discover a sequence of replacements which achieves the generation. Each production rule in the grammar can have a number of actions or *semantic rules* associated with it and then we can ask that these actions be performed during parsing according to the sequence of production rules discovered. In Section 1 we used the example of calculating the value of an arithmetic expression during parsing: the actions were to perform addition and multiplication on attributes. In terms of the arithmetic grammar above these actions can be represented in terms of the production rules themselves. Thus, if parsing discovers that the rule $E \to E \times E$ has been used then the corresponding action is to "obtain the value of the expression by multiplying the values of the first and second subexpressions". Symbolically, the rule $E \to E_1 \times E_2$ has associated with it the action $E.x := E_1.x \times E_2.x$. If all the parsing actions are concerned solely with manipulating attribute values in this way then the production rules and their accompanying actions together form an *attribute grammar*[4].

A full attribute grammar for evaluating simple arithmetic expressions is given in Table 1.

We shall introduce the notation

$$\text{Expression Value}(E) \longrightarrow \text{Expression Value}(E)$$

to denote the sense "the value of expression E may be defined recursively in terms of the expression value". As observed in Section 1, the computational complexity of an arithmetic expression may be defined recursively in terms of two attributes, value and computational complexity. This is denoted as:

---
[4]A full treatment of this subject can be found in the classic text of Aho, Sethi and Ullman's [1], which is the source of our terminology and notation.

Production	Semantic Rules
1. $E \to E_1 + E_2$	$E.x := E_1.x + E_2.x$
2. $E \to E_1 \times E_2$	$E.x := E_1.x \times E_2.x$
3. $E \to$ **number**	$E.x :=$ **number**

Table 1: arithmetic evaluation.

Production	Semantic Rules
1. $E \to E_1 + E_2$	$E.x := E_1.x + E_2.x$ $E.y := A\beta(E_1.x, E_2.x) + E_1.y + E_2.y$
2. $E \to E_1 \times E_2$	$E.x := E_1.x \times E_2.x$ $E.y := B[\beta(E_1.x, E_2.x)]^2 + E_1.y + E_2.y$
3. $E \to$ **number**	$E.x :=$ **number** $E.y := 0$

(where $\beta(a, b)$ denotes the number of bits in the binary representation of the larger of a and b, and A and B are constants).

Table 2: computational complexity.

Computational Complexity(E)
$\longrightarrow$ (Expression Value, Computational Complexity)(E).

The attribute grammar which achieves this definition is given in Table 2.

Now let us carry out a similar exercise for flowgraph arithmetic. Again there are three rules in the grammar:

1. $F \to F; F$
2. $F \to F \uparrow F$
3. $F \to$ **prime flowgraph**

As it stands, this grammar is ambiguous. This worry can be removed by invoking the 'unique decomposition' theorem of [7] which, paraphrased in the terminology of grammars, confirms that there is a non-ambiguous grammar which generates the same language[5]. For our purposes it is not necessary to construct this grammar explicitly; rather we will present it in the form of a 'template' attribute grammar which conveys as much detail as we shall need:

Production	Semantic Rules
1. $F \to F_1; \ldots; F_n$	
2. $F \to P \uparrow F_1, \ldots, F_n$	
3. $F \to$ **prime flowgraph**	

Rule 1 denotes a maximal sequence of flowgraphs, so none of $F_1, \ldots, F_n$ are allowed to be replaced using Rule 1. Rule 2 denotes simultaneous nesting of flowgraphs into a prime flowgraph P, so P is not allowed to be replaced using Rule 2. We shall also allow parentheses in flowgraph expressions.

We are now ready to define an unlimited number of structural flowgraph metrics by choosing semantic rules for our attribute grammar template. As with the arithmetic grammar these instantiated attribute grammars will be classified according to the dimensional complexity of the attribute values in the semantic rules. The following sections present a range of examples with different complexities. We conclude this section with a well known example, McCabe's metric $\nu(F)$[13]. If $d^+(x)$ denotes the outdegree of node x, then $\nu(F)$ is defined by

$$\nu(F) = 1 + \sum_{x \neq \text{stop}} (d^+(x) - 1).$$

The attribute grammar demonstrating that $\nu(F)$ is one-dimensional,

$$\text{McCabe's } \nu(F) \longrightarrow \text{McCabe's } \nu(F),$$

is given in Table 3 and is implicit in [7].

Fig. 7 shows the attribute values for this grammar for the decomposition tree in Fig. 6.

4 Metrics defined using one-dimensional attributes

In this section we give four examples of one-dimensional metrics, whose dimensionality was at least implicit in the literature.

---

[5]There is another difficulty with the grammar. It is not clear what are the terminal and nonterminal symbols since prime flowgraphs can be sequenced or have other flowgraphs nested into them. This difficulty can be overcome by using the theory of graph grammars but for our purposes it is not necessary to be so rigorous; by appealing to the decomposition tree representation of parsing and only using the grammar in attributed form we can avoid any pitfalls.

Production	Semantic Rules
1. $F \to F_1; \ldots; F_n$	$F.x := 1 - n + \sum_{i=1}^{n} F_i.x$
2. $F \to P \uparrow F_1, \ldots, F_n$	$F.x := P.x - n + \sum_{i=1}^{n} F_i.x$
3. $F \to$ **prime flowgraph**	$F.x := 1 + \sum_{x \neq \text{stop}} (d^+(x) - 1)$

Table 3: McCabe's ν.

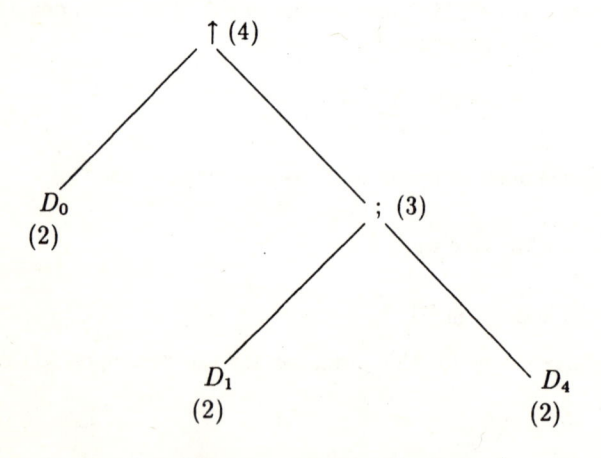

```
              ↑ (4)
             /    \
            /      \
          D₀        ; (3)
          (2)      /    \
                  /      \
                D₁        D₄
                (2)       (2)
```

Figure 7: calculation of McCabe's $\nu(F)$.

Production	Semantic Rules
1. $F \to F_1; \ldots; F_n$	$F.x := 1 - n + \sum_{i=1}^{n} F_i.x$
2. $F \to P \uparrow F_1, \ldots, F_n$	$F.x := P.x - 2n + \sum_{i=1}^{n} F_i.x$
3. $F \to$ **prime flowgraph**	$F.x :=$ number of nodes in F

Table 4: Number of Nodes.

Production	Semantic Rules
1. $F \to F_1; \ldots; F_n$	$F.x := \max_{i=1}^{n} F_i.x$
2. $F \to P \uparrow F_1, \ldots, F_n$	$F.x := 1 + \max_{i=1}^{n} F_i.x$
3. $F \to$ **prime flowgraph**	$F.x := \begin{cases} 0 & \text{if } F = P_1 \text{ (Fig. 3)} \\ 1 & \text{otherwise} \end{cases}$

Table 5: Depth of Nesting.

4.1 Number of Nodes

Most simple of all is a count of the number of nodes in a flowgraph

Number of Nodes$(F) \longrightarrow$ Number of Nodes(F).

The grammar is given in Table 4.

This metric will prove very useful in later sections, where higher dimensional metrics are produced by combining Number of Nodes with some other calculation.

4.2 Depth of Nesting

The depth of nesting of a flowgraph counts the height of its syntax tree, for example how many **if** and **while** statements are nested inside each other. The attribute grammar in Table 5 showing one-dimensionality,

Depth of Nesting$(F) \longrightarrow$ Depth of Nesting(F),

is again taken from [7].

Production	Semantic Rules
1. $F \to F_1; \ldots; F_n$	$F.x := \min_{i=1}^{n} F_i.x$
2. $F \to P \uparrow F_1, \ldots, F_n$	$F.x := \min(P.x, F_1.x, \ldots, F_n.x)$
3. $F \to$ **prime flowgraph**	$F.x := \begin{cases} 1 & \text{if } F \text{ appears in Fig. 3} \\ 0 & \text{otherwise} \end{cases}$

Table 6: Dijkstra Metric.

4.3 Dijkstra Metric

The one-dimensional attribute grammar given in Table 6,

$$\text{Dijkstra Metric}(F) \longrightarrow \text{Dijkstra Metric}(F)$$

yields 1 or 0 according to whether a flowgraph F is D-structured or not [3].

4.4 Testability metrics

An interesting class of metrics are those which capture testability in terms of the least number of inputs required for various kinds of flowgraph coverage. Several such metrics have been shown to be one-dimensional. Perhaps the NPATH metric definition given in [14] is the closest to our attribute grammar formulation: NPATH is a testability measure which is defined for D-structured programs in terms of the BNF syntax of the C language. Metrics similar to this are given by Bache and Müllerburg in [4] and are extended to general program structures in [18].

The elegant format used in the following example,

$$\text{Statement Coverage}(F) \longrightarrow \text{Statement Coverage}(F),$$

uses an ambiguous grammar, Table 7, and is due to R. Lockhart. A more complex format using the non-ambiguous grammar is given by Prather [16].

It was of particular interest to Prather [16] that metrics of this type require extra information about the left-hand argument of the '$\uparrow$' operator in Rule 2. Thus the attribute $F.x$ is calculated using $P.x$ and also information about P itself, namely, the location of v in P. Prather referred to one-dimensional metrics as 'hierarchical' and distinguished the subclass of metrics which do not require P but only $P.x$ in their calculation. He called this subclass 'recursive' and used the testability metrics to prove that it was a proper subclass of the hierarchical metrics.

Production	Semantic Rules
1. $F \to F_1; \ldots; F_n$	$F.x := \max_{i=1}^{n} F_i.x$
2. $F \to P \uparrow_v Q$	$F.x := A + B$
3. $F \to$ **prime flowgraph**	$F.x :=$ Minimum number of walks between start and stop of F which collectively pass every process node.

where A is the number of walks from start to stop counted in $P.x$ which do not pass v, and $B = \max(P.x - A, Q.x)$. Note that P and Q need not be prime flowgraphs.

Table 7: Statement Coverage Metric.

5 Two-dimensional metrics

5.1 The VINAP metrics

The only metrics to have been shown previously to be two-dimensional are the VINAP metrics of Bache [3]. This family of metrics was designed with Depth of Nesting incorporated as a factor to help guarantee that certain axioms for structural metrics would be satisfied (VINAP is an acronym for "Value Increases with Nesting as an Arithmetic Progression"). So an attribute pair is required, the first ordinate being used to record the Depth of Nesting, as given in Section 4, while the second ordinate carries the VINAP value:

$$\text{VINAP}(F) \longrightarrow (\text{Depth of Nesting, VINAP})(F).$$

The grammar for the 'product' member of the family is given in Table 8.

Fig 8 illustrates the calculation of the VINAP Metric for Fig. 6.

5.2 Prather's Example

Prather [16] observed that the following metric was not one-dimensional ('non-inductive') for distinct primes R and S:

$$\nu(F) = \begin{cases} 1 & \text{if the decomposition tree of } F \text{ has more occurrences of } R \text{ than } S \\ 0 & \text{otherwise} \end{cases}$$

Production	Semantic Rules
1. $F \rightarrow F_1; \ldots; F_n$	$F.x := \max_{i=1}^{n} F_i.x$ $F.y := \sum_{i=1}^{n} F_i.y$
2. $F \rightarrow P \uparrow F_1, \ldots, F_n$	$F.x := 1 + \max_{i=1}^{n} F_i.x$ $F.y := P.y \times F.x + \sum_{i=1}^{n}(F_i.y - 1)$
3. $F \rightarrow$ **prime flowgraph**	$F.x := \begin{cases} 0 & \text{if } F = P_1 \text{ in Fig. 3} \\ 1 & \text{otherwise} \end{cases}$ $F.y := \begin{cases} 0 & \text{if } F = P_1 \\ \prod_{x \neq \text{stop}} d^+(x) & \text{otherwise} \end{cases}$

Table 8: VINAP Metric (product version).

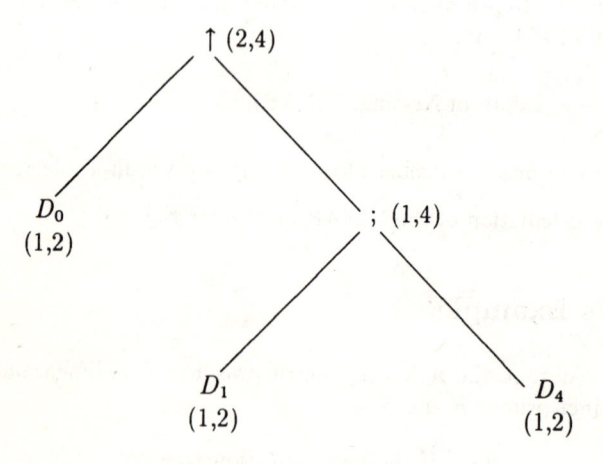

Figure 8: calculation of the VINAP Metric

Production	Semantic Rules
1. $F \to F_1; \ldots; F_n$	$F.x := \sum_{i=1}^{n} F_i.x$
	$F.y := \max(0, F.x)$
2. $F \to P \uparrow F_1, \ldots, F_n$	$F.x := P.x + \sum_{i=1}^{n} F_i.x$
	$F.y := \max(0, F.x)$
3. $F \to$ prime flowgraph	$F.x := \begin{cases} 1 & \text{if } F = R \\ -1 & \text{if } F = S \\ 0 & \text{otherwise} \end{cases}$
	$F.y := \max(0, F.x)$

Table 9: Prather's Non-Inductive Metric.

In fact, the metric is easily seen to be two-dimensional, by taking an attribute pair, the first ordinate of which is used to record the difference between number of Rs and number of Ss:

Prather's Non-Inductive Metric(F)
$\longrightarrow$ (No. of R - No. of S, Prather's Non-Inductive Metric)(F).

The grammar is given in Table 9.

Fig 9 illustrates the calculation of the Prather's Metric for Fig. 6.

5.3 Dunsmore-Gannon Average Nesting

Dunsmore and Gannon [6] have proposed an average nesting metric defined as the average depth at which a node is nested in F. This can be shown to be two-dimensional with the first ordinate recording the number of nodes:

Dunsmore-Gannon(F)
$\longrightarrow$ (Number of Nodes, Dunsmore-Gannon)(F).

The grammar is given in Table 10. Note that the x-attribute is calculated exactly as in Table 4.

Fig 10 illustrates the calculation of Dunsmore-Gannon for Fig. 6.

5.4 Harrison-Magel Scope Metric

The Harrison-Magel Scope metric [11] is a two-dimensional metric which captures the range of influence of each decision within a flowgraph. Again the first ordinate

```
        ↑ (0,0)
       / \
      /   \
     /     \
   D₀      ; (1,1)
 (-1,0)    / \
          /   \
         /     \
        D₁      D₄
       (0,0)   (1,1)
```

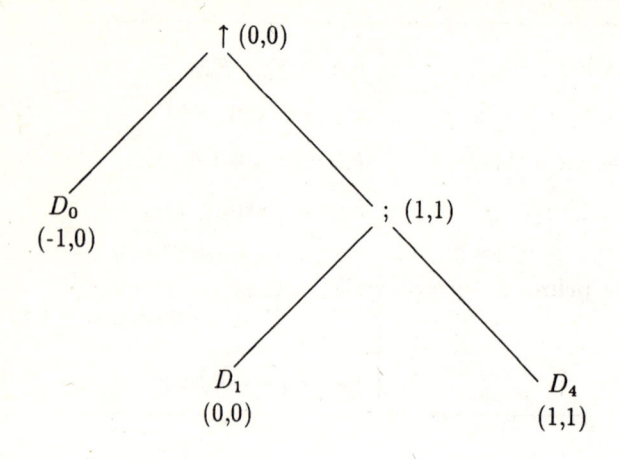

Figure 9: calculation of the Prather's Non-Inductive Metric for $R = D_4$ and $S = D_0$.

Production	Semantic Rules
1. $F \rightarrow F_1; \ldots; F_n$	$F.x := 1 - n + \sum_{i=1}^{n} F_i.x$ $F.y := (1 - n + \sum_{i=1}^{n}(F_i.x \times F_i.y))/F.x$
2. $F \rightarrow P \uparrow F_1, \ldots, F_n$	$F.x := P.x - 2n + \sum_{i=1}^{n} F_i.x$ $F.y := (P.x - 3 + \sum_{i=1}^{n} F_i.x(F_i.y + 1))/F.x$
3. $F \rightarrow$ **prime flowgraph**	$F.x :=$ number of nodes in F $F.y := 1$

Table 10: Dunsmore-Gannon Metric.

```
           ↑ (8, 7/4)
          /        \
         /          \
        /            \
      D₀            ; (7,1)
     (3,1)          /    \
                   /      \
                  /        \
                D₁          D₄
               (4,1)       (4,1)
```

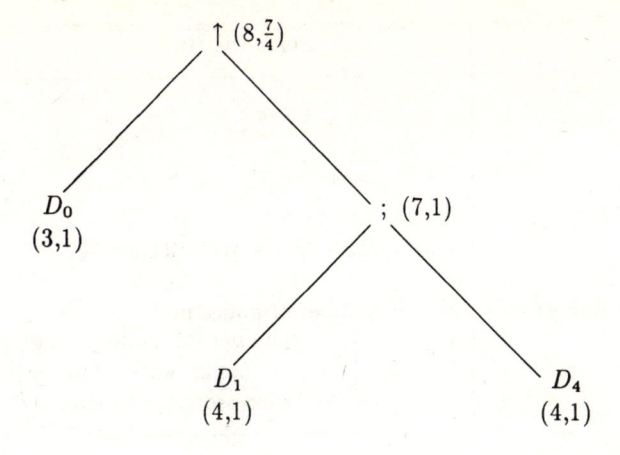

Figure 10: calculation of Dunsmore-Gannon.

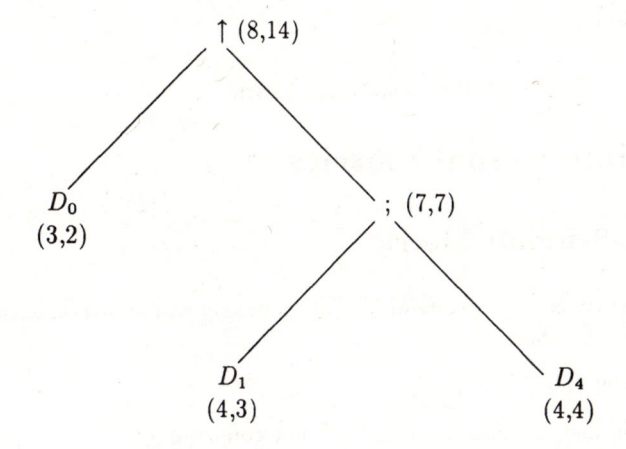

```
           ↑ (8,14)
          /        \
         /          \
        /            \
      D₀            ; (7,7)
     (3,2)          /    \
                   /      \
                  /        \
                D₁          D₄
               (4,3)       (4,4)
```

Figure 11: calculation of Harrison-Magel.

records the number of nodes:

Harrison-Magel(F)
$\longrightarrow$ (Number of Nodes, Harrison-Magel)(F).

In Prather's terminology this is a non-recursive metric and it is convenient to use Lockhart's ambiguous grammar format, as shown in Table 11.

Fig 11 illustrates the calculation of Harrison-Magel for Fig. 6.

A refinement of the scope metric is the Harrison and Magel Scope Ratio measure which is obtained by dividing the number of nodes of a flowgraph by its Scope Number. This is still a two-dimensional metric: the attribute grammar in Table 11 defines the Scope Number using Number of Nodes, so this grammar could be adapted to give the Scope Ratio measure.

Production	Semantic Rules
1. $F \to F_1; \ldots; F_n$	$F.x := 1 - n + \sum_{i=1}^{n} F_i.x$ $F.y := \sum_{i=1}^{n} F_i.y$
2. $F \to P \uparrow_v Q$	$F.x := P.x + Q.x - 2$ $F.y := P.y + Q.y + \gamma(P,v)(Q.x - 2)$
3. $F \to$ prime flowgraph	$F.x :=$ number of nodes in F $F.y := \sum_{d^+(v) \geq 2} \begin{pmatrix} \text{number of nodes lying} \\ \text{on some walk from a} \\ \text{successor of } v \text{ to stop} \end{pmatrix}$

where for process node v in P, $\gamma(P,v)$ denotes the number of control nodes in P having a walk to stop via v. Note that P and Q need not be prime flowgraphs.

Table 11: Harrison-Magel Metric.

6 Higher-dimensional metrics

6.1 The Gong-Schmidt Metric

The Gong-Schmidt metric is a composite of McCabe's metric and an averaged scope metric: $C(F) = \nu(F) + e$, where

$e = (e_1 + \cdots + e_{D(F)})/D(F)$,

$D(F)$ is the number of control nodes in F not counting the stop node,

$e_i = 1 - \frac{1}{d_i}$ and

d_i is the number of control nodes, not counting the stop node, in the subgraph defined by all walks between the i-th control node and its immediate postdominator.

(Recall that the immediate postdominator of a node v, ipd(v), is the nearest node to v, other than v itself, lying on all walks from v to the stop node of F).

$C(G)$ is a three-dimensional, non-recursive metric:

Gong-Schmidt(F)
$\longrightarrow$ (McCabe's ν, Number of Control Nodes, Gong-Schmidt)(F).

The grammar is given in Table 12.

Fig 12 illustrates the calculation of Gong-Schmidt for Fig. 6.

Production	Semantic Rules
1. $F \to F_1; \ldots; F_n$	$F.x := 1 - n + \sum_{i=1}^{n} F_i.x$ $F.y := \sum_{i=1}^{n} F_i.y$ $F.z := F.x + (\sum_{i=1}^{n} F_i.y(F_i.z - F_i.x))/F.y$
2. $F \to P \uparrow_v Q$	$F.x := P.x + Q.x\text{-}1$ $F.y := P.y + Q.y$ $F.z := F.x + \dfrac{\left(P.y(P.z - P.x) + \sum \dfrac{Q.y}{d_w(d_w + Q.y)} \right)}{F.y}$ where the sum is over all control nodes w having v between w and ipd(w) in P.
3. $F \to$ **prime flowgraph**	$F.x := \nu(F)$ $F.y := D(F)$ $F.z := C(F)$

Table 12: Gong-Schmidt Metric.

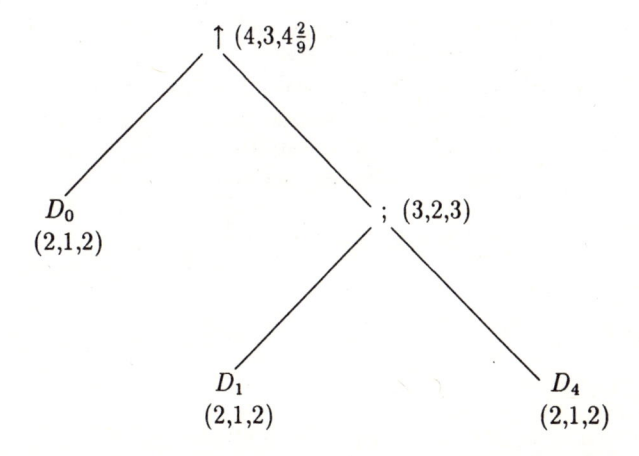

$\uparrow (4,3,4\tfrac{2}{9})$

D_0 (2,1,2)

; (3,2,3)

D_1 (2,1,2)

D_4 (2,1,2)

Figure 12: calculation of Gong-Schmidt.

```
              ↑ (1,2,2,14)
             / \
            /   \
           /     \
          /       \
         /         \
    D₀             ;  (1,2,1,11)
   (1,2,2,5)      / \
                 /   \
                /     \
               /       \
              D₁        D₄
           (1,2,2,6)  (0,1,1,5)
```

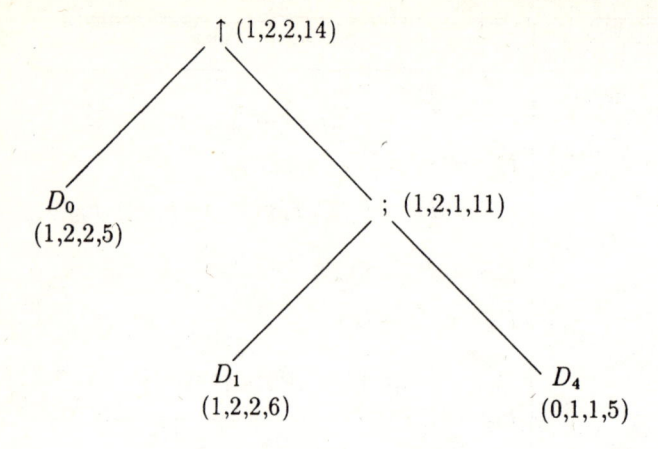

Figure 13: calculation of the Fan-in Fan-out metric.

If we only consider flowgraphs of maximum outdegree 2, then Gong-Schmidt becomes a two-dimensional metric because in this case McCabe's metric can be defined by $\nu(F) = D(F) + 1$.

6.2 Fan-in Fan-out Metric

The following 'information flow'-type metric has been proposed as a measure of complexity of dependency networks in project planning [2]:

$$\nu(F) = \sum_{\text{nodes } x} (\text{fan-in}(x) \times \text{fan-out}(x))$$

where $\text{fan-in}(x) = \max(1, d^-(x))$ and $\text{fan-out}(x) = \max(1, d^+(x))$ (where $d^-(x)$ and $d^+(x)$ denote the indegree and outdegree of x respectively). This is an example of a four-dimensional (non-recursive) metric in which local information about the in- and outdegrees of start nodes and the indegrees of stop nodes must be recorded for sequencing and nesting. We use $s(F)$ and $t(F)$ to denote the start and stop nodes of a flowgraph F respectively and define the following function on flowgraphs F:

$$\alpha(F) := \begin{cases} 1 & \text{if } d^-(s(F)) = 0 \\ 0 & \text{otherwise} \end{cases}$$

Then the metric is denoted:

Fan-in Fan-out(F)
$$\longrightarrow (\alpha, d^-s, d^+t, \text{Fan-in Fan-out})(F).$$

The grammar is given in Table 13.

Fig 13 illustrates the calculation of the Fan-in Fan-out Metric for Fig. 6.

Production	Semantic Rules
1. $F \to F_1; \ldots; F_n$	$F.w := F_1.w$ $F.x := F_1.x$ $F.y := F_n.y$ $F.z := \sum_{i=1}^{n} F_i.z + \sum_{i=1}^{n-1}(F_{i+1}.x(F_i.y - \alpha(F_{i+1})) - F_i.y)$
2. $F \to P \uparrow_v Q$	$F.w := \begin{cases} min(P.w, Q.w) & \text{if } v = s(P) \\ P.w & \text{otherwise} \end{cases}$ $F.x := \begin{cases} Q.x & \text{if } v = s(P) \\ P.x & \text{otherwise} \end{cases}$ $F.y := \begin{cases} P.y + Q.y - 1 & (v, t(P)) \text{ is an edge of P} \\ P.y & \text{otherwise} \end{cases}$ $F.z := P.z + Q.z$ $\quad + Q.x(d^-(v) - \alpha(Q)) - d^-(v)$ $\quad + Q.y(\text{fan-out}(w) - 1)$ $\quad - \text{fan-out}(w)$ where w is the successor of v in P.
3. $F \to$ **prime flowgraph**	$F.w := \alpha(s(F))$ $F.x := d^+(s(F))$ $F.y := d^-(t(F))$ $F.z := \sum_{\text{nodes } x}(\text{fan-in}(x) \times \text{fan-out}(x))$

Table 13: Fan-in Fan-out Metric.

If the fan-in fan-out metric is replaced by a sum of squares:

$$\nu(F) = \sum_{\text{nodes } x} (\text{fan-in}(x) \times \text{fan-out}(x))^2,$$

the dimension of the metric goes up to 5, since both in- and outdegrees need to be recorded for both start and stop nodes.

6.3 Remarks

By taking a composite metric formed from an arbitrarily large number of unrelated flowgraph parameters, we can produce artificial metrics of arbitrarily high dimension. We should stress that we would not claim to be able to prove that these or any of the metrics we have given are actually of an exact dimension. We have only demonstrated that fan-in fan-out, for instance, is *at most* dimension four; we have not eliminated the possibility that there is some way of expressing it in three dimensions. In fact to tackle this issue we would need some concept of 'acceptability of expression', because any n-dimensional metric could be expressed as a one-dimensional metric using Gödel numbering.

Another source of confusion would be the possibility of defining flowgraph metrics in a non-graph-theoretic manner. Thus McCabe's measure can be calculated by lexical analysis, by counting the number of decision statements and how many outcomes they have. We do not regard this a weakness in the concept of structural dimension; it is analogous to the well-known trade-off in compiler design between what information is captured by a lexical analyser and what is considered more appropriately left to the parser.

It is relevant to note that Prather did actually prove, in [16] that there are metrics which are non-recursive.

7 Dimensionality as a complexity ranking

The main issue in making practical use of product metrics is the interpretation of observations. If a range of metric values are represented as a box plot [5], or if two metrics are plotted against each other, then outliers can be used to flag unusual modules. In some circumstances this may be useful even though no interpretation can be attached to the occurrence of an outlier. More often, we need at least some intuition to guide us in choosing which metrics to look at, otherwise 'rogue' modules may be flagged almost at random and all our effort may be spent in making unnecessary checks.

The dimension of a metric seems to relate in some way to how easy it is to interpret the metric. As a convenient convention, we will refer to lexical analysis metrics as having zero dimension, writing, for example,

$$\text{Halstead's Effort}(P) \longrightarrow P.$$

Plotting two zero-dimensional metrics against each other gives results which offer only trivial interpretations: "this module has an unusual number of different operators relative to its size", or "the vocabulary tails off against size according to a log-type curve". By contrast, plotting two high dimensional metrics against each other, say, fan-in fan-out against the Gong-Schmidt metric, is not likely to lead to any more sophisticated level of interpretation. This is despite the fact that very subtle structural relationships are being displayed.

The higher dimensional metrics have generally been devised to overcome obvious short-comings in the simpler metrics. For instance, Depth of Nesting overcomes the problem that McCabe's metric fails to distinguish between 'flat' and 'convoluted' logic having the same number of decisions; the Dunsmore-Gannon average depth of nesting removes the danger that one small area of high nesting may give a false impression about a program as a whole. The concept of dimension helps to quantify this increase in sophistication. We are suggesting that it can also warn of a corresponding decrease in interpretability.

The simple lesson to be inferred from a relationship between dimension and interpretability is that use of a high dimension metric should be supported by a correspondingly high level of understanding of the programming process: to use a high dimension metric you need a correspondingly elaborate theory based on a large body of experience about the way in which the metric relates its parameters. We do not expect zero-dimensional metrics to give rise to a deep theory of programming; it is probably justified to say that Halstead's Software Science is a little grandiose for the very simple metrics on which it is built. But it is even more justified to criticise the use of, say, a three-dimensional metric *without* a fairly elaborate theoretical and empirical understanding of the attributes it purports to address.

The preceding discussion has been couched in rather vague terms (perhaps this is necessarily the case since, until software engineering is equipped with well-defined measurables, we cannot express ourselves other than vaguely!). We can make things a little more precise by making the distinction between *internal* and *external* attributes of software products, as discussed by Fenton [8] and Fenton and Kitchenham [9]. Internal attributes are those which can be measured purely in terms of the product itself. External attributes can only be measured with respect to how the product relates to its environment — its development process, its application domain, its users and so on. For example, size, structuredness and modularity, when precisely defined, are internal measures. The 'ilities': reliability, testability, maintainability and so on, are external measures. Software metrics research generally is motivated by the assumption that external measures, which are the ones we are ultimately interested in, can be captured through indirect measurement using internal measures.

We can now make our proposals regarding metric dimension more precise:

1. An internal flowgraph attribute can be measured by a metric having a well-defined dimension.

2. High-dimensional metrics are capable of measuring more sophisticated internal attributes than low-dimensional metrics.

3. High-dimensional metrics capture internal attributes which are more difficult to understand than low-dimensional metrics.

4. High-dimensional metrics are more difficult to relate to external attributes than low-dimensional metrics.

8 Hypotheses

Proposals 1—4 in Section 7 are still ill-defined and vague. To avoid the criticism that we are offering no tangible contribution to software metrics, we have hit on the idea of summarising our proposals in terms of a list of concrete, *refutable* hypotheses:

Hypothesis One: applicability of attribute grammars. Every metric defined for flowgraphs has a finite upper bound on its dimension.

Hypothesis One is more in the nature of a theoretical conjecture. It is 'hypothetical' in the sense that it probably cannot be confirmed (even, as we mentioned at the end of Section 6, for individual metrics), but should be possible to refute, perhaps by a diagonalisation construction.

In the following hypotheses, let $m_1, m_2, \ldots$ by any finite collection of flowgraph metrics ranked in order of increasing dimension.

Hypothesis Two: dimensionality captures sophistication. The collection of metrics $m_1, m_2, \ldots$ is given to a sample of software engineers who are asked to find two flowgraphs for each m_i which have the same metric value but different *subjective* complexity. Then the time to find such flowgraph pairs will increase with dimensionality.

Hypothesis Three: dimensionality relates to complexity. For some sample of modules, and for each m_i, draw a box-plot or histogram of the value of m_i for the module's flowgraph. Now ask a sample of software engineers to nominate which flowgraphs if any they would estimate to have unusually high or low values of m_i. Then the number of correctly identified outliers will decrease with dimensionality.

Hypothesis Four: dimensionality relates to interpretability. As for Hypothesis Three, but this time the software engineers' task is to

1. nominate an interpretation of each m_i in terms of some external attribute of the modules,
2. nominate which modules if any they would estimate to have unusually high or low values of the nominated external attribute measures.

Then the number of correctly identified outliers will decrease with dimensionality.

We believe it would be perfectly fair to refute the latter three hypotheses on the basis of experiments using students. This is often not valid in experiments which try to refute a link between some internal and external attributes of software. But in Hypotheses 2–4 there are no implications about the industrial relevance of the attributes.

9 Concluding remarks

We have shown that flowgraph metrics can generally be expressed within the theory of attribute grammars. This classifies them according to the dimensionality of the attribute values involved.

Our method has a practical implication for metrics tools. A tool which is based on a parser for the grammar in Section 3 will (according to Hypothesis One) have unlimited flexibility in terms of the metrics it can calculate. All that is required is a YACC-like notation for expressing attributes and a small amount of effort to find a way of expressing a new metric within the attribute grammar. The QUALMS tool [12] is an example of this approach and QUALMS has recently been provided with a general purpose interpreted attribute notation for one-dimensional recursive metrics by British Telecom Research Labs as part of ESPRIT II Project 2686 (COSMOS). For a tool not based on the attribute grammar to incorporate a totally new two- or three-dimensional metric would probably require a fair amount of adaptive maintenance at the code level.

The main motivation for this paper, however, was to provoke thought on the relationship between dimensionality and interpretability and usefulness of metrics. If we have not offered anything concrete on this subject, we have at any rate proposed a number of specific hypothesis which are susceptible to refutation. These may form a basis for further investigation of structural measurement.

Acknowledgement

The presentation of flowgraph theory in Section 2 is largely due to Bob Lockhart of Goldsmiths' College University of London. The paper has also benefited from the comments and suggestions of members of the Grubstake Group: Jim Bieman (Colorado State University), Dave Gustafson and Austin Melton (Kansas State University) and Norman Fenton (City University, London), and of Dr Horst Zuse of the Technical University of Berlin.

References

[1] Aho, A. V., Sethi, R. and Ullman, J. D., *Compilers. Principles, Techniques and Tools*, Addison-Wesley Publishing Company, 1986.

[2] Appiah, S., *Complexity of Project Planning Structures*, MSc Thesis, CSSE, South Bank Polytechnic, Borough Road, London SE1 0AA, 1990.

[3] Bache, R., Structural metrication within an axiomatic framework, in *Structure-based Software Metrics, Collected Papers*, (Elliott, J. J. et al, eds), CSSE, South Bank Polytechnic, Borough Road, London SE1 0AA, UK, 1988.

[4] Bache, R., and Müllerburg, M. Measures of testability as a basis for quality assurance, *Software Engineering Journal*, vol. 5, no. 2, pp. 86–92, 1990.

[5] Bowerman, B. L. and O'Connell, R. T., *Linear Statistical Models: an Applied Approach, 2nd Ed.*, PWS-Kent Publishing Co., Boston, 1990.

[6] Dunsmore, H. E. and Gannon, J. D., Analysis of the effects of programming factors on programming effort, *The Journal of Systems and Software*, vol. 1, no. 2, pp. 141–153, 1980.

[7] Fenton, N. E. and Whitty, R. W., Axiomatic approach to software metrication, *The Computer Journal*, vol. 29, pp. 330–339, 1986.

[8] Fenton, N. E., Software metrics: theory, tools and validation, *Software Engineering Journal*, vol. 5, no. 1, pp. 65–78, 1990.

[9] Fenton, N. E. and Kitchenham, B., Software metrics validation, in *Proc. Dundee Software Quality Workshop, July 1990*, Dundee Institute of Technology, Bell Street, Dundee DD1 1HG, UK, pp. 15–35, 1990.

[10] Gong, H. and Schmidt, M., A complexity measure based on selection and nesting, *ACM SIGMETRICS, Performance Eval. Rev.*, vol. 13, no. 1, pp. 14–19, 1985

[11] Harrison, W. A. and Magel, K. I., A complexity measure based on nesting level, *ACM SIGPLAN Notices*, 16 (3), pp. 63–74, 1981.

[12] Leelasena, L. and Whitty, R., Structure-based software metrics using the QUALMS tool, Internal Report, CSSE, South Bank Polytechnic, Borough Road, London SE1 0AA, UK, 1990.

[13] McCabe, T., A complexity measure, *IEEE Transactions on Software Engineering*, vol. SE-2, pp. 308–320, 1976.

[14] Nejmeh, B. A., NPATH: a measure of execution path complexity and its applications, *Commun. ACM*, vol. 31, no. 2, pp. 188-200, 1988.

[15] Prather, R. E., An axiomatic theory of software complexity measure, *The Computer Journal*, vol. 27, pp. 340–347, 1984.

[16] Prather, R. E., On hierarchical software metrics, *Software Engineering Journal*, vol. 2, no. 2, pp. 42–45, 1987.

[17] Whitty, R. W., Fenton, N. E. and Kaposi, A. A., Structured programming: a tutorial guide, *Software and Microsystems*, vol. 3, no. 3, pp. 54–65, 1984.

[18] Whitty, R. W. and Lockhart, R., Structural metrics, *COSMOS Project Report COSMOS/GC/WP1/REP/7.3*, TechForce BV, Leiden, Netherlands, 1990.

[19] Wilson, R. J., *Introduction to Graph Theory, 3rd Edition*. Longman Scientific and Technical, England, 1985.

3. Measurement Validation/Verification

A Critique of Validation/Verification Techniques for Software Development Measures

David A Gustafson[1], Ramon Mata Toledo[2], Richard E Courtney[1] and Naim Temsamani[3]

Abstract

Both validation and verfication of software measures are essential. Validation checks the predictive abilities of a measure against a dependent variable while verification checks the reasonableness of the measure. The software community has developed many measures but has usually failed to properly validate and/or verify the measures. This paper critiques current verification and validation methods including the **shotgun approach**, which correlates many measures against one or more dependent variables; the **dependent variable approach**; the **controlled experiment approach**; the **foundation approach**, which views software measures as mathematical entities to be studied and analyzed; the **intuitive approach**; the **exploratory approach**, which uses factor analysis; the **goal-oriented approach**, which produces measures of the quantities to optimize; and the **defacto approach**.

---

1. Kansas State University, Computing and Information Sciences, Nichols Hall, Manhattan, KS 66506   (913) 532-6350
2. James Madison University, Math and Computer Science, Harrsionburg, VA 22807 (703) 568-3364
3. 30 Rue Massena 1MB, Douma 1 appt 5-A Moari, Casablanca, Morocco

Introduction

In software development, validation refers to checking the final product against the requirements, while verfication refers to checking the consistency between the products of adjacent phases of the life cycle. In terms of software measures, validating should refer to checking the predictive abilities of a measure against a dependent variable, (the variable of interest). For example, validation might be correlating a proposed error-predicting measure against the number of errors in the final software. Verification should refer to checking the characteristics of a measure during the life cycle, for example, checking that lower values of a design structure measure correlates with better structure of the design. Researchers often fail to properly validate their measures. Both verification and validation are important.

The term "software measures" refers to mappings from software documents to real numbers [Bak87].[1] It includes measures called by various names, such as, complexity metrics, software metrics, design metrics, etc. Although most work in software measures has been done in code measures (which map source code to real numbers), the validation techniques are applicable to both measures that map source code to reals and measures that map software design documents to real numbers. The validation techniques are also applicable to measures that map process data, such as error histories or development time, to real numbers.

Whereas it is now widely acknowledged that software measures have the potential to help control increasing software costs, the software measures field still suffers from a lack of proper validation and verification. Verifying and validating existing measures is fundamental to the development of sound engineering tools. Both are essential to ensuring that the measures behave properly and are useful.

The software community has shown no lack of ingenuity in developing all sorts of exotic measures. There are measures to determine or predict software

---

1. Metrics more properly refer to mappings from pairs of software documents to the real numbers, much like the standard distance metric in the real plane.

characteristics at all different phases of a software's life-cycle, from requirements to testing and from design to maintenance [Ram85]. However, the "correctness" of most of these measures is poorly, if at all, proven.

Among the reasons that lead to this is the fact that many software measures have been developed without any desireable characteristics or any particular use in mind [Kear86]. First, the researchers create an equation to quantify what they consider to determine complexity (only vaguely defined) in a program, and then they study programs with the hope of finding some relationship between the values from the equation and some property of the programs. A better approach is to develop a theory that provides a foundation for the presumed causal relationship before trying to validate the relationship or to develop desireable characteristics of the measure and then to verify these characteristics.

Validating the relationship between the measure and some property of the software is a difficult task. There are numerous factors that may influence the outcome of an experiment (programmer skill, language used, programming task, type of algorithm studied, etc.), and it is hard to find experimental samples that differ in only one factor. Often the validation is valid for only that sample and cannot be generalized to all software.

Discrepancies among the results reported by researchers have also discouraged many an advocate of rigorous methods. For example, Sheppard [She79] concludes that Halstead's software science measures are better that McCabe's metric, whereas Kafura [Kaf81] concludes the reverse. The inability to carry out controlled experiments, and the difficulty to isolate various factors, makes it very difficult to validate measures and to generalize any conclusion drawn from one software project to all other projects.

What we will attempt to do in this paper is to report on a number of validation and verification approaches used by researchers throughout the years. We would like to summarize their methods in a practical and easily referable fashion. By gathering this mass of information into a unique document, comparisons of validation and verification techniques and findings become immediate and systematic. Future researchers will also find it useful to have a set of "precedents" at hand.

Since various approaches can be used for these experiments, we will classify these approaches into categories. The following paragraphs will present the different categories and the results relevant to each category.

Shotgun Approaches

Among the various validation techniques, statistical validation seems to be the most popular among researchers. It has the security of established mathematical techniques and researchers seem to seek confirmation of their intuition in the mathematical rigour. The standard shotgun approach is to correlate as many measures as possible against one or more dependent variables. Because of the large number of interacting factors and the limited amount of data, the likelihood of finding accidental relationships is high [Kea86]. Also, because of the nature of software data, fluctuations are often too high and deviations are too big to lend credibility to the results. Because of the large number of experiments necessary to achieve statistical significance, rarely is the data sufficient to justify the claims. Practically, the findings must be taken with caution and one can hardly use them for prediction.

Standard Dependent Variable Validation

This is the approach of trying to validate a measure against a dependent variable that is measurable after the project is completed. This approach requires that the researcher develop an underlying theory that supports the causal relationship that is intended to be validated. This approach sometimes is not very popular because the number of factors that can influence this relationship is very large and care in the analysis of data is required. Other factors than the factor being studied may be causing the relationships. Thus, the results can be inconclusive if the theory is not good or the data is not analyzed carefully.

Controlled-Experiment Approaches

Having developed an underlying theory that suggests a casual relationship between some measure of a document and some property, researchers can design controlled experiments that test the theory. The controlled experiment often requires duplicate development efforts. The experiments can be very expensive. Due to the number of possible factors and the cost of software development, this approach is not taken as often as it should. However, if care is taken in designing the experiments the results will be conclusive and generalizable. The controlled-experiment approach is the only sure way to validate a measure.

Verification Approaches

Developers can view software measures as mathematical entities which have properties that can be studied and analyzed. Thus software measures can be studied without dependence on a set of programs. For example, properties of measures can be derived from a set of axioms and definitions. Weyuker [Wey86] adopts such an axiomatic approach. She reviews Halstead's and McCabe's measures in light of mathematical properties.

Melton, et al. [Mel88] develop a mathematical paradigm for software measures. The mathematical paradigm involves identifying an abstraction of the software document, developing a partial ordering of the abstraction, and finding an order-preserving mapping from the abstraction to the real numbers. For example, if the abstraction maps code to control flow diagrams and the partial order relates flowgraphs, McCabe's measure can be used as the order-preserving mapping to the real numbers[Mel88]. This verifies that McCabe's complexity measure is a "containment-based structural complexity measure." This means that it is based on a constructive partial order. Among other properties, this guarantees that adding to a program will never cause a decrease in the complexity measure.

Work in measurement theory [Zus88] gives insight into intrinsic characteristics of software measures. One characteristic is the type of scale of the measure.

Measures can have nominal, ordinal, interval, ratio or absolute scales. For example, measures that have a ratio scale can be averaged and give a meaningful result. Measures with an ordinal scale can not be averaged.

The foundation approaches verify that the measure has certain desireable properties. Thus, the measures will still require validation against the desired predictors. However, the measures will be guaranteed to behave properly.

Exploratory approaches

Because of the enormous number of parameters that can affect the outcome of an experiment, and the uncertainty of how measures relate to one another on one hand and to quality measures on the other, some validators prefer to adopt an exploratory approach. The prefered technique [Mata 84] [Tems88] is factor analysis of a large set of software measurements. This mathematical technique allows the reduction of an initial set of measures into an equivalent smaller set. Moreover, as shown in [Tems88], this method allows the grouping of measures into classes (called loading groups), which seem to form a basis of the complexity space. The measures in a class are highly related and only one measure from a class should be used in further validation efforts.

Exploratory approaches produce understanding about which values may be useful in developing software measures. The resultant measure still needs to be validated against the desired predictors.

Intuitive approaches

Because of the big number of interacting factors in software development, some researchers have traded the dependent variable validation methods for a subjective, more intuitive approach. What these researchers attempt to do is to correlate software measures to the judgement of "experts" who are familar with the system being studied. This avoids some of the problems of validating against the dependent variable. In their paper [Kaf87], Kafura give an example of such an approach. A possible motivation behind this method is the desire to provide managers with measures that agree with experts' opinions.

Intuitive approaches do not address the question of the validity of the experts' opinions. For example, consider the arguments over GOTO-less programming. Whichever side the experts take gets propagated into the measure. Thus folklore becomes encoded into a software measure.

Goal-Oriented Approaches

When a goal of optimizing a particular quantity exists, then it may be appropriate to develop measures that are closely related to that quantity. For example, if customer satisfaction is the goal to optimize, then a measure such as number of customer complaints is generally considered appropriate. Management can then use this measure as the quantity to optimize. Goal-oriented approaches often produce measures that are based on the "process data". A difficulty with this approach is that the results are valid only in this environment. Transferring the measures to another environment will require revalidation.

DeFacto Approaches

Some methods used for validation software measurements fail to fall completely within one of the previous categories. The defacto approach is one of these methods. A researcher focuses on a quantity which in his opinion determines complexity. He or she devises an equation to compute the quantity and then proceeds to compute the quantity for a set of programs. The computed quantities are then compared with the actual quantities, When the observed quantities fall repeatedly within "acceptable" margins of the expected values then the equations (or model) will be considerd to hold, otherwise they will be dismissed. Such an approach has been used by Halstead to validate the length and intelligence content equations, as well as the program level equation and to determine a Stroud number for his effort equation [Hal77]. It has also been used by [Ban81] to estimate the number of conceptually unique operands in an algorithm.

Summary of approaches

Table 1 summarizes the approaches to validation and verification. The columns indicate whether the approach achieves validation or verification, whether the approach produces a dependent variable that can then be predicted, whether there is an underlying theory used or produced and whether the results of the approach are generalizable to other data or environments.

approach	verification	validation	dependent variable	underlying theory	generalizable
shotgun	no	no	no	no	no
dependent variable	no	yes	yes	necessary	can be
controlled	no	yes	yes	yes	possibly
foundation	yes	no	no	may result	yes
exploratory	yes	no	no	may result	yes
intuitive	no	no	opinions	folklore	no
goal oriented	no	yes	no	no	no
defacto	no	no	no	no	no

Table 1 : validation methods

Shotgun approaches produce measures that are specific to that particular set of data. The results are not generalizable beyond the specific set of data. The experiments will need to be repeated many times before they can claim any generalizability. This approach neither verifies or validates the measure. Dependent variable validation is expensive but is the best approach for validating a well-understood relationship that is built on an underlying theory.

Foundational approaches produce measures that have guaranteed properties. This approach has promise as being the first step in selecting measures to be used in further study and in verifying that existing measures have the necessary properties to be useful.

Exploratory approaches produce measures that are promising but need further validation. This approach may also serve as the first step in identifying possible relationships between variables.

Initutive approaches produce measures that are very specific to the data used and are not generalizable. The results produced have usually been contradicted when the experiments have been repeated on different data.

Goal oriented approaches produce measures that are specific to the particular problem and the particular environment. Although very useful in the specific application, they need to be redeveloped in every environment and for each goal.

DeFacto approaches produce measures that have little support or justification. This approach has little justifcation for its use since it neither verifies or validates measures nor provides any additional insight into the measurement task.

Specialization to Design

Design measures are further from the final result than code measures, thus they are harder to validate. Correlations between the measurements and the results are fuzzier because of the intervening processes that must occur. A new question must be answered: is the effect seen a result of the design or the result of a process occurring between the design and the effect? One of the interesting effects of calculating a design measure is that it requires a person to carefully examine the design while obtaining inputs for the measure. For example, in calculating DeMarco's Design Weight [DeM85] which determines the number of tokens and the number of decisions, the user is forced to analyze the design very throughly. The better results obtained in later phases may be the side effect of having done the analysis.

Additionally if the effect wasn't a direct effect of the design, was it an indirect effect? That is, did changing the design cause some other change that resulted in a better implementation. This suggests that verification of design measures and the development of the underlying theory are even more important in design measures.

Validation of any measure is generally done with completed projects. To validate design measures, the measurement should be done at the end of the design phase. If the measure indicates a recommended change then the changes may be made before progressing into the next phase, but care must be taken that any improvement in the final product is due to the improvement in the design and not a side effect of the changes.

For example, to validate a measure that forecasts the cost of maintenance, a set of designs is needed that have forecast maintenance costs higher than reasonable. Then the design must be changed so that the forecast cost of maintenance is lower. Then if the cost of maintenance is lower than originally predicted the measure is validated. Of course this takes several years to collect the data along with all the uncertainty that the actual maintenance requests aren't significantly different than what the model assumed.

Almost all of the current design measures add the terms of the measure which are calculated on parts of the design. Since most measures also say that less is better, the measures often promote fewer modules. Recognizing that the whole design is an art of balancing all of the factors known to the project, it seems somewhat amiss of design measures not to incorporate terms reflecting the whole design. In too many measures the best design structure according to the measure is a single module.

Conclusions

Effective use of measures in the area of software design requires good validation and verification. Lack of planning for validation in the development of design measures will result in measures that have limited usefulness and questionable validity. Measures that will have general applicability need to be developed with a good foundation. Measures that will only be used in limited areas can be developed empirically but still need good validation.

Bibliography

[Bak87]: A. Baker, J. Bieman, D. Gustafson and A. Melton, "Modeling and Measuring the Software Development Process", **Proc HICSS Conf 1987** pp. 23-40.

[Ban81]: S.K. Bandyopadhyay, "Theoretical relationships between potential operands and basic measurable properties of algorithm structures", **ACM Sigplan Notices**, Vol. 16, No. 2, February 1981.

[Con86]: S.D. Conte, H.E. Dunsmore, V.Y. Shen, **Software Engineering Metrics and Models**, The Benjamin/Cummings Publishing Company, Inc., Menlo Park California, 1986.

[DeM85]: Tom DeMarco, **Controlling Software Projects**

[Hal77]: Maurice H. Halstead, Elements of Software Science, New York: Elsevier, 1977.

[Kaf81]: Dennis Kafura et al, "On the Relationship Among Three Software Metrics", Performance Evaluation Review, Vol. 10, No. 1, pp. 3-10,

[Kaf87]: Dennis Kafura et al, "The Use of Software Complexity Metrics in Software Maintenance", IEEE Transactions on Software Engineering, Vol. 13, No. 3, pp. 335-343, March 1987.

[Kea86]: Joseph K. Kearney et al, "Software Complexity Measurement"CACM, Vol. 29, No. 11, November 1986.

[Mat84]: Ramon Mata-Toledo, "A Factor Analysis of Software Complexity Metrics", Ph.D. Dissertation, Kansas State University, Manhattan, Kansas 1984.

[Mel88]: Austin Melton, et al "A Mathematical Perspective on Software Measures Research" Kansas State University, Tech Report TR-CS 88-6

[Ram85]: C.V. Ramamoorthy, et al, "Metrics guided Methodology", IEEE COMPSAC 85, pp. 111-120, 1985.

[She79]: Curtis D. Sheppard, et al, "Third Time Charm: Stronger Replications of the Ability of Software Metrics to Predict", Proceedings ICSE, Vol. 4, pp. 356-360, September 1979.

[Tem88]: Naim Temsamani, "Automating and Refining Software Measurements", Master's Thesis, Florida Institute of Technology, Melbourne, Florida, 1988.

[Wey86]: Elaine J. Weyuker, "Evaluating Software Complexity Metrics", IEEE Transactions on Software Engineering, 1986.

[Zus88]: Horst Zuse and Peter Bollman, "The Use of Measurement Theory to Describe the Properties and Scales of Static Software Complexity Measures"

Algebraic Models and Metric Validation*

Martin Shepperd
Dept. of Computing and Cognition,
Bournemouth Polytechnic,
Talbot Campus,
Fern Barrow,
Poole, BH12 5BB, England

Abstract

A major problem in the field of software metrics is that much of the work can be characterised as speculative: that is, it requires considerably less effort to propose a metric than it does to produce a convincing validation of its utility. The outcome is a plethora of what might be regarded as putative metrics and a corresponding scarcity of properly validated metrics. This paper outlines a method for the formal evaluation of a software metric and its underlying model. This is based upon the specification of the model as an algebra and its desired behaviour as an associated axiom set. If these axioms can be proved to be invariant across the model, then the model may be considered to be valid with respect to its axioms. Where an axiom cannot be shown to be invariant this implies that either the model is anomalous or that the axiom was inappropriate. This approach is demonstrated with respect to a design metric based upon inter-module coupling. It is argued that this method of metric validation is a general one, which is capable of increasing confidence in the correctness of a metric particularly during the early stages of its development when empirical data may either be sparse or unavailable. A further benefit of this approach is that there exists a trivial transformation process from the algebra into OBJ, thus enabling the model to be animated. It is intended as a practical means whereby metrics workers can eliminate pathological models prior to embarking upon costly and time consuming empirical validation exercises. Finally, it must be emphasised that this method should not supplant empirically based means of validation, rather that it should be employed as a complementary technique.

Keywords: Software metrics, measurement, validation, algebraic specification, software design.

---

*This work has been supported by British Telecom Research Labs., Martlesham Heath, Ipswich, IP5 7RE, England

1. Introduction

Although there has been no shortage of software metrics proposed over the past 20 years, validation of these metrics has proved difficult. However, without satisfactory evaluation it is unreasonable to expect widespread adoption by the software engineering industry. Yet this is a frustrating situation, given the need to bring quantitative methods to bear upon the task of controlling large scale software engineering projects [deMa82, Boeh84, Gilb88].

There appear to be several barriers to metric evaluation. The first is the poor definition of a metric and its underlying model or theory. Meaningful validation is difficult until clear counting rules are provided and assumptions made explicit. An example of a metric validation hampered by inadequately articulated model is given by Ince and Shepperd [Ince89] in their analysis of the classic Henry and Kafura information flow metric [Henr81]. Indeed, many of the peculiarities and anomalies within the information flow metric arise, precisely because the model is defined in extremely vague terms.

The second area of difficulty is that of empirical analysis — the usual approach to metric validation — is often a difficult, expensive and protracted business. In [Ince88] we describe some of the ideal requirements for a convincing empirical study. These include large numbers of data points, use of industrial subjects in an industrial environment dealing with large scale artifacts and the need for appropriate statistics. The fact that many of these are difficult to achieve — other than the proper use of statistics — is borne out by our survey of approximately 50 published validations of design metrics. Of these 50 studies only four came close to fulfilling our desiderata. This not due to the perversity of metrics researchers but the difficulty of carrying out studies in industrial environments. Consequently, most work is of a passive or observational form which tends to suffer from factors that are outside the experimenter's control, or worse still outside his or her knowledge. Even the appropriate use of statistics to interpret empirical results, has lead to difficulties — *vide* the re-interpretation of many of the early "confirmations" of Halstead's software science by Hamer and Frewin [Hame82] or the re-appraisal of the support for McCabe's cyclomatic complexity metric [McCa76] by Shepperd [Shep88].

In this paper we present an alternative approach to metric validation based upon a formal specification of the metric model which eliminates much ambiguity. In addition the desired model behaviour is described as a set of invariants, for example one might stipulate that adding an additional entity to data design must always increase the value of the metric. The validation then consists of demonstrating that the axioms remain invariant for all model behaviours. This method is then applied to a design metric that captures some notion of inter module coupling [Stev74] and can be derived from a standard module hierarchy chart. Our findings suggest that this is a feasible approach and one which has potential for future metrics research.

2. Algebraic validation

Our method of algebraic validation of software metrics comprises three steps:

- formal definition of the model;
- identification of desired model behaviour as an axiom set;
- proving the axioms are invariant.

Each of these steps will be described in turn.

For the first step we formally define the model behind the metric. The approach that we have adopted is to do this by means of algebra [Gutt77, Ehri85], which yields several advantages. The notation is unambiguous, it focuses attention upon the constructor or composition operations [Geha82] thereby providing a framework for defining meaningful and meaningless objects for measurement, and lastly it can easily be animated using OBJ[1]. The outcome of this step are the signatures defining the operations to build and manipulate a model of the object of measurement, combined with a set of equations that define the semantics of these operations. The equations may be regarded as a term rewriting system.

In the second step, the desired behaviour of the metric and its model must be described as a set of axioms. An example of such an axiom is the removal of a shared data structure from a software design cannot increase a maintainability metric value. Isolating these axioms is a skilful process that requires some insight into the measurement domain, however, our method provides certain guide-lines to aid this process, which are described later in this section.

The third step is to formally prove whether the axioms are invariant over the model defined. When an axiom cannot be shown to be invariant one must infer either that the metric is flawed or that the axiom describing desired model behaviour was inappropriate.

We now examine the issue of identifying axioms of model behaviour in more detail. There has been some work in the arena of axiomatic validation of software metrics, for example that of Prather [Prat84] and Weyuker [Weyu88]. The axioms proposed by Prather are rather weak and unrestricted whilst those proposed by Weyuker are on the contrary highly constraining. The problem with the former is that one tends to accept metrics that ought to be rejected, whilst with the latter the reverse pertains. Consequently, our solution is to adopt a flexible approach whereby the axioms are specific to a given model and metric[2]. Given the potential diversity of software metrics it is hard to envisage any other alternative! Our approach is also novel in that whilst there is some interest in the axiomatic treatment of metrics [Zuse89, Melt90] no other work deals with a formal definition of the model.

Returning to the axioms, observe that measures must satisfy three classes of axioms:

- those axioms that are fundamental to all measurement;
- axioms necessary for the type of scale adopted;
- axioms specific to the model underlying the measure.

It will be noted that the axiom classes decrease in scope of application from universal to specific for a single, or small family of metrics. Each class will be reviewed in turn.

The following are axioms that must hold for all measurement for it to be meaningful.

---

[1] The algebra defining the coupling metric later in this paper, has been implemented with a minimum of effort.

[2] An alternative flexible approach has been presented by Zuse and Bollmann [Zuse89] in the form of viewpoints which allow for the specification of varying sets of fundamental requirements for different metrics, or even the same metric. The method described in this paper differs in that it employs an equational rewrite system to define and reason with the axioms.

Axiom 1: It must be possible to describe, even if not formally, the rules governing the measurement [Pfan68][3]. This axiom is somewhat difficult to apply in practice, but in essence, once the error-proneness of the measuring process has been accounted for, all measurements of the same object or process attribute must assign it to the same equivalence class.

Axiom 2: The measure must generate at least two equivalence classes in order that, as Weyuker [Weyu88] points out, the measure be capable of discrimination.

Axiom 3: An equality relation is required[4]. Without an empirical equality operation each measurement, if it could be called that, would generate a new equivalence class with exactly one member.

Axiom 4: The previous axiom is further strengthened, such that if an infinite number of objects or events are measured, eventually two or more must be assigned to the same equivalence class. This is a restatement of Weyuker's third axiom [Weyu88]. We note that some forms of measurement using a nominal scale, for example car number plates, do not satisfy this axiom — a hardly surprising observation when one considers that such a process must lie at the limits of what could reasonably be called measurement.

Axiom 5: The metric must not produce anomalies (i.e. the metric must preserve empirical orderings). In other words the Representation Theorem [Supp71, Kran71] must hold, where:

$$\forall\ p,q : \text{object} \cdot P\ r_e\ Q \rightarrow |P|\ r_n\ |Q|$$

where r_e is any empirically observable relation and r_n is the equivalent relation within the number or measurement system.

To apply this axiom however, it does require that there is agreement upon the empirical orderings and that possibility of erroneous measurement is disregarded. Unfortunately, in the arena of software engineering, such agreement is not always forthcoming.

Axiom 6: The Uniqueness Theorem must hold [Supp71] for all permissible transformations for the particular scale type, that is, there exists a homomorphism between the transformed and the measurement structures.

Regarding the second class of axioms, those that are sufficient for different measurement scales, these are well documented in the classical measurement literature, for example Stevens [Stev59] and Krantz *et al* [Kran71]. Clearly, our axiom set must be tailored to take account of scale and this is an important decision for any metric. Refer to [Zuse90] for a detailed discussion of the impact of scale upon software metrics.

The third class of axioms are those that relate to the specific model underlying the measure in question. Again, it is possible to provide categories under which axioms may be selected. These are:

---

[3]This does not imply that the rules must always be applied correctly, since there is the possibility of error in the measurement process — a point eloquently made by Henry Kyberg [Kybe84] amongst others.

[4]This is not dissimilar in impact to Weyuker's third axiom [Weyu88].

- resolution;
- empirically meaningless structures;
- model invariants.

Under resolution it may be desirable to include Weyuker's second axiom that asserts that there only exist a finite number of objects of a given measurement score. This would be important if metrics, that are insensitive in certain respects[5], are to be avoided. One has certain reservations as to whether there is a practical distinction between infinite and a very large number but there are, nevertheless, occasions when the axiom may emphasise required metric behaviour.

Having chosen the axioms necessary for the type of measurement one must consider the composition operations available for the objects or processes under scrutiny. The importance of composition is that it is the constructor operator, and allows us to describe different objects or processes, in a recursive [Fent86] or hierarchical [Prat87] manner. What the existing approaches fail to embrace is the possibility of metrics where there is no composition closure[6]. It is an important aspect of any axiomatisation that we define meaningless structures for which measurement is undefined. In other words, we need to know when we should *not* measure as well as when to measure.

Model invariants are clearly going to be extremely diverse. Examples include Prather's [Prat84] second and third axioms which relate to measures of control flow structure. This is a difficult aspect of an axiomatic evaluation of a model, because in the end the choice of axioms will be dependant upon intuition and insight. Where it cannot be shown that a model satisfies such an axiom, two conclusions are possible. First, one might infer that the model is deficient in some respect, or second, that the axiom itself is inappropriate. Whatever, this axiomatic method at least draws the attention of the metrologist to such potential problem areas. It does not provide necessarily an answer.

In concluding this section, there are three points of note. Axiomatisations of software metrics are a vital tool for the theoretical validation of metrics and models, as they allow exploration of the model behaviour in a more rigourous fashion. Without doubt, they represent a step forward from merely using one's intuition. They may also permit a more thorough coverage of the model behaviour than the intuitive approach, or for that matter, than many empirical evaluations, particularly where cost or availability of data is a factor.

Second, they provide a mechanism to establish certain foundational properties of the model. These are:

- consistency, so that there exists one and only one outcome for any set of inputs;
- completeness, that the axiom set is sufficiently rich that there is no set of inputs for which no outcome is prescribed;
- the model is not rejected for violation of axioms for empirically meaningless structures.

Consistency is established by showing that the axiom set exhibits the Church-Rosser property. This is unfortunately an undecidable question. There are various notions of

---

[5]The classic example, is of course, McCabe's cyclomatic complexity [McCa76] where one may infinitely vary the number of procedure nodes for a fixed number of predicate nodes, for a program flow graph.

[6]This will be the case for any syntactic software metric.

completeness, including the concept of sufficiently complete [Gutt78] which is weaker than the more usual mathematical definitions of completeness[7], but these are still undecidable.

Third, theoretical evaluation provides early feedback for the design and development of metrics and models. Given that empirical validation is a costly and time-consuming enterprise, any technique that helps identify models that are manifestly inadequate must be lauded.

3. Examples of algebraic validation

This section illustrates, with two examples, the algebraic validation method described above. The first example is a trivial design metric based upon a count of modules in a system architecture in order to illustrate the underlying principles rather than to offer a serious metric. The algebraic specification [Gutt77, Ehri85] comprises two parts. The first part describes the signatures of the various operations needed to build (new and add) and to measure (metric) system architectures. The second part defines the meaning of the operations as a set of rewrite equations.

new: $\rightarrow$ design
add: mod $\times$ design $\rightarrow$ design
metric: design $\rightarrow$ nat

m: mod
D: design

1. metric(new) = 0
2. metric(add(m,D)) = 1+metric(D)

In this example all add operations are permissible - in other words there are no restrictions upon this operation. However, it is a frequent occurrence that we wish to restrict the range of the constructor operations as it might be meaningless to measure some objects. For example, it might be desirable to restrict the add operation so as to enforce unique module names. This may be accomplished as follows. An additional operation *add?* is included within the specification, the result of which depends upon whether the module to be added already exists within the architecture.

add?: mod $\times$ design $\rightarrow$ design $\cup$ {duplicate_module}

3. add?(m,D) = IF exists(m,D) THEN (duplicate_error} ELSE add(m,D)

This then requires the definition of an internal operation *exists*.

exists: mod $\times$ design $\rightarrow$ boolean

4. exists(m,new) = FALSE
5. exists(m,add(n,D)) = IF m=n THEN TRUE ELSE exists(m,D)

---

[7]An axiom set is usually said to be complete if it is impossible to add an independent axiom because *all* well formed formulae either follow from, or are inconsistent with, the existing axiom set.

This then completes the specification of our simple module counting metric. The next step is to identify properties of the metric and its underlying model that we wish always to remain true. For example, we might demand that adding a module to an arbitrary system architecture must always increase the metric value. This may be restated as:

$$\forall D: \text{design} \bullet \text{metric}(D) < \text{metric}(\text{add}(m,D))$$

The last step is to prove that the above axiom holds. In this case, this is trivially true since the metric is a simple count and the axiom merely demands a positive monotonic function. Since the axiom is true, this demonstrates that the metric behaves as required, and consequently increases our confidence in it.

Next, we examine a more complex and realistic example of a metric. The following is an algebraic specification of a simple design metric, C, that is a measure of the degree of connectivity between modules within a system architecture. Such information will be of value to software designers because it will enable them to control these couplings, leading to more maintainable designs. This is similar in concept to the work on ripple analysis by Yau *et al* [Yau80], in that couplings are viewed as channels which potentially enable maintenance changes to propagate through a system. Designs with few couplings contain this propagation potential and are therefore regarded as more maintainable.

The C metric may informally be defined as follows. A *coupling* between two modules is defined to occur whenever a data structure is shared between the modules such that one module writes to the data structure and the other modules retrieves from the data structure — refer to Figure 1.

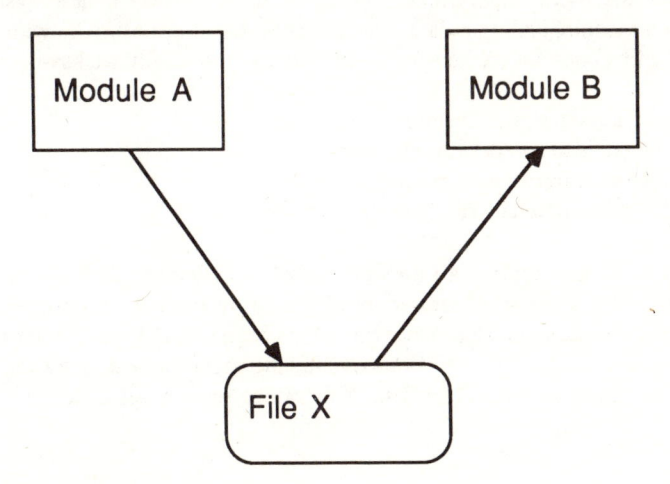

Figure 1: Example Module Coupling

Thus one module is able to influence the behaviour of the other. From an analysis of module couplings it is possible to compute the *fan_in* and *fan_out* of each module where the fan_in is the count of flows that terminate at a module and the fan_out the count of flows that emanate from a module. The product[8] of these two terms gives the C metric for the ith module.

$$C_i = \text{fan\_in} \cdot \text{fan\_out}$$

If these are summed across the system this gives a value for C,

$$C = \sum_{i=1}^{i=n} C_i$$

where there n modules in a system.

Although this coupling metric could be extended — for example it ignores parameterised communication between modules — it is still potentially useful for software designers, and in fact forms a major subset of system architecture metrics as IF4 [Ince89, Shep90] and is indirectly related to the information flow metric due to Henry and Kafura [Henr84]. In any case the simplicity is for reasons of brevity and elsewhere we have successfully applied this method to more complex metrics, for example the Information Flow metric and the 'work' metric [Shep91].

We will now develop a formal, algebraic specification of the behaviour of the coupling metric and its underlying model in terms of equations. This will be defined step by step; for a complete specification refer to the Appendix. The first part of the algebraic specification defines the model operations. These include creating a new system architecture, adding a module, adding a data structure access and so forth. As with the previous example, we first consider the constructor operations. Informally we have:

new - creates a null system architecture
addm - adds a module to a system architecture
rd - defines a retrieval from a data structure by a module
wr - defines an update of a data structure by a module

These are necessary to build or define all possible system architectures for which our metric is defined. Note that some architectures are illegal, for instance we cannot have a design with two modules of the same name since this would create an ambiguity, nor can a nonexistent module access a data structure. Consequently the operations *addm, rd* and *wr* can all fail and instead return an error condition. This can be seen by reference to their signatures.

new: → sys
addm: mod × sys → sys ∪ {duplicate_error}
rd: mod × ds × sys → sys ∪ {missing_mod_error}
wr: mod × ds × sys → sys ∪ {missing_mod_error}
addm': mod × sys → sys
rd': mod × ds × sys → sys
wr': mod × ds × sys → sys

---

[8] A product is taken since this is equivalent to the number of information paths across a module linking the couplings in and out.

The semantics of these operations are given by the following equations, where *m* and *n* are type mod and *S* is type sys:

1. exists?(m,new) = FALSE
2. exists?(m,addm(n,S)) = IF m=n THEN TRUE ELSE exists?(m,S)
3. exists?(m,rd(n,d,S)) = exists?(m,S)
4. exists?(m,wr(n,d,S)) = exists?(m,S)

5. addm(m,S) = IF exists?(m,S) THEN {duplicate_error} ELSE addm'(m,S)

6. rd(m,d,S) = IF exists?(m,S) THEN rd'(m,d,S) ELSE {mod_not_found}

7. wr(m,d,S) = IF exists?(m,S) THEN wr'(m,d,S) ELSE {mod_not_found}

Figure 2 shows an example software architecture which can be unambiguously defined using the following sequence of constructor operations.

rd(A,d,rd(B,d,wr(A,d,addm(A,addm(B,new)))))

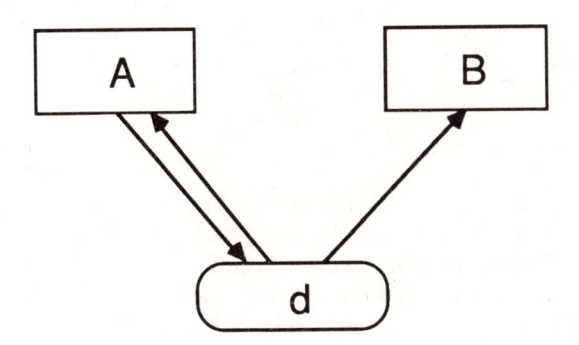

Figure 2: A Simple Software Architecture

The operations fall into two categories, external and internal, the latter being indicated by a prime. The latter are required in order to restrict the range of the constructor operations although their presence is transparent to the behaviour of the model, hence their name. Equation 5 defines the relationship between the external, unrestricted add module operation and its internal, restricted counterpart. The latter is guaranteed to succeed because we have already tested for the possibility of duplicate modules. The next step is to define the metric operations C, for the entire system and C_i for a specified module. Both these operations have internal equivalents, to generate a dummy argument to mimic a state in the case of C and prevent a metric value being returned for a module that does not exist in the case of C_i.

C_i: mod × sys → nat ∪ {mod_not_found}
C: sys → nat
C_i': mod × sys → nat
C': sys × sys → nat

8. C(S) = C'(S,S)

9. $C'(new,S) = 0$
10. $C'(addm'(m,T),S) = C_i'(m,S) + C'(T,S)$
11. $C'(rd'(m,d,T),S) = C'(T,S)$
12. $C'(wr'(m,d,T),S) = C'(T,S)$

13. $C_i(m,S) = $ IF exists(m,S) THEN $C_i'(m,S)$ ELSE {mod_not_found}
14. $C_i'(m,S) = $ fan_in(m,S,S)*fan_out(m,S,S)

Equation 10 indicates that the system wide metric C is defined as the sum of the C_i for each module which in turn is the product of the fan_in and fan_out for each module. Next the fan_in and fan_out operations are given as:

fan_in: mod × sys × sys → nat
fan_out: mod × sys × sys → nat

15. fan_in$(m,new,S) = 0$
16. fan_in$(m,addm'(n,T),S) = $ fan_in(m,T,S)
17. fan_in$(m,wr'(n,d,T),S) = $ fan_in(m,T,S)
18. fan_in$(m,rd'(n,d,T),S) = $ IF $m=n$ THEN #wr$(d,n,S) + $ fan_in(m,T,S) ELSE fan_in(m,T,S)

19. fan_out$(m,new,S) = 0$
20. fan_out$(m,addm'(n,T),S) = $ fan_out(m,T,S)
21. fan_out$(m,rd'(n,d,T),S) = $ fan_out(m,T,S)
22. fan_out$(m,wr'(n,d,T),S) = $ IF $m=n$ THEN #rd$(d,n,S) + $ fan_out(m,T,S) ELSE fan_out(m,T,S)

These equations state that the fan_in of a module is a function of the number of data structures that it retrieves or reads from. It is also dependant upon the modules, other than itself, that write to the data structure, which will be determined by the operation #wr. An advantage of a formal model definition is that it removes all ambiguity, so in this instance it is clear that a global flow is not counted when a module both reads and writes to a data structure itself, since the operation explicitly tests for $m \pi n$. It is also evident that this metric will count duplicate flows between modules, either via more than one shared data structure or by means of multiple reads and writes, to the same data structure. One might debate the desirability of such a counting strategy but at least it is made explicit.

#rd: ds × mod × sys → nat
#wr: ds × mod × sys → nat

23. #rd$(d,n,new) = 0$
24. #rd$(d,n,addm'(m,S)) = $ #rd(d,n,S)
25. #rd$(d,n,wr'(e,m,S)) = $ #rd(d,n,S)
26. #rd$(d,n,rd'(e,m,S)) = $ IF $d=e$ AND $m \pi n$ THEN $1 + $ #rd(d,n,S) ELSE #rd(d,n,S)

27. #wr$(d,n,new) = 0$
28. #wr$(d,n,addm'(m,S)) = $ #wr(d,n,S)
29. #wr$(d,n,rd'(e,m,S)) = $ #wr(d,n,S)
30. #wr$(d,n,wr'(e,m,S)) = $ IF $d=e$ AND $m \pi n$ THEN $1 + $ #wr(d,n,S) ELSE #wr(d,n,S)

This completes the definition of the metric and its underlying model. Next, we turn to *desired* model behaviour. To demonstrate the method of validation we will only consider two axioms, although clearly, in practice there are other model characteristics which one would wish to establish.

Using the framework described earlier for identifying model axioms, we focus upon the third class of axiom — that is those specific to this model. A characteristic that one might demand for our *first axiom* is: that as additional global flows or couplings are introduced to an arbitrary software design, this must increase the value of the C metric. This can more formally be stated as:

$\forall$S:sys; d:ds; m,n:mod • C(S) < C(wr'(n,d,S))
where #rd(m,d,S) $\geq$ 1 and m$\neq$n

and:

$\forall$S:sys; d:ds; m,n:mod • C(S) < C(rd'(n,d,S))
where #wr(m,d,S) $\geq$ 1 and m$\neq$n

The *second axiom* that we will investigate is the requirement that the metric supports the development of designs that exploit reusable components, a characteristic that is not commonplace amongst design metrics as one might expect — *vide* the graph impurity measure due to Yin and Winchester [Yin78] which penalises reuse. A formal restatement of this axiom is:

$\forall$m,n,r_1,r_2:mod; S:sys d,e:ds •
C(wr'(r_1,d,rd'(r_1,d,wr'(r_2,e,rd'(r_2,e,wr'(m,d,rd'(m,d,wr'(n,e,rd'(n,e,addm'(r_1,addm'(r_2,addm'(n,addm'(m,S)))))))))))))) >
C(wr'(r_1,d,rd'(r_1,d,wr'(m,d,rd'(m,d,wr'(n,d,rd'(n,d,addm'(r_1,addm'(n,addm'(m,S))))))))))

where r_1 and r_2 are functionally equivalent.

The architecture of two such designs are given in Figure 3.

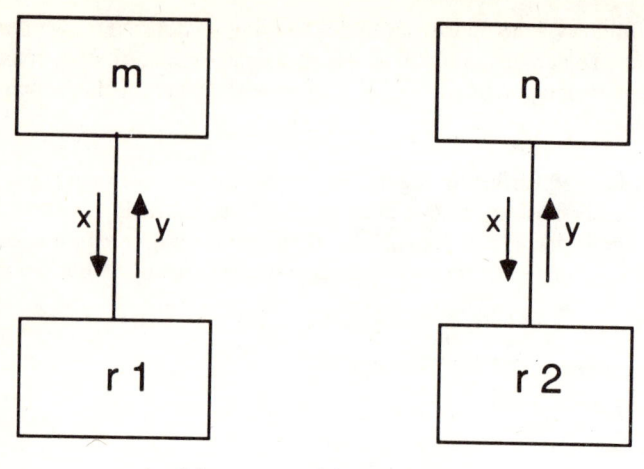

Architecture with duplication

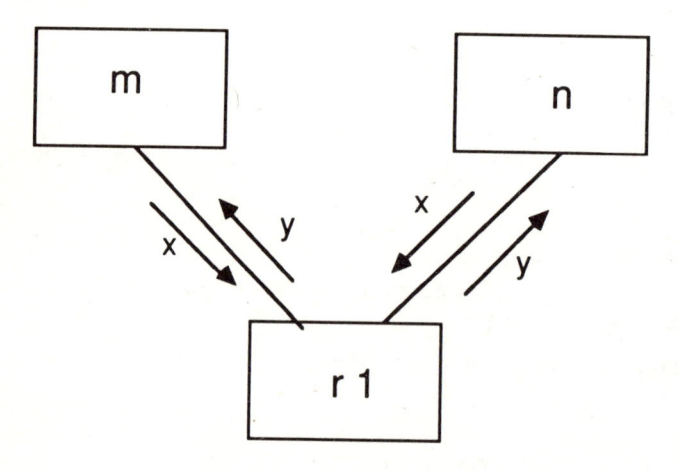

Architecture with re-use

Figure 3: The Impact of Re-use upon a Metric

It goes without saying that there are many other axioms which one might derive for this model of module coupling. For instance one might wish to demonstrate that it is not a simple size measure by showing that the metric is not merely a positive monotonic function of the module count. Another possibility would be to show that adding modules to an arbitrary design can never decrease the metric value. However, in order to demonstrate our approach we will focus upon the above two axioms. Since the formal proofs are rather lengthy we give an abbreviated view in this discussion. For a more exhaustive treatment the reader is referred to [Shep91].

Returning to *Axiom One* we note that it is universal in nature, consequently we only need a single counter-example in order to refute the axiom. On the other hand, to establish a universal truth we will need to reason inductively. Here the base case will be with *fan_in$_m$*, *fan_in$_n$*, *fan_out$_m$* and *fan_out$_n$* set to zero, and that by incrementing *fan_in$_m$*

and *fan_out$_n$* the C metric will be increased. From Equation 14 we have that the C_i metric is the product of *fan_in$_i$* and *fan_out$_i$* and from Equation 10 that C is the sum of all C_i values. This means that we must show that at least one of C_m and C_n are increased by the action of incrementing *fan_in$_m$* and *fan_out$_n$*.

However, we see that for module m:

$$(0+1)*0 = 0*0$$

and that likewise, for n:

$$0*(0+1) = 0*0$$

Clearly, neither C_i value has been increased by the action of introducing an additional coupling between the two modules, and as a result the C metric value is not increased. Consequently, Axiom One does not hold.

The reason for the rather curious behaviour of our model is not hard to determine. Since the metric is founded upon the product of module fan_in's and fan_out's the effect of incrementing a fan_in, is in part dependent upon the value of the fan_out, and of course, *vice versa*. Thus if a module has a zero fan_in, then irrespective of the size of its fan_out, the value of C_i will always be zero. Should the reader consider this to be a rather contrived example, it is worth noting that such well known metrics as the Henry and Kafura information flow measure [Henr81] would also fail to satisfy this axiom.

Axiom Two is based upon the view that a design metric should not have the side effect of encouraging the duplication of modules when reuse is an alternative. In other words, as designers minimise module coupling they also minimise module redundancy. Figure 3 depicts two functionally equivalent architectures, the second one of which re-uses component r_1 instead of duplicating it as component r_2. As with Axiom One, this is a universal axiom.

The simplest case — and also the base case for an inductive argument — is with S set to an empty design or equal to *(new)*. Adopting a similar approach to Axiom One, we note that C is the sum of, in this case C_m, C_n, C_{r1} and C_{r2} for the first design and C_m, C_n, and C_{r1} for second design.

We now seek to show that the C metric for the first design is greater than that for the second. This we can do by tabulating the fan_in and out values for each module in Table 1.

Duplication				Re-use			
Mod	F_I	F_O	C_i	Mod	F_I	F_O	C_i
m	1	1	1	m	2	2	4
n	1	1	1	n	2	2	4
r_1	1	1	1	r_1	2	2	4
r_2	1	1	1				
			C=4				C=12

Table 1: Coupling metric values for the architectures in Figure 3

By summing the C_i values for each system it is clear that the value for the design that duplicates r_1 as r_2 is lower than that for the design that re-uses r_1, and therefore the second axiom falls. The reason for this anomalous behaviour is that the model behind the metric does not adequately distinguish between a module invocation and a module interface; a module has a single interface but may be invoked many times. Similar problems are discussed in respect of information flow metrics in [Ince89]. This is an example of a metric that has a potentially dangerous side effect built into it, if it were not applied with considerable caution in an industrial environment. It is, therefore, imperative that metrics be fully understood prior to their application and the algebraic approach described in this paper enables this to be accomplished in a rigourous and inexpensive fashion.

So, to recap. The algebraic approach is a method of formally validating a metric at an early stage in its development and may be employed to filter out weaker candidates prior to deploying costly empirical validation resources. It comprises three stages.

Stage One is to turn an informal description of metric and its supporting model into a formal specification by identifying the constructor operations and the measurement function; defining their signatures and by giving their semantics as a set of rewrite equations. This is a technique known as algebraic specification.

Stage Two is to determine the desired model behaviour using the various categories under which the behaviour may be described, for example measurement resolution. These must then be formally stated as axioms that characterise properties that are invariant over the model, for example, adding a data structure to a given system architecture must never result in a decrease in a metric value.

Stage Three is to demonstrate that the axioms are indeed invariant over the model. This can be accomplished by rigourous argument or by formal proof. Note that the use of term rewriting systems such as OBJ can considerably facilitate the derivation of such proofs. Where an axiom does not hold, one may draw one of two possible inferences: either the axiom was not well chosen and that the model behaviour is in actual fact acceptable, or that model is deficient in this particular respect and will need to be modified.

Having gained confidence in a model, by means of this algebraic validation technique, it is still necessary to empirically validate the model, as it is probable that there are model properties that are important, yet that have been omitted from the set of model axioms due to oversight. Thus, the two validation approaches are complementary. Last, it must be stressed that it is not intended that practising software engineers become involved in this process, rather it is the province of research and development staff, who need to satisfy themselves that a metric is well founded, before incorporating it into organisation and software engineering processes.

4. Summary

Clearly, further work is required to complete the algebraic validation of our example metric, particularly to explore such issues as the relationship between these metrics and other data metrics such as Henry and Kafura's metric [Henr81] and the type of design strategies that the metric favours, for instance when to hide information [Parn72]. Work using this technique on the design metric IF_4 has revealed three flaws previously unknown to its progenitor, notwithstanding the considerable amount of empirical evaluation that it had been subjected to [Shep91].

The theoretical evaluation has been stressed since it has not been given great attention in the past. Its particular value is, of course, that such techniques are almost invariably a good deal less resource consuming, than empirical studies. This is not to decry empirical work, but merely to observe that if we are expend considerable effort in an empirical validation of a model it should at least be internally consistent and satisfy certain elementary criteria. Furthermore, theoretical analysis may uncover different problems with a model to those found by empirical investigation. Where it is possible to articulate a required model behaviour, mathematical proofs offer a higher degree of confidence than empirical studies. This is because the latter are in many ways akin to sampling from a large, and probably heterogeneous, population, with no certainty that the sample is representative. On the other hand, there are many situations where it is not possible to state *a priori* what model behaviour is required. In such circumstances empirical investigation is likely to be more effective. Empirical evaluation is also likely to be more effective at highlighting models that are insufficiently broad in scope or that make unrealistic assumptions. To repeat then, both forms of model evaluation are complementary and necessary.

One might also add, that as a by-product, an algebraic specification of metric is an effective way of unambiguously defining the counting rules for a metric. This alone has been the source of considerable confusion in the past, see for example [Lass81]. Likewise, it might also be argued that a formal specification provides a better foundation for the development of metric based software tools [Kitc86].

Although the flavour of this paper has been theoretical, formality alone is not sufficient. Indeed the essence of measurement is the mapping of empirical relations, drawn from an inherently informal world, into a formal model [Stev59]. However, the application of a little more rigour will make the development, refinement, validation and application of metrics a considerably less fraught process than is the present case.

References

[Boeh84] Boehm, B.W. 'Software engineering economics'. *IEEE Trans. on Softw. Eng.* 10(1) pp4-21. 1984.

[deMa82] deMarco, T. *'Controlling software projects. Management, measurement and estimation'.* Yourdon Press. NY. 1982.

[Ehri85] Ehrig, H. Mahr, B. *Fundamentals of algebraic specification*, EATCS, Vol.6 Springer-Verlag, 1985.

[Fent86] Fenton, N.E. Whitty, R.W. 'Axiomatic approach to Software metrification through program decomposition'. *Computer J.* 29(4) pp330-340. 1986.

[Geha82] Gehani, N.H. 'Specifications formal and informal - a case study', *Softw. Pract. & Experience,* **12**, pp433-444, 1982.

[Gilb88] Gilb, T. *Principles of software engineering management,* Addison-Wesley, 1988.

[Gutt77] Guttag, J.V. 'Abstract data types and the development of data structures'. *CACM* 20(6) pp397-404. 1977.

[Gutt78] Guttag, J.V. Horning, J.J. 'The ALgebraic Specification of Abstract data types', *Acta Informatica,* 10, pp27-52, 1978.

[Henr81] Henry, S. Kafura, D. Harris, K. 'On the relationship among three software metrics' *ACM SIGMETRICS Performance Evaluation Review* 10, Spring pp81-88. 1981.

[Hame82] Hamer, P.G. Frewin, G.D. 'M.H. Halstead's Software Science - A Critical Examination'. *Proc. IEEE 6th Int. Conf on Softw. Eng.* pp197-206. 1982.

[Ince88] Ince, D.C. Shepperd, M.J . 'System design metrics: a review and perspective.' *Proc. IEE / BCS Conf. Software Engineering '88* July 12- 15, Liverpool University, pp23-27. 1988.

[Ince89] Ince, D.C. Shepperd, M.J. 'An empirical and theoretical analysis of an information flow based design metric'. *Proc. European Software Eng. Conf.,* Warwick, England. Sept. 12-15, 1989.

[Kitc86] Kitchenham, B.A. McDermid, J.A. 'Software metrics and integrated project support environments'. *Softw. Eng. J.* 1(1) pp58-64. 1986.

[Kran71] Krantz, D.H. Luce, R.D. Suppes, P. Tversky, A. *Foundations of measurement.* Academic Press, London. 1971.

[Kybe84] Kyburg, H.E. *Theory and measurement.* Cambridge Univ. Press, Cambridge, England. 1984.

[Lass81] Lassez, J-L. van der Knijff, D.J.J. Shepherd, J. Lassez, C. 'A critical examination of software science'. *J. of Syst. & Softw.* 2, pp105-112. 1981.

[Lisk86] Liskov, B. Guttag, J. *Abstraction and specification in program development.* MIT Press, MA.. 1986.

[McCa76] McCabe, T.J. 'A complexity measure' *IEEE Trans. on Softw. Eng.* 2(4) pp308-320. 1976.

[Melt90] Melton, A.C. Gustafson, D.A. Bieman, J.A. Baker, J.A. 'A mathematical perspective for software measures research', *Softw. Eng. J.* 5(4) pp246-254, 1990.

[Parn72] Parnas, D.L. 'On the criteria to be used in decomposing systems into modules'. CACM 15(2) pp1053-1058.

[Prat84] Prather, R.E. 'An axiomatic theory of software complexity metrics'. *The Comp. J.* 27(4) pp340-347. 1984.

[Prat87] Prather, R.E. 'On hierarchical software metrics'. *Softw. Eng. J.* 2(2) pp42-45. 1987.

[Shep88] Shepperd, M.J. 'A critique of cyclomatic complexity as a software metric' *Softw. Eng. J.* 3(2) pp30-36. 1988.

[Shep90] Shepperd, M.J. 'An empirical study of design measurement'. *The Softw. Eng. J.* Jan. 1990.

[Shep91] Shepperd, M.J. System Architecture Metrics: An Evaluation, PhD Dissertation, Open University, 1991.

[Stev59] Stevens, S.S. 'Measurement, psychophysics and utility' in Churchman, C.W. Ratoosh, P (eds.) *'Measurement: definitions and theories'*. Wiley, N.Y.. 1959.

[Stev74] Stevens, W.P. Myers, G.J. Constantine, L.L. 'Structured design' *IBM Sys. J.* 13(2) pp115-139. 1974.

[Supp71] Suppes, P. Zinnes, J.L. 'Basic measurement theory'. In Lieberman, B. (ed.) *'Contemporary problems in statistics'* O.U.P. 1971.

[Weyu88] Weyuker, E.J. 'Evaluating software complexity measures'. *IEEE Trans. on Softw. Eng.* 14(9) pp1357-1365. 1988.

[Yau80] Yau, S.S. Collofello, J.S. 'Some stability measures for software maintenance'. *IEEE Trans. on Softw. Eng.* 6(6) pp545-552. 1980.

[Yin78] Yin, B.H. Winchester, J.W. 'The establishment and use of measures to evaluate the quality of software designs' *Proc. ACM Softw. Qual. Ass. Workshop* pp45-52. 1978.

[Zuse89] Zuse, H. Bollmann, P. 'Software metrics: using measurement theory to describe the properties and scales of static complexity metrics'. *ACM SIGPLAN Notices* 24(8), pp23-33, 1989.

[Zuse90] Zuse, H. *Software Complexity, Measures and Methods*, deGruyter, Berlin, 1990.

Appendix - An Algebraic Specification of a Coupling Metric

syntax

external operations

new: $\rightarrow$ sys
addm: mod sys $\rightarrow$ sys $\cup$ {duplicate_error}
rd: mod $\times$ ds $\times$ sys $\rightarrow$ sys $\cup$ {mod_not_found}
wr: mod $\times$ ds $\times$ sys $\rightarrow$ sys $\cup$ {mod_not_found}
C_i: mod $\times$ sys $\rightarrow$ nat $\cup$ {mod_not_found}
C: sys $\rightarrow$ nat

internal operations

exists?: mod $\times$ sys $\rightarrow$ boolean
addm': mod $\times$ sys $\rightarrow$ sys
rd': mod $\times$ ds $\times$ sys $\rightarrow$ sys
wr': mod $\times$ ds $\times$ sys $\rightarrow$ sys
fan_in: mod $\times$ sys $\times$ sys $\rightarrow$ nat
fan_out: mod $\times$ sys $\times$ sys $\rightarrow$ nat
#rd: ds $\times$ mod $\times$ sys $\rightarrow$ nat
#wr: ds $\times$ mod $\times$ sys $\rightarrow$ nat
C_i': mod $\times$ sys $\rightarrow$ nat
C': sys $\times$ sys $\rightarrow$ nat

semantics

vars

S, T: sys
m,n: mod
d,e: ds

equations

1. exists?(m,new) = FALSE
2. exists?(m,addm(n,S)) = IF m=n THEN TRUE ELSE exists?(m,S)
3. exists?(m,rd(n,d,S)) = exists?(m,S)
4. exists?(m,wr(n,d,S)) = exists?(m,S)

5. addm(m,S) = IF exists?(m,S) THEN {duplicate_error} ELSE addm'(m,S)

6. rd(m,d,S) = IF exists?(m,S) THEN rd'(m,d,S) ELSE {mod_not_found}

7. wr(m,d,S) = IF exists?(m,S) THEN wr'(m,d,S) ELSE {mod_not_found}

8. C(S) = C'(S,S)

9. C'(new,S) = 0
10. C'(addm'(m,T),S) = C_i'(m,S) + C'(T,S)
11. C'(rd'(m,d,T),S) = C'(T,S)
12. C'(wr'(m,d,T),S) = C'(T,S)

13. C_i(m,S) = IF exists(m,S) THEN C_i'(m,S) ELSE {mod_not_found}

14. C_i'(m,S) = fan_in(m,S,S)*fan_out(m,S,S)

15. fan_in(m,new,S) = 0
16. fan_in(m,addm'(n,T),S) = fan_in(m,T,S)
17. fan_in(m,wr'(n,d,T),S) = fan_in(m,T,S)
18. fan_in(m,rd'(n,d,T),S) = IF m=n THEN #wr(d,n,S) + fan_in(m,T,S) ELSE
    fan_in(m,T,S)

19. fan_out(m,new,S) = 0
20. fan_out(m,addm'(n,T),S) = fan_out(m,T,S)
21. fan_out(m,rd'(n,d,T),S) = fan_out(m,T,S)
22. fan_out(m,wr'(n,d,T),S) = IF m=n THEN #rd(d,n,S) + fan_out(m,T,S)
    ELSE fan_out(m,T,S)

23. #rd(d,n,new) = 0
24. #rd(d,n,addm'(m,S)) = #rd(d,n,S)
25. #rd(d,n,wr'(e,m,S)) = #rd(d,n,S)
26. #rd(d,n,rd'(e,m,S)) = IF d=e AND m≠n THEN 1 + #rd(d,n,S) ELSE
    #rd(d,n,S)

27. #wr(d,n,new) = 0
28. #wr(d,n,addm'(m,S)) = #wr(d,n,S)
29. #wr(d,n,rd'(e,m,S)) = #wr(d,n,S)
30. #wr(d,n,wr'(e,m,S)) = IF d=e AND m≠n THEN 1 + #wr(d,n,S) ELSE
    #wr(d,n,S)

4. Foundations

Properties of Software Measures

Dr. David A. Gustafson
Baba Prasad

Department of Computing and Information Sciences,
Kansas State University, Manhattan, KS 66506

July 23, 1991

ABSTRACT

Software measures (or metrics) are important in managing software development. Selecting which metrics to use is difficult. This paper describes desireable properties of software metrics that have been mentioned in the literature. The subsumes relationship between properties is investigated. A partial order of the properties is presented. Knowledge of these properties should help in selecting software metrics.

1 Introduction

Software metrics have great potential. Their use in managing software development is important. However, selecting which software metrics to use is difficult. There are many software metrics that have been suggested. Most articles on software metrics promote the author's favorite metric as the best. There are no approaches to objectively selecting which metric is the best for a specific purpose.

Important work has been done on the foundations for software metrics [6]. This foundational work helps to identify the characteristics or properties of specific metrics. Investigating these properties of software metrics is important. Identifying which properties imply other properties will allow managers to decide which properties are important or necessary for metrics being selected for particular tasks.

2 Properties in the literature

The literature has a number of properties of software metrics that are identified as being useful. Some of these properties are very informal, some are formally defined. We will start with the informal properties.

2.1 Informal Properties

Almost as soon as software metrics were produced, people were describing the properties that metric should have. These early properties were informal. They also tended to be extrinsic in the sense that they depended on how the metric was being used than on any intrinsic property of the metric.

- Properties from Basili and Reiter [1]
  Basili and Reiter claimed that for a metric to be useful it had two have the two properties. Both of these properties are subjective and informally defined.

  B1 - Sensitivity A metric has to be "sensitive to externally observable differences" It is not specified to which observable differences in the source code it had to be sensitive.

  B2 - Intuitiveness Second, a metric had to correspond to intuitive notion about differences. Again, this is very subjective because the intuition is not specified.

- Properties from *Software Engineering Metrics and Models* [3]

    In their book on software metrics, Conte, Dunsmore and Shen give a set of "meta-metrics that can be used to evaluate a proposed metric"

    - **C1 - Simplicity** The metric must be easily interpreted(C1a). The metric should produce a single value(C1b).
    - **C2 - Validity** The metric should measure what it should measure. This implies that there is intuition about what a metric measures and the metric should match this intuition.
    - **C3 - Robustness** This property implies that the metric should not allow cheating. That is, there should not be a way to "improve" the value of the metric without improving the source code. Part of this notion is a notion of monotonicity(C3a), that is adding to the program should not lower values. A second aspect is that changes that do not increase the program should only lower the values if they are good changes(C3b). This latter aspect is not well defined and is probably impossible to verify.
    - **C4 - Prescriptiveness** This property has two aspects: it can be used to guide management of development(C4a) and it should be available during development(C4b)
    - **C5 - Analyzability** This property requires that the values can be analyzed with standard statistics.

- Properties from Kearney [5]

    Kearney, etal. lists properties that they feel all useful metrics should possess. Again, the properties are not formally defined.

    - **K1 - Robustness** This property implies that the metric should not allow cheating. That is, there should not be a way to "improve" the value of the metric without improving the source code. Again, this is really two properties: monotonicity(K1a) and changes that lower the value should be good(K1b).
    - **K2 - Normativeness** This property is related to how users view the values obtained. There should be a "normal" value that discriminates between "good" programs abnd "bad" programs. For example, the cyclomatic complexity metric comes with the value 10;

good programs have complexity less than 10 and bad programs have complexity greater than 10.

K3 - Specificity Specificity relates to how well the user can understand what attributes of the source code influence the value of the metric. For example, in the cyclomatic complexity metric it is clear that the number of decisions determines the value.

K4 - Prescriptiveness Prescriptiveness relates to how well the user understands how to change the source code to improve the value of the metric. For example, in the cyclomatic complexity metric creating a subprogram that contains some of the decisions will decrease the value of the metric on the calling program. Since the cyclomatic complexity is based on just the module, this will decrease the value of the metric.

2.2 Axiom-based properties

There are been a number of attempts to formalize software measurement through the use of axioms. The following articles and their axioms imply certain properties.

- Properties from Prather [7]

  P1 - Wholeness Wholeness is intended to imply that the whole has at least the complexity of the sum of the complexities of the component pieces. Prather describes three axioms that a *proper metric* must satisfy. In the discussion, he says that the reason for the axioms is to ensure that the whole is at least as big as the sum of the parts.

  P2 - Combination Prather includes a requirement that the linear combination of proper metrics is also a proper metric.

  P3 - Inductive Prather says an inductive metric is one that can be defined inductively over the class of simple statements. More generally this should be over the components in the model.

  P4 - Structuredness Prather's third requirement is that any inductive metric gives a lower value on the structured version of a program than on the unstructured (using goto's) version of the same program.

- Properties from Fenton and Whitty [4]
  Fenton and Whitty discuss problems with Prather's approach and suggest a generalization beyond the limitation to structured flowgraphs. In terms of properties, there are two properties suggested that are listed below:

  F1 - Sequential Determinism The complexity of a sequential flowgraph should be uniquely determined by the complexities of the components.

  F2 - Nonsequential Determinism The complexity of a non-sequential flowgraph should be determined by both the complexities of the components and the complexity of the nonsequential structure.

  F3 - Linear Combination A proper axiom scheme will have specific upper and lower bounds. They state and prove that if a metric satisfies a proper axiom scheme than any positively weighted linear combination also satisfies that axiom scheme. This property requires that there is such a proper axiom scheme.

- Properties from Weyuker [8]
  The article by Weyuker describes axioms or properties that software metrics should have. The list below consists of properties extracted from those axioms or properties. The names associated with the properties were chosen by the author; Weyuker identified the properties only by number.

  W1 - Distribution The first property that Weyuker presents indicates that not all the programs should have the same metric value. That is, the metric should distribute the value of the metrics.

  $$(\exists P)\,(\exists Q)\ such\ that\ |P| \neq |Q|$$

  W2 - Fineness The second property requires that the metric is "not too coarse"

  $$\forall c \geq 0,\ there\ are\ only\ finitely\ many\ programs\ of\ complexity\ c$$

  W3 - Coarseness This property requires that the metric is "not too fine"

  $$\exists\ distinct\ programs\ P, Q\ such\ that\ |P| = |Q|$$

W4 - Implementation Dependence This requires that implementation details affects the metric.

$$\exists \ programs \ P \ and \ Q \ such \ that \ P \equiv Q \ and \ |P| \neq |Q|$$

W5 - Monotonicity This is the monotonicity property. Adding to the source code can not decrease the metric.

$$\forall \ P \ and \ Q, |P| \leq |P;Q| \wedge |Q| \leq |P;Q|$$

Not all metrics have this property. For example, Halstead's effort metric does not. Generally, any metric that involves division or averaging will not have the property of monotonicity.

W6a,W6b - Interaction There is a complexity that is not inherent in the individual pieces but it has do to with the combination of pieces. This property requires that for at least three programs, combining two of them will produce a different value than combining the other two.

$$\exists \ P, Q, R \ such \ that \ |P| = |Q| \ but \ |P;R| \neq |Q;R|$$

$$\exists \ P, Q, R \ such \ that \ |P| = |Q| \ but \ |R;P| \neq |R;Q|$$

W7 - Ordering This property requires that for at least one program, re-ordering the statements of the program will produce a different value of the metric.

$$\exists \ P \ and \ Q \ such \ that \ Q \ is \ formed \ by \ permuting \ P \ and \ |P| \neq |Q|$$

W8 - Renaming This property requires that metrics are insensitive to the renaming of variables.

$$If \ Q \ is \ formed \ by \ renaming \ the \ variables \ in \ P, \ then \ |P| = |Q|$$

W9 - Strict Wholeness The property of the whole being bigger or equal to the sum of the parts is a common notion. Weyuker requires a strict wholeness, that is, there is at least one program such that the value on the whole is greater than the sum of the values on the parts.

$$\exists \ P \ and \ Q \ s.t. \ |P| + |Q| < |P;Q|$$

2.3 Formal Properties

- Properties from Zuse's *Software Complexity* [9]

    Z1 - Sensitivity The sensitivity of the metric to atomic changes to the underlying model (e.g. control flow graph) is called a partial property by Zuse. [9, page 52]
    The complete set of the partial properties that a metric is sensitive to is called the property s of the metric.

- Properties from Grubstake [6, 2]

    G1 - Well-founded Structural Metric A well-founded structural metric [6] is a metric that has a mapping to anmodel that captures the aspect to be measured(G1a), a partial ordering on the model that preserves the relationships of the aspect(G1b) and an order-preserving mapping from the model to the real numbers(G1c).

    G2 - Constructive Structural Metric A constructive structural metric is a metric that has properties G1a, G1b, and G1c and has additionally a set of constructive operations on the model that allows the image of any program to be constructed and additionally that the result of applying the transform is greater than that the original element (G2d).

    G3 - Monotonicity A metric has the property of monotonicity if a new program is created by adding to a program, then the value of the metric on the old program is less than the value of the metric on the new program.

- Additional Grubstake Properties
  These following properties have not been previously published.

    G4 - Nontrivial Model A metric has this property if the model on which it is built is not trivial. That is, the model must have more than one instance. For example, using a singular object as the model would be trivial since all documents would map to the same object.

G5 - Nontrivial Ordering A metric has a nontrivial ordering if every instance in the model has a relation with at least one other instance other than top and bottom.

G6 - Nontrivial Mapping A metric has a nontrivial mapping if the order-preserving mapping does not map all the instances to the same value in the answer set. This is a weaker property than G7.

G7 - Strict Order Preserving Mapping A metric has this property if the order preserving mapping keeps distinct any two elements that have a relationship in the ordering but are not the same element.

$$a \leq_m b \land a \neq b \Rightarrow m(a) \leq m(b)$$

G8 - Ratio-Preserving Mapping A metric has a ratio-preserving mapping if the distance between instances in the model is proportional to the distance between the values in the answer set.

G9 - Relation-Preserving Mapping A metric has a relation preserving mapping if any two instances that have the same value in the answer set also had the same instance in the model.

$$a = b \Leftrightarrow m(a) = m(b)$$

G10 - Dataflow Oriented Model A metric has a dataflow-oriented model if the model includes information about the flow of data and the ordering on the model distinguishes instances that are only different in their dataflows.

G11 - Name Independent Model A metric has a name-independent model if the model does not contain information on the names used in the program.

- Scale Properties

The scales in measurement theory are defined in terms of the transformations that are allowed while the result still is valid.

S1 - Ordinal Scale The transformation can be any strictly increasing monotonic function. With an ordinal scale it is not meaningful to talk of the average of a set of value.

S2 - Interval Scale The transformation can be of the form ax + b where a $\geq$ 0. Temperatures in fahrenheit and celsius are examples of interval scales. In fact, the transformation between the two scales is of the form ax + b. For example, it is meaningful to talk of the average temperature for a day, but it is not meaningful to talk of one day being twice as hot as another day.

S3 - Ratio Scale The transformation can be only of the form ax where a $\geq$ 0. It is meaningful to take averages and percentages of values on a ratio scale. For example, it is meaning ful to say that x is twice as big as y. Temperatures expressed in the Kelvin (absolute) scale are an example of a ratio scale. It now makes sense to talk about one temperature being twice as hot as another temperature.

3 Orders on the Properties

It is possible to define an ordering on the properties that were identified in the previous section. The ordering (relation) will be a subsumes relation, $\geq_s$. That is, property A $\geq_s$ property B if any metric that has property A also has property B. Two properties are equal if each $\geq_s$ the other.

Proposition 1 *K1 = C3*

Both of these properties are "robustness" Although they are not well-defined, they are obviously equivalent.

Proposition 2 *K4 $\geq_s$ C4*

Kearney's prescriptiveness requires that the user understand how to change the source code to manipulate the values. Conte's prescriptiveness requires that it should be available during development and be useful to manage. Although this is a value judgement, we feel that if it is understandable enough to be able to manipulate the source code, than it will be available early and could be used for management.

For example, the cyclomatic complexity metric seems to satisfy these two properties. The developer knows that it is the number of decisions, these can be estimated early and can be used to control the "size" of the modules.

Proposition 3 $S3 \geq_s C5$

A ratio scale implies that averages, percentages and other statistical operations can be performed. Thus, Conte's analyzability would seem to be satisfied.

Proposition 4 $G1b \geq_s B1$

A partial order that preserves relationships of attributes is sensitive to any externally observable difference. This is assuming that the model chosen captures the attributes of interest and that the observable differences are in terms of these attributes.

Proposition 5 $G1a \geq_s B2$

A valid model captures the aspects that need to be measured, and therefore, intuitively reflects differences.

Proposition 6 $G1a \geq_s C2$

By ensuring that the mapping to the model captures the aspect to be measured, we can guarantee that the metric is valid.

Proposition 7 $G1c \geq_s C1$

Any order preserving mapping can be formally defined, and is therefore, easily understood. Since it preserves an order, it produces a single value.

Proposition 8 $G1 \geq_s K3, K4$

The mapping to a model captures what is to be measured, and hence is both specific and prescriptive.

Proposition 9 $G3 = C3a = K1a = W5$

These are all specifying monotonicity.

Proposition 10 $G2 \geq_s P3$

The grubstake property of being a containment-based structural metric subsumes the idea of being inductive over a structure.

Any constructive partial order that is mapped into R (the set of real numbers) with an order preserving mapping is inductive over the set of simple components (statements).

Proposition 11 $G2 \geq_s G1$

Obviously, G2 subsumes G1 because G1 plus containment-based ordering is G2.

Proposition 12 $G2 \geq_s G3$

Constructive operations increase the value of the metric and therefore imply monotonicity (G3).

Proposition 13 *G4 and G7 $\geq_s$ W1 and W2*

A non-trivial model and a non-trivial mapping on this model ensures that the distribution is not too fine or too coarse. Thus, the combination of G4 and G7 subsume both W1 and W2.

Proposition 14 *G4 and G7 $\geq_s$ W4*

A non-trivial model guarantees that the implementation of the program is reflected in the model. Thus, two programs performing the same function can have different abstract representations (or instances in the model). A non-trivial mapping of these different instances can yield different values.

Proposition 15 *G5 $\geq_s$ W1*

Since G5 yields an ordering that is more complex than a flat lattice, we know that G5 can distribute values of the metric.

Proposition 16 *G8 $\geq_s$ W6*

Weyuker obviously designed this axiom for data flow meaures. When the model provided by G8 is dataflow-oriented, it automatically accounts for W6.

Proposition 17 *G5 $\geq_s$ G1*

A nontrivial ordering automatically subsumes a partial ordering.

Proposition 18 $G5 \geq_s Z1$

A non-trivial ordering is sensitive to changes in the structure of the program.

These propositions about the subsumes relationships are displayed in a graph structure (see figure 1). The properties at the top of an arc subsume those properties at the bottom of the arc.

4 Conclusions

This paper presents a survey of many properties of software measures that have been presented in the literature. Although many of the early properties mentioned were informally defined and subjective, it has been argued that the more recent properties are both formally defined and subsume most of the earlier properties. Thus, by selecting metrics that have the objective properties, we can also be assured of having the subjective properties.

Understanding these properties and the relationships of the properties to each other will make it easier to evaluate proposed software measures. The problem still exists to decide which properties are useful or necessary for the desired application.

Research is continuing in evaluation of properties, specification of metrics, and the automation of determining the properties of metrics from their specifications.

References

[1] V. R. Basili and Jr. R. W. Reiter. Evaluating automatable measures of software development. *Proc. Workshop on Quantitative Software Models*, pages 107–116, 1979.

[2] James Bieman, Norm Fenton, David Gustafson, Austin Melton, and Robin Whitty. Moving from philosophy to practice in software measurement. *Proceedings of FACS Workshop on Software Metrics*, 1991.

[3] S. Conte, H. Dunsmore, , and V. Shen. *Software Engineering Metrics and Models*. Benjamin Cummings, Menlo Park, CA, 1986.

[4] N. Fenton and R Whitty. Axiomatic approach to software metrication through program decomposition. *computer journal*, 29(4):329–339, 1986.

[5] Joseph Kearney, Robert Sedlmeyer, William Thompson, Michael Gray, and Michael Adler. Software complexity measurement. *C. ACM*, 29(11):1044–1050, 1986.

[6] A. Melton, D. Gustafson, A. Baker, and J. Bieman. A mathematical perspective for software measures research. *IEE Softare Engineering Journal*, 5(5):246–254, 1990.

[7] R. E. Prather. An axiomatic theory of software complexity measure. *The Computer Journal*, 27(4):340–347, 1984.

[8] Elaine Weyuker. Evaluating software complexity measures. *IEEE Trans on Software Engineering*, 14(9):1357–1365, September 1988.

[9] Horst Zuse. *Software Complexity*. de Gruyter, New York, 1991.

POSet of Properties of Measures

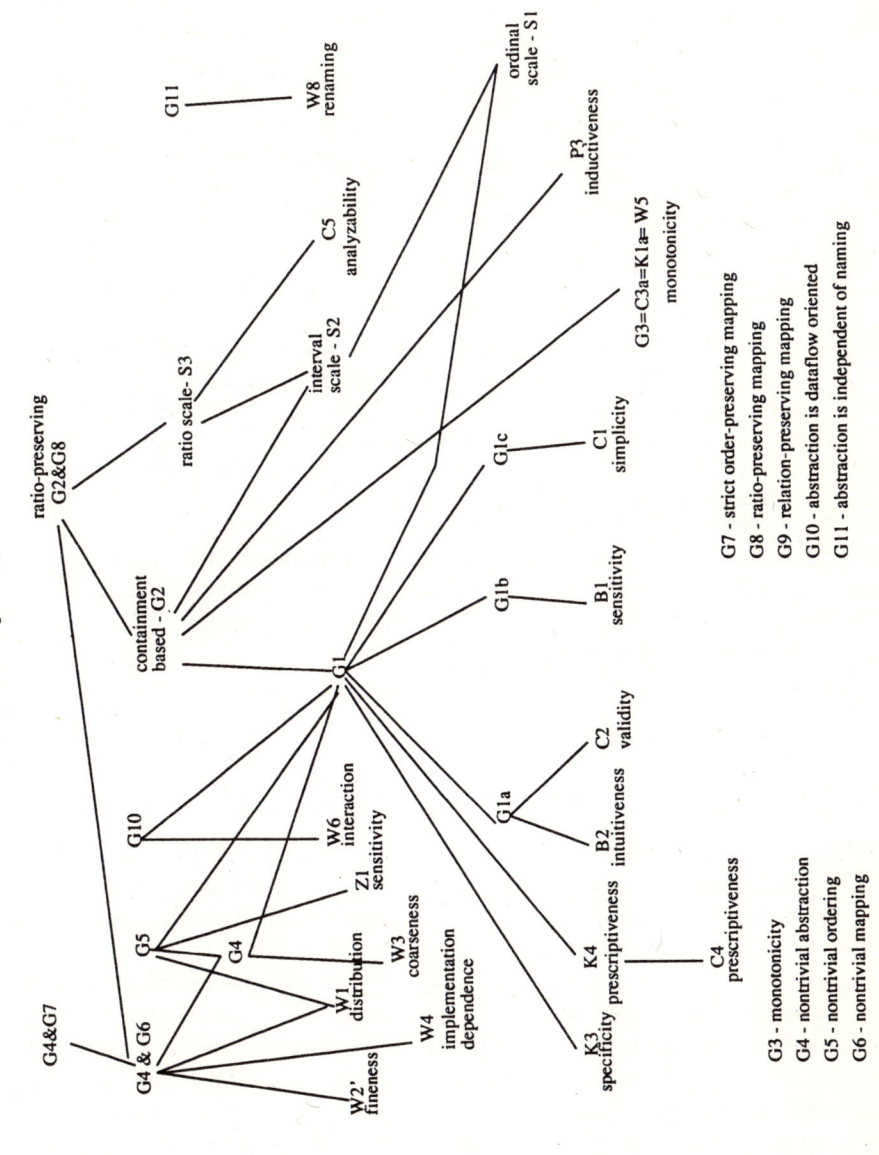

(rotated figure, page 193)

Nodes and labels:
- G4 & G7
- W2' fineness
- G4 & G6
- W4 implementation dependence
- W1 distribution
- G5
- W3 coarseness
- G4
- Z1 sensitivity
- G10
- W6 interaction sensitivity
- K3 specificity
- C4 prescriptiveness
- K4 prescriptiveness
- B2 intuitiveness
- G1a
- C2 validity
- C1
- B1 sensitivity
- G1b
- C1 simplicity
- G1c
- G3=C3a=K1a=W5 monotonicity
- P3 inductiveness
- interval scale - S2
- ratio scale - S3
- C5 analyzability
- containment based - G2
- ratio-preserving G2&G8
- ordinal scale - S1
- G11
- W8 renaming

Legend:
- G3 - monotonicity
- G4 - nontrivial abstraction
- G5 - nontrivial ordering
- G6 - nontrivial mapping
- G7 - strict order-preserving mapping
- G8 - ratio-preserving mapping
- G9 - relation-preserving mapping
- G10 - abstraction is dataflow oriented
- G11 - abstraction is independent of naming

Specifying Internal, External, and Predictive Software Metrics*

Austin Melton
Department of Computing and Information Sciences
Kansas State University
Manhattan, Kansas 66506 USA
austin@cis.ksu.edu

Abstract

We investigate three types of software metrics which we call internal, external, and predictive software metrics. These three types of software metrics allow for a complete classification of all software metrics. In this paper, however, our main purpose is not to classify metrics; our main purpose is to explain what the specification of a metric should include. One of the main ideas which is behind this paper but which is not fully developed here is that software metrics should be developed in much the same manner as programs are developed. This development should include requirement documents, specification documents, design documents, the definition of the metric itself, testing documents, and a user's manual. In this paper we give a specification template for internal, external, and predictive software metrics.

1 Introduction

1.1 Background and Informal Definitions

In this paper software metrics are divided into three classes; they are internal, external, and predictive software metrics. These classes are not entirely disjoint; a metric may, for example, be both external and predictive in which case we call it an external-predictive metric. However, every software metric is internal, external, and/or predictive. It should be emphasized that a software metric may be defined on any software document; we do not restrict software metrics by requiring them to be defined only on source code. (Later in the Introduction we discuss the notion of a *software document* more fully.) Informally, an *internal software metric* measures a static characteristic or attribute of a software document; these measurements – and thus the definition of the internal software metric – dependent solely on the software documents themselves. Examples of internal metrics are lines of code and coupling metrics. Internal software metrics should be highly accurate and reliable. Informally, an *external software metric* measures a characteristic or an attribute which

---

*Research is supported in part by NATO Collaborative Research Grant 034/88 and by ONR Grant N00014-88-K-0455.

is simultaneously a characteristic of a software document and something external to the document, e.g., a machine on which the document must run or a person who must work with the document. Examples of external metrics are costs and functions which measure maintainability. Since it is not usually possible to get accurate measurements of all machines on which a software document will run or of all humans who will work with a software document, external software metrics can not be expected to be as reliable as internal metrics. Informally, a *predictive software metric* estimates a characteristic or attribute of a software document which does not exist or which for some other reason is not available at the time of the measuring (estimating). Examples of predictive metrics are estimating lines of source code from a specification and estimating testing costs from high-level design documents. Since a predictive software metric may by its nature only produce estimates, it can not be as reliable as an internal metric. It is clear that an external-predictive metric must be used with caution because its measurements are potentially fragile and unreliable.

We feel that our presentation of predictive metrics gives insight into how such metrics may be defined and into the some of the problems associated with them. However, we also feel that more research is needed before these metrics will be completely understood. For a somewhat different perspective on predictive metrics, see [1].

1.2 A Software Project Model

As mentioned above we assume that a software metric may be defined on any software document. To clarify what we mean by a software document, we briefly describe the software project model which is developed in [2].

A software project model instance consists of a finite collection of interdependent, directed, acyclic graphs. Each graph consists of documents of a common type; examples of such graphs include specification graphs, pseudo-code graphs, and user manual graphs. It is left to the determination of the software project manager(s) as to which *software document types* are included in a particular project. Each document in each graph is called a *software document* or *document* for short. Each software document is a self-contained entity which could fully describe the type's aspect for the project at the time of the document's creation. We say "*could* fully describe" because in fact there may be parallel versions of a particular document type being developed, and thus, a single document would not fully describe its type's aspect for the whole project. The possible development of parallel versions is the reason why the graphs are not trivial non-branching trees. The graphs are interdependent because all the latest documents of all types may be used in the creation of the next document of any type. The graphs are directed by time of creation of the documents. Although the graphs are acyclic, the same document may appear more than once in a graph. Having the same document appear twice in a graph would probably mean that the persons working on the documents of this type prefer to start again with an earlier document and continue developing from that earlier point on – essentially saying that the most recent work on this document type has seemingly yielded no useful results.

Figure 1 represents a simple software project. Similar figures are found in [2]. The main difference between Figure 1 and the figures in [2] is the orientation of the axes. In Figure 1 the time axis is the horizontal axis; in [2] the time axes are the vertical axes.

The software project model emphasizes that software is developed in parallel and that each activity – modeled by different document types – influences all the other activities. Each "*" in Figure 1 represents a software document of the type listed on its immediate left.

1.3 Definitions

The following definitions are used in defining software metrics.

Definition 1.1 Let X be a set, and let $\leq$ be a relation on X, i.e., $\leq$ is a subset of $X \times X$. $\leq$ is a *preorder* on X if

i. $(x,x) \in \leq$ for each $x \in X$ and

ii. whenever $(x,y) \in \leq$ and $(y,z) \in \leq$, then it must follow that $(x,z) \in \leq$.

Property i. is called *reflexivity*, and property ii. is called *transitivity*.

$\leq$ is a *partial order* if it is a preorder and

iii. whenever $(x,y) \in \leq$ and $(y,x) \in \leq$, then $x = y$.

Property iii. is called *antisymmetry*. (In a sense antisymmetry says that the order is strong enough or sensitive enough to determine the identity of the elements.)

$\leq$ is a *total* or *linear order* if it is a partial order and

iv. for every $x, y \in X$, it is either the case that $(x,y) \in \leq$ or $(y,x) \in \leq$.

If $\leq$ is a preorder, then $(X, \leq)$ or just X is called a *preordered set*; if $\leq$ is a partial order, then $(X, \leq)$ or X is called a *partially ordered set* or *poset* for short; and if $\leq$ is a linear or total order, then $(X, \leq)$ or X is called a *linearly* or *totally ordered set*.

We will normally use $\leq$ as an infix operator; and thus, we will usually write $x \leq y$ instead of $(x,y) \in \leq$.

Each linearly ordered set is also a poset, and each poset is also a preordered set. Linearly ordered sets are so-called because their elements can be "lined up" according to the order. The natural numbers with their usual order are a linearly ordered set. If X is a set with at least two elements, then the power set of X, i.e., the set of all subsets of X, with the subset order is a poset which is not a linearly ordered set because there are subsets of X which are not comparable. If X is the set of all people in London and if these people are ordered by height measured to the nearest millimeter, then X is a preordered set which is not a poset because there are distinct people with the same height, i.e., there are different persons x and y with $x \leq y$ and $y \leq x$ (but $x \neq y$. Equality is not determined by the order.)

Definition 1.2 Let $(X, \leq_X)$ and $(Y, \leq_Y)$ be preordered sets, and let $f : X \longrightarrow Y$ be a function with domain X and range Y. f is an *order-preserving function* if it is the case that whenever $x_1 \leq_X x_2$ then $f(x_1) \leq_Y f(x_2)$, i.e., f *preserves* the order from X into Y.

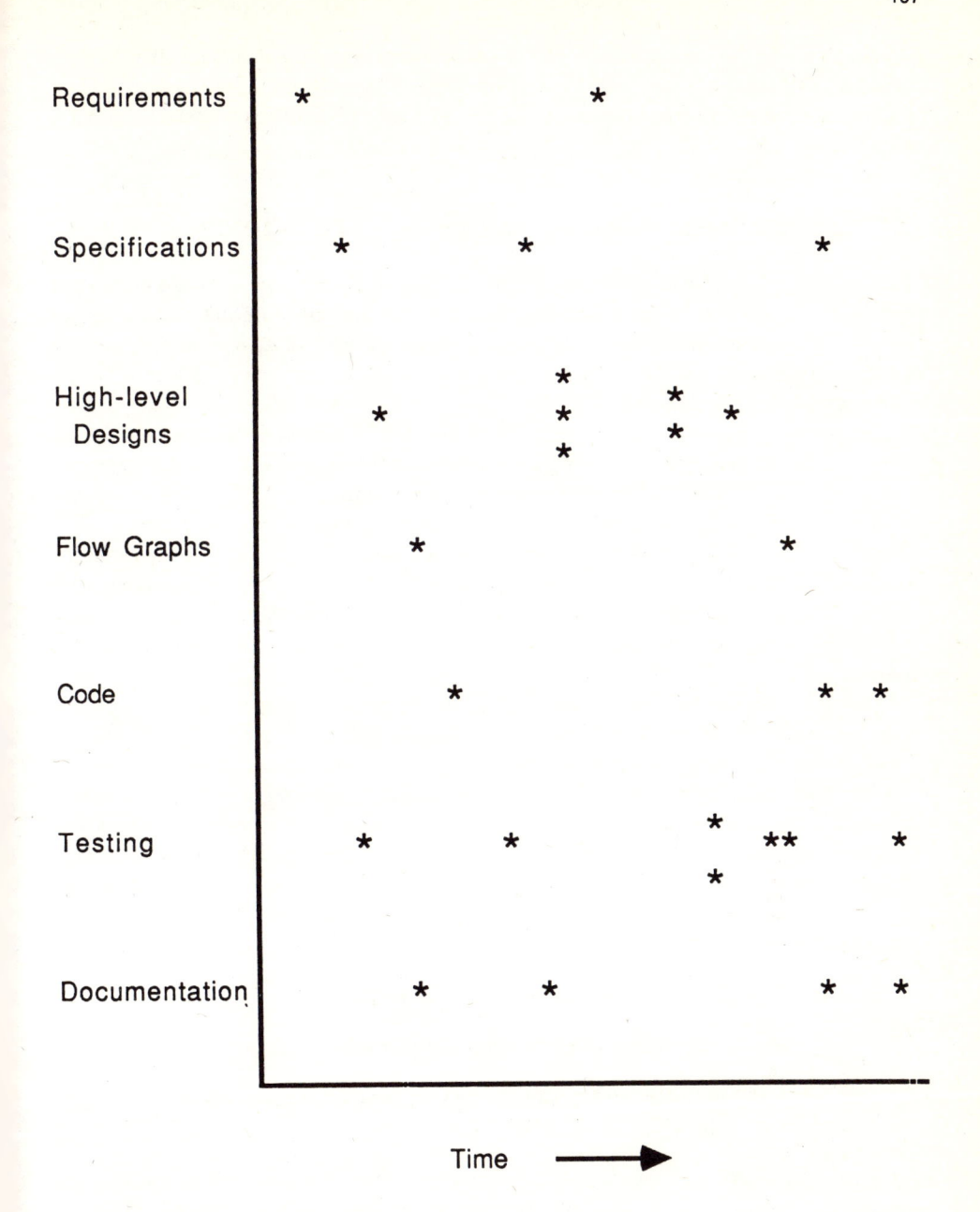

```
Requirements   *              *

Specifications    *         *                *

High-level                  *
Designs         *           *       *  *
                            *       *
                            *

Flow Graphs        *                     *

Code               *                        *  *

Testing       *         *        *    **      *
                                 *

Documentation      *       *                *  *
```

Time →

Life of Typical Software Project

Figure 1

We will use the expression *software document type set* for a set of software documents of the same type.

Since software metrics are functions, we will talk of a software metric's domain and range.

2 Characteristics of All Software Metrics

The domain of a software metric may be (or may include) any software document type set. We do not assume that software metrics may only be defined on sets of source code documents. We may define metrics on sets of specifications, sets of design documents, sets of testing documents, and even on sets of documentation documents to name some possibilities.

In the early days of software metrics' research it was hoped (and believed) that there existed at least one metric which would reveal everything about the (relative) complexity of programs – where a program meant source code. It has been shown (see, for example, [4]) that such an all-encompassing metric can not exist. Such a metric would have to be self-contradictory because programs have many different and conflicting aspects or attributes of complexity. From this early misconception we have learned that the specifications for a software metric must include not only a software document type set but also an attribute which is to be measured by the metric.

However, we can do even better. Most documents for any document type are complex, and it is often hard to focus on a fixed attribute in a complex document. Thus, when specifying a software metric, we require a document type, an attribute of that type, and a model type for documents of that type. (We use the terms *model type* and *model instance* for clarity. For example, we call flowgraphs a model type, and we call a particular flowgraph a model instance.) The model type must clearly reveal the attribute being measured; each model instance is simply an abstraction of the document which highlights the attribute being measured. The models have a number of uses in software measurement:

- They allow us to focus on the attribute in question.

- They help us determine when metrics are related.

- And equally important they can prevent us from trying to compare incomparable measurements.

When designing and validating metrics, researchers often do the following – or a variation thereof. A few sample documents of the specified type are given to experts who are asked to rank the documents based on increasing complexity. (A much better request would of course be: to rank the documents based on increasing amount or presence of a specific attribute.) Then the ranking of the documents as determined by the experts is compared with the ranking of the documents as determined by the proposed metric. The metric has credibility if the experts' ranking closely matches the metric's ranking. An example would be if a particular document is ranked as the fifth most complex by the experts, then its measurement, i.e., the value which the metric assigns to it, should be (about) the fifth largest measurement value.

This validation procedure assumes that there is an order on the set of documents being measured, and it further assumes that this order is preserved by the metric, i.e., that the metric is an order-preserving function. (The conclusion that a metric should be an order-preserving function is also obtainable via measurement theory. According to measurement theory, for a function to properly measure something the function must preserve all pertinent relations from the domain to the range.)

It is an important area of research to find good model types for different document types and to see what orders these model types impose. (See [4] for more information concerning software measurement orders.) For the remainder of this paper, we assume that for each document type and for each attribute, there is a corresponding model type and a partial order on the set of models instances. Once we have a partial order on the set of model instances for a given document type set D, we can easily define a corresponding order on D itself by saying $d_1 \leq d_2$ if and only if

(the model instance of d_1) $\leq$ (the model instance of d_2).

The order on D is usually only a preorder because in general there exist distinct documents in D with the same abstraction.

As stated above the models can help us determine when metrics (and their corresponding measurements) are related and when they are not related. If the attributes being measured by different metrics have the same or related model types, then we may be able via the model types to establish that the metrics are comparable. However, if the model types for the two metrics are not related, then we should not expect that the metrics and their corresponding measurements are related.

We have not addressed the question as to what kinds or types of measurements our software metrics should produce, i.e., we have not addressed the question as to what set or sets we should use for the ranges of our software metrics. The usual range sets are subsets of the nonnegative real numbers or subsets of the natural numbers. In this paper we will not specify particular range sets; we simply call our range sets *answer sets*. The question as to what are good and appropriate answer sets is not trivial nor has it been satisfactorily answered. According to measurement theory the important orders of the domains of our metrics should be preserved by the metrics into the answer sets. However, we know that some important software measurement orders are partial and not total, the best known example being the "inclusion" order on flowgraphs [4]. Thus, according to measurement theory the answer set for a metric whose domain order is based on the flowgraph order should not be total. But any subset of the reals or the natural numbers is a totally ordered set.

3 Internal Software Metrics

Definition 3.1 An *internal software metric* is an order-preserving function from a document type set to an answer set. The order on the document set is determined by the order on the corresponding set of model instances of a model type which highlights the documents' attribute which the metric is measuring. The purpose of an internal software metric is to measure the presence and "amount" of the designated attribute in the software documents. The measurements (or answers) of an internal software metric are completely determined by the (static) documents themselves; and thus, internal metrics should be highly reliable.

We are now ready to give the specifications for an internal software. When we use an expression like "an attribute of a type", we mean "an attribute of a document of that type".

Figure 2 depicts in part the major components of an internal software metric.

Specification 3.2 The specification of an *internal software metric* consists of

- a document type,

- an attribute of the type,

- a model type of the document type and this model type must highlight the attribute,

- a partial order on the model instances and this partial order must reflect the relative "amount" of the attribute in each document,

- an answer set and this set must have (at least) a partial order defined on it, and

- an order-preserving function from the set of model instances to the answer set.

The characteristics of the order-preserving function from the set of models to the answer set determine the type of measurement (in the sense of measurement theory) which the metric will produce. In the vocabulary of measurement theory, the characteristics of the function determine the type of scale. Thus, these characteristics determine how we can use the measurements which the metric produces – whether we can take, for example, mean averages or if we must settle for medians or modes.

Let D be the document type set; let M be the set of model instances; and let AS be the answer set. If we let $abs : D \longrightarrow M$ be the function which maps a software document to its model instance or abstraction and if we let $m' : M \longrightarrow AS$ be the order-preserving function from the set of model instances to the answer set, then the actual metric being defined is the composition $m' \circ abs$. Let's call this function m; thus, $m = m' \circ abs$.

A natural question to ask is: Is m an order-preserving function? The answer is "yes". Recall there is a natural preorder defined on D by
$$d_1 \leq_D d_2$$
if and only if
$$abs(d_1) \leq_M abs(d_2)$$
(For clarity we sometimes subscript the "$\leq$" symbol. For example, $\leq_M$ is the partial order defined on the set of model instances M.) The order $\leq_D$ inherits reflexivity and transitivity ¿from $\leq_M$. However, since the function abs is in general many-to-one, there will in general be distinct, i.e., unequal, documents d_3 and d_4 in D with $abs(d_3) = abs(d_4)$; thus, $d_3 \leq_D d_4$ and $d_4 \leq_D d_3$; but $d_3 \neq d_4$. Since this natural order on D – and note that this order does indeed reflect the "amount" of the attribute in each document – is defined as it is via abs and $\leq_M$, abs is order-preserving. And thus, m is also order-preserving because the composition of order-preserving functions is an order-preserving function.

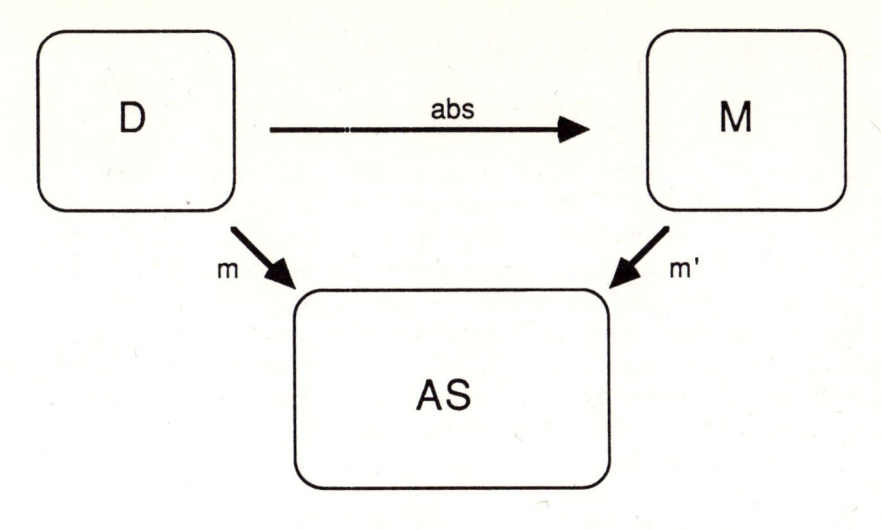

Internal Software Metric

Figure 2

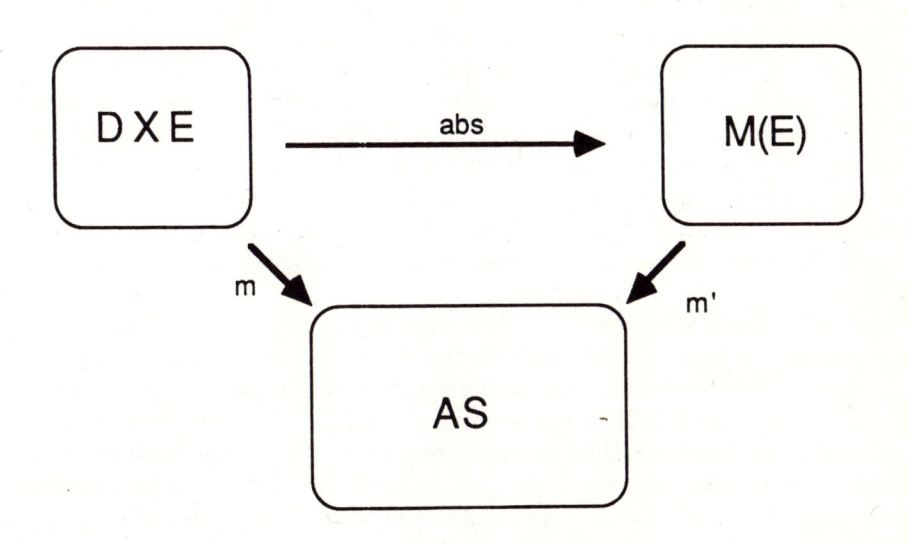

External Software Metric

Figure 3

4 External Software Metrics

Definition 4.1 An *external software metric* is an order-preserving function whose domain is a Cartesian product of a document type set and an *external set*. The external set does *not* contain software documents. The order on the Cartesian product is determined by the order on the corresponding set of model instances of a model type which highlights the attribute which the metric is trying to measure. The ideal purpose of an external software metric would be to measure the presence and "amount" of the designated attribute in the ordered pairs consisting of a software document and an external element – which might be, for example, a person or a machine. Since the measurements (or answers) of an external software metric are not completely determined by the documents themselves, it is not expected that such measurements can in general be as accurate as the measurements produced by an internal software metric.

Figure 3 shows the basic setup for an external metric.

When we discuss external metrics, the situation immediately becomes much more complicated than for internal metrics. Most of the complications arise because because of the presence of the *external set*. This external set may be a set of people, e.g., a set of programmers in charge of maintaining programs, or a set of programs, e.g., a set of compilers; or the external set may itself be a Cartesian product, e.g., a Cartesian product of a set of programmers and a set of compilers. The external set is so-called because it consists of elements which are external to the sets of software documents; thus, the name *external* software metric. For simplicity in our discussions, we'll assume that the external set consists only of humans.

Let D denote a document type set, and let E denote the external set (of humans). Possibilities for the attribute include readability, modifiability, maintainability; such attributes clearly depend on both a document and a human.

What kinds of model types are needed for $D \times E$? This question can probably not be answered well at this time; this seems to be a good area for future research. About the best we can now do is make a few comments/suggestions on such model types.

One possibility is to *pretend* that the domain of our metric, i.e., the set $D \times E$, contains only documents, i.e., pretend that the E doesn't exist. Thus, we could use a model type for D as our model type. On the one hand this suggestion seems ludicrous because it is obvious that for many attributes the human (or whatever external) factor will be very influential in the measurement. On the other hand there are cases in which we only have the documents upon which to base the measurements. In these cases it is clear why our measurements are often not highly reliable. In some cases we must realize that the very nature of what we are trying to do with external metrics means that we have to expect and live with potentially large inaccuracies.

Another possibility for handling the E in $D \times E$ is to attempt to explicitly measure the human factor. Thus, our model instances will contain not only abstractions of the documents but also abstractions of the humans – abstractions which highlight the human characteristics needed for the attribute in question. However, there potential problems in trying to explicitly measure the documents and the humans. These potential problems include:

1. we would need to have each human who will be using the documents made available for measuring and

2. we would need to know how to measure humans regarding such factors as understanding, problem solving, etc.

Concerning the first item, it would be difficult to get the humans (or for their managers to allow them) to sit through these measurement sessions; and concerning the second item, we don't in general know how to measure such human characteristics.

Is there an other possibility for handling the E in $D \times E$? Maybe we don't have to either completely ignore the E component or completely measure it. We could make some simplifying assumptions regarding the E component, and then incorporate these assumptions into our model type. For example, if we are measuring understandability, we could assume in our model type that there are three kinds of humans: those who have keen understanding, those who have average understanding, and those who don't know what understanding is. Then without having the humans undergo extensive testing we could with a high degree of accuracy map each (document, human) ordered pair to an ordered pair consisting of the model instance of the document and one of the three intelligence levels.

These three possibilities (of which only the first and third are probably reasonable) for handling the E coordinate help explain two long observed phenomena of software metrics. These phenomena are

1. it is very hard to get external metrics that are reliable over a wide range of applications and

2. sometimes individual companies develop external metrics that are quite reliable for in-house projects.

The first phenomenon is (in many situations) explicable because when an external metric is defined without regard to the E coordinate, i.e., by assuming that the E coordinate does not exist, then such a metric will of course only have a small range of reliability. The second phenomenon is explicable because in some companies the E component is relatively constant for certain attributes. Thus, if one of these attributes is being measured and if in the definition of the metric these relatively constant values are taken into consideration, then the metric should be reliable when applied in-house or even when applied in another company in which the E component has approximately the same constant values.

We are now ready to specify an external software metric.

Specification 4.2 The specification of an external software metric includes

- a Cartesian product whose first component is a document type and whose second component is an external set,

- an attribute of the Cartesian product,

- a model type of the Cartesian product and this model type must highlight the attribute,

- a partial order on the model instances and this partial order must reflect the "amount" of each attribute in each order pair from the Cartesian product,

- an answer set and this set must have a partial order defined on it, and

- an order-preserving function from the set of model instances to the set of answers.

As in the case of an internal software metric, the actual external software metric is simply the composition of the functions $abs : D \times E \longrightarrow M$ and $m' : M \longrightarrow AS$, i.e., $m = m' \circ abs$. We denote the set of model instances by $M(E)$ to emphasize that there are various ways to handle the E-component.

5 Predictive Software Metrics

In this section we use the term *predictive software metric* more precisely than we have in the earlier sections. From our early uses of the term, a predictive metric could be used to predict either an internal or an external attribute. However, in this section we assume that a predictive metric is only used to predict internal attributes. If we want to predict external attributes, we will use an external-predictive metric.

Definition 5.1 A *predictive software metric* is an order-preserving function ¿from a software document type set to an answer set. The order on the document type set is determined by the order on the corresponding set of model instances of a model type which highlights an attribute. However, the purpose of the metric is not to measure an attribute of the domain document type set itself. The purpose of an external software metric is to measure an attribute in software documents which are not currently available. Since these documents are not available, the metric must be defined on another document type set, and we must have a "theory" which relates the two document type sets or the corresponding model type sets. Since the measurements of a predictive software metric are not determined by the documents we actually want to measure, we should not expect a predictive metric to be as reliable as an internal metric. The reliability is in part dependent on the "theory", but even with a good theory there is a built-in degree of unreliability.

Since both external and predictive metrics have built-in unreliability factors, whenever we define a predictive-external metric, we should not expect a high degree of reliability. It may be the case that only internal metrics can produce real measurement in the formal sense of measurement theory or even in the intuitive, everyday sense in which we normally use the term "measurement".

Although we do not have access to the documents we really want to measure, we do know their document type, and we can determine an appropriate model type for the attribute we would like to measure. For example, we may want to measure an aspect of control flow in source code, but we only have specifications or high-level designs. We still know that a model type for the source code is the flow graph model, and we know how to define an abstraction function from the source-code set to the set of flowgraphs. As we will see below, it is sufficient to find a theory which tells us how to associate the documents which we have with the documents we would like to have or to find a theory which tells us how to associate model instances for the documents we have with model instances of the documents we would like to have.

For ease of reference we let D_1 be the document type set of the documents which we have, and we let D_2 be the document type set of the documents we would like to have and measure. Further, att_1 is the attribute in D_1, and att_2 is the attribute we would like to measure in D_2. M_1 is the set of model instances for D_1 and att_1, and M_2 is the set of model instances for D_2 and att_2.

For predictive software metrics it is often the case that the D_2-attribute which we are estimating is (at best) only partially developed in the D_1-documents; and thus, there are usually several possibilities for how the full development might continue. The existence of these possible developments is what produces the built-in imprecision in predictive metrics. There is of course also the imprecision which arises if the theory relating the two document types or the the two model types is not good. An example of a predictive metric is a function whose domain type is specifications and whose answers are natural numbers which are to represent lines of source code.

Figure 4 gives the basic setup for a predictive software metric.

The specifications for a predictive software metric include two document type sets, two attributes, and two models. Further, we need a "theory" which explains and justifies why the document set D_1 with attribute att_1 can be expected to be helpful in predicting the attribute att_2 in document set D_2 or why the model instances in M_1 should be related to model instances in M_2. Further, our theory should tell us how to associate documents in D with documents in D_2 or how to associate model instances in M_1 with model instances in M_2. (As we will see later, it does not matter whether we associate documents with documents or model instances with model instances; we do not need to be able to do both.) This theory is probably not a theory in a formal sense though we are not sure how developed these predictive metric theories might become.

Figure 4 shows our situation. The maps abs_1, mod, doc, and abs_2 essentially (see next paragraph) form what is called a commuting diagram; that is, the composition functions $mod \circ abs_1$ and $abs_2 \circ doc$ are equal. In going from D_1 to M_2 it does not matter if one uses the function $mod \circ abs_1$ or the function $abs_2 \circ doc$; both functions give the same results. This is why we do not need both the functions doc and mod; either one is sufficient for our work. The fact that the diagram commutes is clearly of practical importance because it means that we do not need to define both doc and mod; we do not need to develop two theories – one for relating the documents and an other for relating the model instances. We can develop whichever theory is easier to develop, and then we can use the corresponding function doc or mod.

In the above paragraph is the statement that abs_1, mod, doc, and abs_2 "essentially" form a commuting diagram. Since if we define both doc and mod we are doing so from possibly two different theories and since both doc and mod are only estimating functions, it is probably not the case that $mod \circ abs_1$ and $abs_2 \circ doc$ are exactly equal, i.e., it is probably not the case that abs_1, mod, doc, and abs_2 exactly form a commuting diagram. However, $mod \circ abs_1$ and $abs_2 \circ doc$ should be equal within the limits of the estimating. In other words for a given D_1-document d, $(mod \circ abs_1)(d)$ and $(abs_2 \circ doc)(d)$ may not be the very same M_2-model instance, but they should be M_2-model instances of two D_2-documents which could both be the completion of d. Thus, for our predicting purposes $mod \circ abs_1$ and $abs_2 \circ doc$ are equal, i.e., for our purposes abs_1, mod, doc, and abs_2 do form a commuting diagram.

Now we are ready to give the specifications for a predictive software metric.

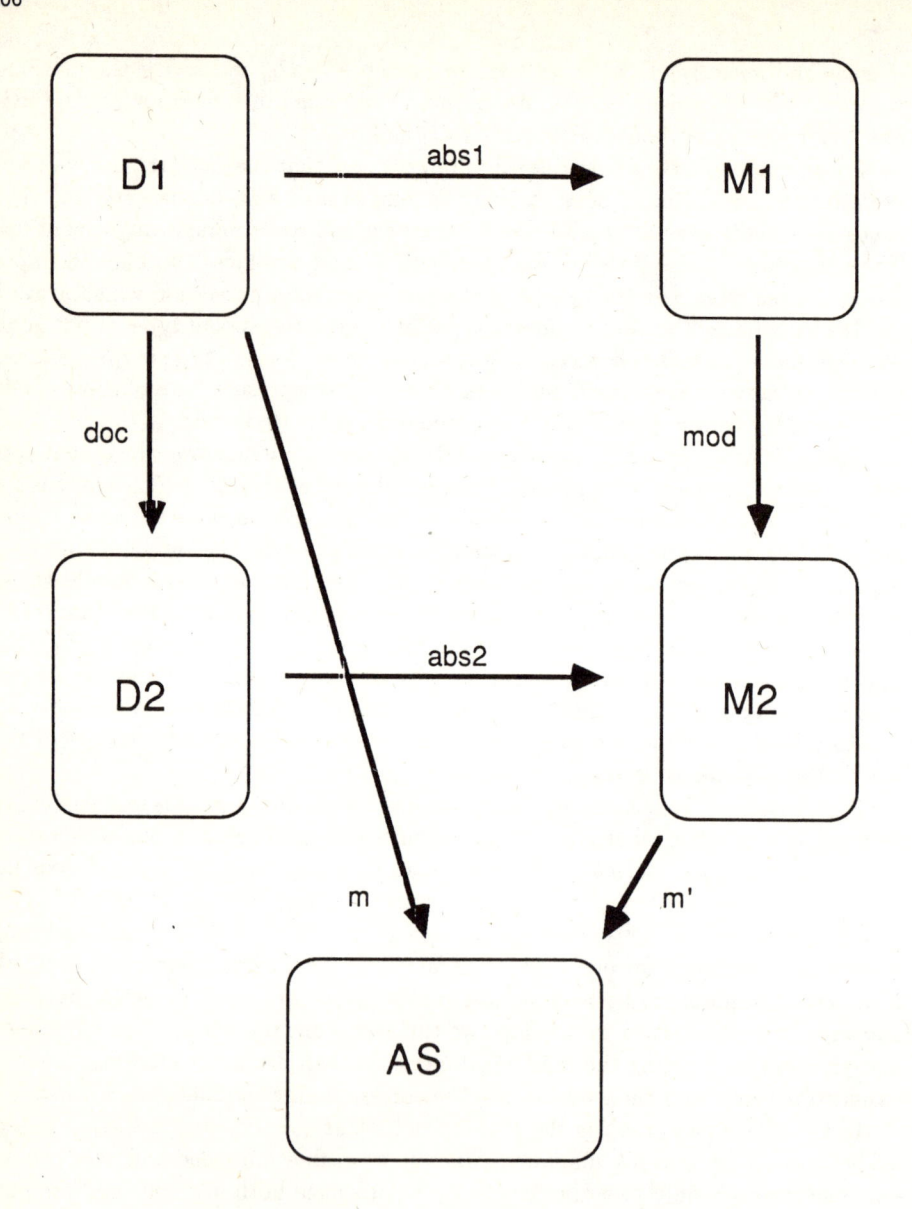

Predictive Software Metric

Figure 4

Specification 5.2 The specification of a predictive software metric includes

- a document type set the documents of which we for some reason do not have access to (we call this document type set D_2),

- an attribute of document type set D_2 (we call this attribute att_2; it is this attribute we would like to measure if we had access to the documents in D_2),

- a model type for the D_2-document type and att_2-attribute (this model type which we call M_2 must highlight the attribute att_2),

- a partial order on M_2 (this partial order must reflect the "amount" of attribute att_2 in each document in D_2),

- a document type set (we call this type set D_1 and we have access to the documents of this type),

- an attribute of the document type set D_2 (we call this attribute att_1),

- a model type for the D_1-document type and att_1-attribute (this model type which we call M_1 must highlight the attribute att_1),

- a partial order on M_1 (this partial order must reflect the "amount" of attribute att_1 in each document in D_1),

- a theory as described above which relates either the D_1- and the D_2-documents or the M_1- and M_2-model instances (this theory must justify why the documents in D_1 with attribute att_1 can be used to estimate the "amount" of attribute att_2 in the D_2 documents or why the model instances in M_1 can be mapped into the model instances in M_2 in such a way that the "amount" of the att_2 attribute in D_2 documents is accurately estimated)

- an answer set with a partial order defined on it, and

- an order-preserving function $m' : M_2 \longrightarrow AS$.

The order-preserving function *doc* or *mod* will be determined by the theory described above, and the desired desired predictive metric is $m' \circ mod \circ abs_1$ or $m' \circ abs_2 \circ doc$. The uncertainty or unreliability in a predictive metric exists because in general there are different valid *doc* and *mod* functions, i.e., there are in general many ways that a D_1 document can be completed into a "correct" D_2 document. The more we development automated programming tools, the more we will limit the possible variations for the functions *doc* and *mod*, and the more accurate our predictive software metrics will become.

6 Conclusions

We have introduced the idea that the design and development of software metrics is a process which should be approached in a manner similar to the design and development of a large software project. In this paper we have only discussed the specifications of software metrics, and we have done so with regard to three types of metrics: internal, external, and predictive metrics. We chose these three types because we feel they are distinctly different from each other and because they include all software metrics.

We have also raised a number of research questions which we feel are interesting and important for the future development of software measurement theory.

References

[1] A. Baker, J. Bieman, N. Fenton, D. Gustafson, A. Melton, and R. Whitty. A philosophy for software measurement. *Journal of Systems and Softare*, 12:277–281, 1990.

[2] A. Baker, J. Bieman, D. Gustafson, and A. Melton. Modeling and measuring the software development process. *Proc. 20th Hawaii International Conference on Systems Sciences (HICSS-20)*, II:23–30, January 1987.

[3] N. Fenton and A. Melton. Deriving software measures throughout the development process. *Journal of Systems and Software*, 12:177–187, 1990.

[4] A. Melton, D. Gustafson, A. Baker, and J. Bieman. A mathematical perspective for software measures research. *IEE Softare Engineering Journal*, 5(5):246–254, 1990.

The Mathematics of Measurement in Software Engineering

Meg Russell

Centre for Systems and Software Engineering, Department of Electrical Engineering, South Bank Polytechnic, London, UK.

1 INTRODUCTION

This paper gives an outline of the mathematics included in a new course on measurement for software engineering. This is a relatively new subject which is currently being promoted within the European Community. The work described is part of a collaborative project called 'METKIT', funded by the European Commission under their 'ESPRIT' programme. The mathematics included can be broadly divided between measurement theory and statistics.

2 SOFTWARE ENGINEERING MEASUREMENT

Ever since the 'software crisis' was identified over 20 years ago, software producers have been searching for new methods to help with the production of quality software. The crisis came about when the informal development methods previously used became inappropriate for new complex software systems. The software produced was of poor quality, and cost and time overruns became common.

In the 1990's software plays a part in many peoples' lives, controlling not only business systems, but also safety critical systems such as those for air traffic control. However, many of the symptoms of the software crisis persist. Newspapers frequently report disasters where the failure of a software system is the suggested cause, and we often hear of huge systems which have been cancelled due to time overruns of years, or cost overruns of millions of dollars.

Ever since the software crisis began, software producers have been trying to introduce an engineering approach into their work, believing this to be the only way to solve the crisis. This has been a partial success. Methods such as formal specification techniques and structured programming are well-known and widely used. However, one part of engineering which is not yet widely accepted is the vital role of measurement. Traditional engineering disciplines state requirements in measurable terms, use measurement to predict project costs and timescales, and monitor projects against these requirements and predictions throughout the life-cycle. This approach is rarely taken in software engineering. In fact recent surveys have shown that 40-50% of software producers record no data at all on the progress of their projects [HEEMSTRA88], [MANCINI90]. Much research into the use of measurement in software engineering has been carried out over recent years. One major reason that measurement methods have not been taken up is the lack of technology transfer between researchers and practitioners.

3 THE METKIT PROJECT

METKIT (Metrics Education ToolKIT) is a technology transfer project. Its aim is to raise awareness and increase usage of software engineering measurement ("metrics") within European industry. It is a three year project which began in February 1989.

METKIT is funded by the European Community under its ESPRIT programme, which has itself been a major source of funding for software engineering measurement research [WHITTY90]. The project was born out of a realisation that

---

This paper was prepared for the Mathematics in Engineering Education conference, held in Budapest in April 1991. © METKIT consortium, January 1991.

although much good research had been done, the message about the need to measure had not got through to practitioners in the software industry.

METKIT is producing educational materials about software engineering measurement for managers and engineers in the software industry and for academic students studying software engineering. The project is a collaboration between academic and industrial partners with various areas of expertise, from four European countries. South Bank Polytechnic's role is entirely concerned with materials for academic students. The 'academic package' comprises a number of modules relating to different aspects of software engineering measurement, which may be combined in various ways to create courses. Most of the materials are for traditional classroom teaching, providing overhead projector transparencies for the teacher and notes for the student. Background reading for the whole package is provided in a textbook, whose production has been part funded by the project [FENTON91].

4 Background Studies

The first year of METKIT was spent on various background studies. These included research into software engineering measurement, to find a coherent framework within which to present past research work [BUSH90], and an investigation into the level of use of measurement in industry. Another part of the background work was an investigation into the current amount of software engineering measurement teaching in academic institutions. This same study looked at possible approaches to teaching the subject, and teachers' needs for educational materials. It was made up of two parts: an international postal survey, using a short questionnaire, and a series of in depth interviews with experienced teachers of the subject. Full details of the results can be found in [RUSSELL90].

The questionnaire revealed that the majority of teachers of software engineering include some material on measurement on their courses, but that they are desperately short of materials to use. They used mostly traditional teaching methods, and their main source was textbooks. However, existing textbooks in software engineering contain little material on measurement.

The interviews provided suggestions about the best way to teach the subject. It seemed that it was inappropriate to try and teach students about the use of particular measures without providing a strong motivation to measure, and a range of background knowledge. Teachers wanted to present a generic approach to measurement, which was independent of individual meas-ures. This need can be met by teaching the rudiments of measurement theory. Teachers also stressed that an understanding of basic statistics was vital, if students were to learn how to carry out the measurement process properly. This can be provided by a brief look at experimental design, data collection and data analysis.

5 Measurement Theory

Measurement theory, although perhaps not widely known, is a well-established discipline. It has been researched by scientists, engineers and philosophers since early this century. [CAMPBELL20] is widely cited as the pioneer work; Finkelstein has more recently written many articles with a philosophical bias (eg. [FINKELSTEIN82]); mathematical background is provided in [KRANTZ71], and perhaps best in [ROBERTS79].

Measurement theory provides a formal framework for measurement. It defines the process of measurement as a mathematical function. It tells us how to find whether a measure is valid. It enables us to decide what mathematical operations are meaningful on a given measure - this is reliant on the measurement 'scale type' of the measure. These factors have frequently been overlooked. Many of the 'measures' of the social sciences can be seen, in the light of measurement theory, not to be measures at all, or at best to be measures which are unsuited to sophisticated statistical analysis. However, social scientists are not the only ones to make these mistakes. Many of the proposed measures in software engineering do not stand up to scrutiny. This is why it is particularly important that software engineering students are acquainted with the basic principles of measurement theory.

The following sections describe the subject as it is taught on the course. As the METKIT target audience are not mathematicians, mathematical language and notation in the course are kept to a minimum. Hence the subject is described in slightly more mathematical depth here than it is to METKIT students.

5.1 THE REPRESENTATIONAL THEORY OF MEASUREMENT

Measurement is defined as:

The process of objective, empirical assignment of numbers or symbols to attributes of entities in such a way as to describe them.

An *attribute* is a property or characteristic, and an *entity* is an object or event. Examples of attributes of entities that may be measured include the height of a person, the time taken to complete a journey, the cost of a process and the reliability of a product.

Measurement may be either *direct* or *indirect*. *Direct* measurement of an attribute does not depend on the measurement of any other attribute. *Indirect* measurement involves the measurement of one or more other attributes. For example, measurement of area in terms of width and length, or measurement of reliability as mean-time-to-failure are both indirect. Measurement of a person's height or of the cost of a process may both be made directly.

The two possible uses of measurement are *assessment* and *prediction*. The obvious difference between these is that assessment is about attributes that already exist, whereas prediction is about attributes that do not yet exist. Indirect measurement and prediction are similar, since they both rely on a *model* of one attribute in terms of others. In indirect measurement we model one attribute that exists in terms of another or others. In prediction we model an attribute that does not yet exist in terms of another or others that do.

One important aspect of carrying out measurement properly is clearly defining the attribute of interest in advance of its measurement. Unless an attribute is clearly defined, it cannot be measured objectively, as without a well-defined rule measurement cannot be independent of the person carrying it out. These comments may seem obvious, but the principles are often ignored. Consider measures of intelligence, such as IQ tests, and ask yourself what they really measure. If these 'measures' are measures at all, then they surely do not capture intelligence, but some other attribute, perhaps problem solving skills or verbal reasoning? If IQ were a measure of intelligence then a person who scored zero IQ should be of zero intelligence; but this seems an impossible concept. A far more likely explanation is, for example, that the person couldn't read. In fact, if you asked ten different people to define intelligence, you would probably get ten completely different answers. An attribute as ill-defined as this cannot be susceptible to objective measurement.

Another important part of defining the attribute to be captured by a measure is to define the relations which it imposes on the entities in question. A software attribute which researchers have spent much time trying to measure is *complexity* (see [ZUSE91] for over 100 examples of proposed measures). One aspect of this is the complexity of the program control flow, which is thought to have an impact on how easy the program is to understand, and consequently how easy it will be to amend and maintain. Program control flow can be modelled as a flowgraph, for which many measures claiming to capture complexity have been defined.

Any useful measure of complexity must surely be able to capture the intuitive relation of 'flowgraph A is *more complex than* flowgraph B', or at least that of 'flowgraph A is *of different complexity to* flowgraph B'. Consider the flowgraphs in figure 1. It is probably safe to say that flowgraph (b) is more complex than flowgraph (a), and that flowgraph (c) is more complex than flowgraph (a), but what about the relationship between (b) and (c)? It is hard to say which is the more complex, but equally it is hard to be sure that they are of the same complexity. It seems that we cannot define complexity in such a way that it both satisfies our intuitive understanding and also produces a useful measure. Hence it is a poor candidate for measurement.

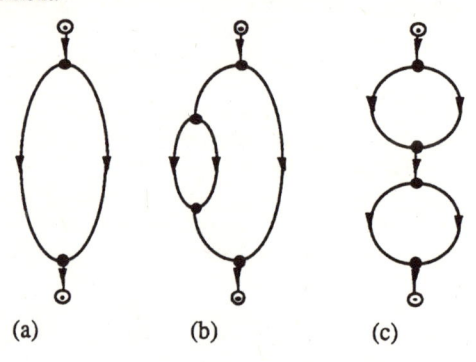

Figure 1: Flowgraphs

If C is the set of entities that we want to measure (eg. flowgraphs), and R is the set of empirical relations (eg. 'is more complex than') imposed by our attribute, then we call (C, R) an *empirical relation system*. A measure, M, is then a *mapping* from the empirical relation system into a *numerical relation system*, which we can denote by (N, P). Here N is a set of numbers or symbols, and P is a set of numerical relations. M maps each entity into a number or symbol, and each empirical relation into a numerical relation.

This can be illustrated with an example of the measurement of height of people. If we are looking for a measure of height, we may in some circumstances be interested in only one empirical relation $r = \{(x, y): x \text{ is a different height to } y\}$. In this case the empirical relation system includes only this one relation ($R = \{r\}$). The numerical relation system will therefore also only contain one relation. The most intuitive measure in this case is the one where each person is mapped into a number in such a way that two people are mapped into the same number *iff* they are of the same height. That is, the numerical relation which is the image of r is $M(x) \neq M(y)$.

A slightly more sophisticated measure of height would be one which captured two empirical relations. That is $R = \{r_1, r_2\}$, where $r_1 = \{(x, y): x \text{ is a different height to } y\}$, $r_2 = \{(x, y): x \text{ is taller than } y\}$. Here the numerical relation system would also contain two relations, which in the most intuitive measure would be $M(x) \neq M(y)$ and $M(x) > M(y)$, corresponding to r_1 and r_2 respectively.

The commonest way to measure height is by equating each person to a number of *units* (eg. centimetres). This kind of height measure is far more sophisticated than either of the two above. It captures many more relations: for example we can say that one person is 1.5 times or twice as tall as another, or that one person is 20cm taller than another.

The *representation condition* of measurement says that, for a measure to be a valid characterisation of an attribute, all empirical relations must be preserved in the numerical relation system. That is to say that the measure must be a *homomorphism*. For example, returning to the measurement of height, if Paul is taller than Sarah, then for any measure M of height, $M(Paul) > M(Sarah)$. It is here that many so-called measures fail. Returning to the flowgraph example, even supposing that we were able to decide the order, in terms of complexity, of a set of flowgraphs; it might be very hard to find a well-defined homomorphism from these into the real numbers. The IQ test could also be shown as an invalid measure of intelligence by using the representation condition. This only requires finding one pair of people where the first is more intelligent than the second, but the second has the higher IQ.

5.2 Scale Types and Meaningfulness

Rarely is a measure of an attribute unique. For example in the measurement of height, we can choose from several scales (eg. centimetres, metres, feet or inches). Here we know that we can transform any scale into another by multiplying by a constant (2.54 to transform inches into centimetres). In fact mult-iplication of any such measure by any non-zero constant will generate another measure which satisfies the representation condition. For example, mult-iplication of the centimetre scale by 3.5 will result in a new scale with 3.5cm as the unit. For this measure of height, we say that multiplication by a non-zero constant is an *admissible transformation* - meaning that it always results in another valid measure.

Other measures have other types of admissible transformation. For example consider the most primitive measure of height mentioned earlier. This only captures one empirical relation - that of *x is a different height to y*. Any assignment of numbers that maps people of distinct heights into distinct numbers will satisfy the representation condition, hence making an acceptable measure. Thus any measure may be transformed into any other by a one-to-one mapping. Also any measure subjected to any one-to-one mapping will generate another measure.

The admissible transformations on a measure define its *scale type*. There are five 'regular' scale types, namely:

- nominal
- ordinal
- interval
- ratio
- absolute.

This list may be said to be in ascending order, with the 'highest' or most desirable scale type being the absolute scale. The higher the scale type, the more mathematical (statistical) operations are valid. The scale type that we can attain with a measure depends on how well we understand the attribute that we are measuring.

Nominal scales are the lowest type. They don't capture any concept of order with respect to the attribute, but simply classify entities. For example, the measure of height which captures only whether people are of the same height, or a measure of gender which assigns 2 to males and 5 to females. The admissible transformations for nominal measures are the one-to-one functions.

Ordinal scales not only classify entities with respect to the attribute, but also place them in order by amount of the attribute. For example, the height measure earlier which captured the relation 'taller than' has ordinal scale type. Similarly the number of stripes on an army officer's arm is an ordinal measure of seniority. Any monotonic increasing function on the number of stripes measure results in a new measure preserving the off-icers' rankings. The admissible transformations for ordinal measures are the monotonic increasing functions.

Interval scales are quite uncommon. They make use of a *unit* of measurement, but have no absolute zero. Interval measures capture not only the order of entities with respect to the attribute, but also some notion of the *distance* between entities with respect to the attribute. For example, this year is 1991. A year being a true unit, it is meaningful to talk about differences (or 'intervals') in years, eg. 'the interval between 1960 and 1980 was double that between 1980 and 1990'. However, the year zero is not an absolute zero, as there were years before this. Temperature measurement in centigrade and fahrenheit is also interval. As with conversion between centigrade and fahrenheit, the admissible transformations for interval scales are the functions of the form $F(M) = aM + b$ $(a > 0)$.

Most well known scientific measures are of ratio scale type. The ratio scale is similar to the interval scale, but has an absolute zero. The ratio scale is so named because the existence of a zero makes it meaningful to take ratios. The measurement of height in centimetres or inches is an example of a ratio measure. Here 0cm really does mean no height, and at the same time the centimetre is a true unit. Hence we can say that person A is twice as tall as person B. As we have seen, the admissible transformations for ratio scales are the functions such that $F(M) = aM$ $(a > 0)$.

The highest scale type is absolute. Absolute measures actually count the number of occurrences of the attri-bute in question. Examples are counting the number of people in a room or the number of lines of code ('LOC') in a program. Note that LOC is not an absol-ute measure of program length (this could also be measured in thousands of LOC ('KLOC'), or in pages). It is only an absolute measure of the number of LOC. An absolute measure of an attribute is unique, ie. the only admissible transformation is the identity function.

Figure 2 summarises measurement scale types:

Scale Type	Characteristics	Admissible Transformations
Nominal	classifies	$M' = F(M)$ (F 1-1 mapping)
Ordinal	classifies and orders	$M' = F(M)$ (F monotonic increasing)
Interval	differences matter, no zero	$M' = aM + b$ $(a > 0)$
Ratio	zero, ratios	$M' = aM$ $(a > 0)$
Absolute	counting	$M' = M$

Figure 2: Measurement Scale Types

Scale types tell us what mathematical operations may meaningfully be applied to measurement results. This is vital when we come to consider statistical analysis. A statement concerning measures is said to be *meaningful* if its truth or falsity remains unchanged when every scale involved is replaced by another that has been obtained via an admissible transformation.

We can see how this works by considering some simple examples of statements using measurement:

(1) The mean age of the population is higher now than it was in 1960.
(2) The mean gender of the population is higher now than it was in 1960.
(3) This program is twice as long as that one.
(4) It is twice as hot today as it was yesterday.
(5) It was 30°C on Monday, 25°C on Tuesday and 20°C on Wednesday. Hence the temperature difference between Monday and Tuesday was the same as that between Tuesday and Wednesday.
(6) A general has 5 stripes on their sleeve, a colonel has 4 and a sergeant 3. Hence the difference in seniority between a general and a colonel is the same as that between a colonel and a sergeant.

(1) is meaningful if the ordinary measure of age in years and months is used. Since this is a ratio measure, any admissible transformation must be multiplication by a (positive) constant. The mean today will remain higher than the mean in 1960, regardless of what constant is used. (2) is not meaningful. Since any measure of gender must be nominal, any 1-1 mapping is admissible. For example the values for male and female could be reversed. This would result in the truth value of the

statement being changed. (3) is meaningful if length is measured by lines of code, or another ratio measure. Multiplication by a positive constant will leave the ratio of length between the programs the same. (4) is not meaningful. Centigrade is only an interval measure of temperature. Since 0°C is not an absolute zero, ratios like this are not meaningful. It is admissible to transform interval scales by adding a non-zero constant. This would change the ratio between the two temperatures. (5), however, is meaningful. The ratio between *differences* in temperature is unchanged by the transformations admissible on interval scales. (6) is not meaningful. The number of stripes on the sleeve is an ordinal measure. Any monotonic increasing function is admissible. However, most monotonic increasing functions would not leave the number of stripes between generals and colonels equal to that between colonels and sergeants.

So the scale type of a measure defines what mathematical operations are meaningful on the measurement data. This clearly has implications for statistical analysis of the data. Many statistical operations are unsuitable for data of the lower scale types as they rely on adding measurement values together or on taking ratios. This is discussed further below.

6 STATISTICS

The statistical material in METKIT is divided into three subjects: experimental design, data collection and data analysis. The material does not teach detailed mathematical techniques, these can be found in any textbook. Rather it concentrates on a common sense approach which allows proper respect to the type of measurement used and produces results which are reliable, whilst being easy to understand.

As the topics covered here are well established, they are not described in the same amount of detail as the previous sections. Interested readers should consult [FENTON91] for full details.

6.1 EXPERIMENTAL DESIGN

One use of measurement in software engineering is for monitoring experiments. For example, an experiment might be set up to compare reliability of code produced using two different programming techniques, or to validate a cost prediction model by comparing predicted costs with actual costs across several projects.

Experiments in software engineering are often very badly designed, making it hard to draw useful and justified conclusions. Students are introduced to the basic concepts of a well-designed experiment. These include identifying the population of interest, articul-ating the hypothesis and choosing a sample. Methods of randomising samples, and the importance of sample size on validity of conclusions is emphasised.

The importance is stressed of understanding the type of data you have before you analyse it. Students are told that general parametric tests for analysing experimental data are unsuitable for many types of data. As well as being normally distributed, data must be of interval scale type or above for parametric tests. In addition, many of the tests make other demands of data, such as the need for measurement outcomes to be mutually exclusive and exhaustive. Although most texts in this subject emphasise the other considerations, it is rare for stress to be put on the measurement theory obligations for data. One text which does is [SIEGEL56].

6.2 DATA COLLECTION

The most important message in the METKIT data collection material echoes an important point from measurement theory. That is, the need to identify clearly in advance what attribute you want to measure. All too often, software companies collect the data that is easiest, rather than that which is the most useful. This results not only in being unable to obtain the results of the most interest, but also in resentment in staff towards data collection in general, if this is seen to be a pointless and time consuming exercise.

Consideration of staff attitudes is important. Software production, unlike that of other engineering products, is largely an intellectual activity. Hence many of the measures of interest relate to peoples' performance. Collection of such data must be carried out carefully. Staff must not feel that data may be used against them. They must be educated about the benefits of meas-urement - for example as a tool to help better under-standing of the process - and results must be fed back to them as soon as possible. They must also be educated in the actual collection of data, for example correct ways to complete forms. Forms themselves must be carefully designed to minimise incorrect recording.

The general message in the data collection material is a simple one. The whole measurement process relies on good data collection. Any amount of sophisticated data analysis cannot retrieve good quality results from poor quality data.

6.3 Data Analysis

Data analysis techniques help us to reduce data to a more useful form and to extract further information from it. For example we may want to find the average productivity of a group of programmers, and how much individual group members vary from it. This could help us to predict time required to complete a new project.

Like statistical tests for experimentation, many data analysis techniques require data to be of at least interval scale type, and to be normally distributed. The *mean* is one example of this. It is not meaningful on ordinal or nominal data. It also does not make a good average when applied to data sets that are non-normal. For example the mean applied to income will produce a misleadingly high average if there are just a few very large values. Such facts are often disregarded by standard texts in statistics, which are only too keen to encourage readers to apply the most complex analysis techniques without discussing their limitations.

Software engineering data is often of only ordinal scale type. This is because a lot of software engineering attributes are not yet very well understood. Even software engineering data which is of interval scale type or above is often not normally distributed, often being skewed (usually towards zero) and with a number of very high values. Hence in software engineering we must often restrict ourselves to the use of robust summary statistics and nonparametric methods.

For representing central tendency, then, the *mean* is often unsuitable for software engineering data. A robust alternative is the *median*. This is the midpoint of the data when it is arranged in increasing order. The median is unaffected by monotonic increasing transformations, so making it suitable for ordinal measures. (It is however unsuitable for nominal data - the *mode* must be used instead). The measures of spread that accom-pany the median are the *quartiles*. These divide the data into four equal parts when arranged in increasing order. The middle quartile is the median, so we talk about the *median* and the *upper quartile* and *lower quartile*.

The median and quartiles can be used to construct a *box plot* which represents the data graphically. Figure 3 is a box plot of lines of code for 17 software modules.

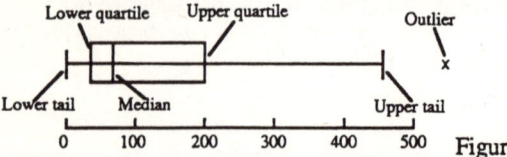

Figure 3: Boxplot

The upper and lower tails are constructed by multiplying the box length by 1.5 and adding and subtracting from the upper and lower quartiles respectively. The lower tail in figure 3 is truncated at zero as negative lines of code are not meaningful.

Values outside the tails are called *outliers*, and are shown explicitly.

Box plots, although simple, can be useful in helping understand the data. For example, in figure 3 we can see that the data is skewed to the left. They are also helpful in allowing outliers to be picked out. Such items, with unusually high or low values may be worth examining as a part of quality control.

It is also often of interest to consider the relationship between two attributes, for example length of software modules and programming effort. The simplest way to investigate this, which is also independent of the type of data, is to draw a scatterplot. Figure 4 shows a scatterplot of length against effort for 17 modules.

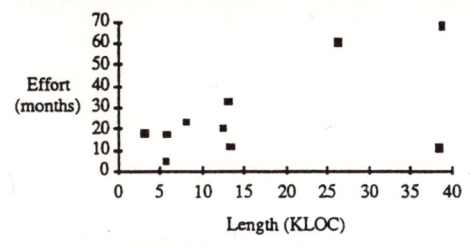

Figure 4: Scatterplot

Scatterplots can also help us to understand our data, by suggesting whether the attributes have, for example a linear relationship, as the ones in figure 4 seem to have. They can also help us to spot outliers. There is an outlier in figure 4 which represents a very long module which has little effort associated with it. Again, it may be worth examining this module as part of quality control. It could be a very simple module, or one that has been reused from another system. On the other hand it could have been sloppily written and could cause problems in the future.

7 SUMMARY AND CONCLUSIONS

The METKIT materials provide a background in measurement theory and basic statistics for software engineering students. These subjects have traditionally been overlooked. Measurement theory is important not only to help us understand the measurement process, but to also as a guide to what analysis techniques may be applied to what data. The statistics that is covered is very simple, but emphasises points often ignored in traditional texts - not least the need to think carefully whether certain techniques are applicable to your data.

The ideas outlined in this paper are not only relevant to software engineering students. An understanding of the frequently-ignored principles of measurement theory and a common sense approach to statistics could be a valuable part any engineer's education.

8 ACKNOWLEDGEMENTS

This work has been funded by the CEC under their ESPRIT programme. I would also like to thank my colleagues at the CSSE for their input, and particularly Norman Fenton of the CSR, City University, whose ideas (now laid down in [FENTON91]) have been vitally important to our work in this subject.

9 REFERENCES

[BUSH90]
Software Measurement: A Conceptual Framework, M. E. Bush and N. E. Fenton, Journal of Systems and Software, vol. 12 pp 223-231, 1990.

[CAMPBELL20]
Physics, The Elements, N. R. Campbell, Cambridge University Press, 1920 (reprinted as *Foundations of Science*, Dover, 1957).

[FINKELSTEIN82]
Theory and Philosophy of Measurement, L. Finkelstein, in *Handbook of Measurement Science, Volume 1: Theoretical Fundamentals*, P. H. Sydenham (ed.), Wiley, 1982.

[FENTON91]
Software Metrics: A Rigorous Approach, N. E. Fenton, Chapman and Hall, 1991.

[HEEMSTRA88]
Controlling Software Development Costs: A Field Study, F. J. Heemstra and R. Kusters, University of Technology, P.O. Box 513, 5600 MB Eindhoven, Netherlands, 1988.

[KRANTZ71]
Foundations of Measurement, Volume 1, D. H. Krantz, R. D. Luce, P. Suppes and A. Tversky, Academic Press, 1971.

[MANCINI90]
Maintenance Cost Estimation: Industrial Point of View, L. Mancini and R. Ciampoli, European COCOMO Users Group Meeting (unpublished), 1990.

[ROBERTS79]
Measurement Theory with Applications to Decision Making, Utility, and the Social Sciences, F. S. Roberts, Addison Wesley, 1979.

[RUSSELL90]
International Survey of Software Measurement Education and Training, M. Russell, Journal of Systems and Software, vol.12 pp.233-241, 1990.

[SIEGEL56]
Nonparametric Statistics for the Behavioural Sciences, S. Siegel, McGraw-Hill, 1956.

[WHITTY90]
METKIT and the ESPRIT Program, R. Whitty, M. Bush and M. Russell, Journal of Systems and Software, vol. 12 pp. 219-221, 1990.

[ZUSE91]
Software Complexity: Measures and Methods, H. Zuse, De Gruyter, 1991.

Measurement Theory and Software Measures

Horst Zuse
Technische Universität Berlin (FR 5-3)
Franklinstraße 28/29
D - 1 Berlin 10 (Germany)

Peter Bollmann-Sdorra
Technische Universität Berlin (FR 5-2)
Franklinstraße 28/29
D - 1 Berlin 10 (Germany)

Abstract

During the last years much attention has been directed toward the measurement process of the properties of software. Many software measures have been developed in order to determine the static complexity of single programs (intra-modular complexity) and entire software systems (inter-modular complexity) and many authors discussed the properties of software measures. Measurement theory gives qualitative conditions for the use of measures. In this paper the properties of software measures related to the ordinal and ratio scale are given and applied to the Measure of McCabe. Furthermore the application of measurement theory to flowgraphs and programs is discussed. Additionally necessary and sufficient conditions for the behaviour of software measures with respect to concatenation operations are investigated. These results make the properties of software measures more transparent.

1 Introduction

Measurement is becoming recognized as a useful way to soundly plan and control the execution of software projects and software development during the software life-cycle. However, doing measurement it is important to know the scale level - like ordinal, interval, ratio and absolute scale - of the measurement process. The knowledge of the scale level is essential for using statistics.

Some authors mention measurement theory and scales related to software measures. Harrison et al. /HARR82/ discuss scales, like ordinal, interval and ratio scales.
Conte et al. /CONT86/ point out (P.129):
It is often difficult to determine to which scale a measure belongs. For example, in the recorded defects for software modules, we notice that there are certain modules with no defects, indicating the presence of absolute zero. But is the number of defects really from a ratio scale?
In Mayrhauser /MAYR90/ we can find a list of correlations coefficients and the scale level which is required (p.572-573):

The Pearson Product Moment is a parametric statistics. It assumes a linear relationship between two variables, and it requires an interval or a ratio scale.

Additionally we can find in the column "applicability" of the correlations of the Pearson Product Moment the statement: *Beware when using with ordinal scale.* Basili et al. /BASI86/ write:

The second phase of experimental process is the study planning phase. The following sections discuss aspects of the experimental planning phase: 1)design, 2)criteria, and 3)measurement...... The required data may include both objective and subjective data and different levels of measurement: nominal, ordinal, interval or ratio.

In Li et al. /LI78/ we can find a discussion of the scale types. Li et al. used the Pearson correlation coefficient for inter-metric correlations.

In the Report of the Alvey Project "Structured-Based Software Measurement" /ALVE88/ and the book of Fenton /FENT91/, many statements about measurement theory and software measurement and scales are discussed.

Although the importance of measurement theory in the context of software measurement has been widely recognized there are not too many detailed measurement theoretic investigations of software measurement. Especially qualitative criteria that a given measure may be used as an ordinal or ratio scale are missing in many approaches. In this paper it is shown how these criteria can be developed.

Another important criterion for the use of software measures are their properties related to concatenation operations. Such proposals of concatenation properties were given for example, by Weyuker /WEYU85/, /WEYU88/, by Jayaprakash, et al. /JAYA87/, by Bache /BACH87/ and by Prather /PRAT84/. The application of measurement theory to concatenations operations is also discussed in this paper.

Using the weak order and the extensive structure criteria can be given for the use of a software measure as an ordinal or a ratio scale. These types of scales for software measures are required in literature. However, the requirement of the extensive structure and the ratio scale for a software measure may be a too strong assumption. For that reason we propose weaker conditions for the concatenations of programs, designs or entire software system. These conditions give the reader informations whether it is possible to calculate the overall complexity of the entire system from the complexities of pieces of software. Hence it is important to know the behaviour of the measure related to concatenation operations.

Many software measures are based on the flowgraph of programs. We ask how measurement scales on flowgraphs are related to measurement scales on programs. The answer is given by four conditions.

In detail the following points are treated in this paper.

In Section 2 foundations of measurement theory are introduced and applied to software measures. In Section 3 operations on programs and the consequences for software complexity measurement are discussed. In Section 4 concatenation operations from the literature are presented and are discussed by many examples. In Section 5 the results of our investigation are presented. In Section 6 the list of references is given. Proofs of theorems can be found in the Appendix I and II. In Appendix III the used software measures are defined.

2 Measurement Theory and Software Complexity

In this Section we introduce basic concepts of measurement theory and show the applications to software measures.

2.1 Basic Concepts of Measurement Theory

First of all we want to introduce the notion of an empirical, a numerical relational system and a scale. Let

A = (A,R1,...,Rn,o1,....om).

be an empirical relational system, where A is a non-empty set of objects, Ri are ki-ary relations on A with i=1,..,n, and oj, j=1,..,m, are binary operations on A.

According to Luce et al. /LUCE90/, p.270, we assume for an empirical relational system **A** *that there is a well-established empirical interpretation for the elements of* **A** *and for each relation Si of* **A**. We also assume the same for the binary operations. In Section 2.4 we present an empirical interpretation of flowgraphs.

Let further

B = (B,S1,....,Sn,•1,....,•m),

be a formal relational system, where B is a non-empty set of formal objects, for example numbers or vectors, Si, i=1,..,n, are ki-ary relations on B, and •j, j=1,..,m, are closed binary operation on B.

We also include the case that there are no relations or no operations.

A **measure** μ is a mapping $\mu: A \rightarrow B$ such that the following holds for all i=1,..,n;j=1,..,m and for all a,b,a1i,...,aki $\in$ A:

$$Ri(a1,....,aki) \iff Si(\mu(a1),....,\mu(aki))$$
and
$$\mu(a \; oj \; b) = \mu(a) \bullet j \; \mu(b)$$

Then the the Triple (**A**, **B**, μ) is called a **scale**. According to this definition we see that measurement assumes a homomorphism.

Given two relational system **A** and **B** we can ask whether there exists a measure μ such that (**A**, **B**, μ) is a scale. This problem is called the representation problem. If such a measure μ exists we can ask how uniqueally the measure μ is defined. This problem is called the uniqueness problem. The uniqueness problem leads to the definition of scale types such as ordinal or ratio scale. We do not discuss the interval scales here because the concatenation of programs is given in a natural way (D-Structures). Hence we think that the discussion of the conditions for the ratio scale has a higher priority.

Let g: X->Y and h: Y->Z be mappings. Then hg denotes the composed mapping hg(x)=h(g(x)) for x∈ X.

Definition 2.1 *(Admissible Transformation):*
Let (A, B, µ) be a scale. A mapping g: µ (A)->B is an admissible transformation iff (A, B, g µ) is also a scale.
♦

Real scales are classified according to the admissible transformations.

Name of the Scale	Transformation g
Nominal Scale	Any one to one g
Ordinal Scale	g: Strictly increasing function
Interval Scale	g(x) = a x + b a > 0
Ratio Scale	g(x) = a x a > 0
Absolute Scale	g(x) = x

Figure 2.1: Scale types of real scales.

Admissible transformations lead to the definitions of meaningful statements /ROBE79/. A statement with measurement values is meaningful iff its truth value is invariant to admissible transformations. Meaningfulness guarantees that the truth value of statements with measurement values is invariant to scale transformations. For example if we say that the distance D1 is twice as long as distance D2, then this statement is true or false no matter whether length is measured in meters or yards. These problems are existing in the area of software measures too. This is the case if we want to make statements with measurement values for example after having applied statistical methods. We want to explain this problem by a statement which was given by Weyuker /WEYU88/.

Example 2.1:
Let P1 and P2 be program bodies combined in some way to P1 o P2. Let µ be a measure. Then the requirement for complexity by Weyuker /WEYU88/ is that there exist P1, P2 such that

$$\mu(P1 \text{ o } P2) \geq \mu(P1) + \mu(P2).$$

This statement is not meaningful for an interval scale. If we apply the admissible transformation of the interval scale g(x)=a x+b, then we get:

$$a \mu(P1 \text{ o } P2) + b \geq a \mu(P1) + b + a \mu(P2) + b,$$

for all a>0 and for all b∈ $\Re$. Hence, the truth of the statement is not invariant to this type of admissible transformation. The statement is meaningful for a ratio scale.

♦

We see that meaningfulness depends on the admissible transformations. The admissible transformations depend on the relational systems under consideration. Hence it is important to study the conditions which should hold on the relational systems in order to have a certain class of admissible transformations or equivalently to have a certain scale type.

Basically the measurement theory approach is as follows: Given a homomorphism into a numerical relational system, which qualitative conditions should hold on the empirical relational system in order to have a scale and secondly what are the admissible transformations? Hence measurement theory yields hypothesises about reality. Whether we have to reject these hypothesises depends on the outcome of empirical investigations. Like statistics, measurement theory does not say how reality looks like. However it says how reality should look like in order to apply a method, for example a statistical test.

2.2 Ordinal and Ratio Scale

In this Section we introduce conditions for the ordinal and ratio scale.

Ordinal Scale

Let us remember that a weak order is a binary relation $\bullet\geq$ that is transitive and complete:

$P \bullet\geq P'$, $P' \bullet\geq P'' \Rightarrow P \bullet\geq P''$ transitivity
$P \bullet\geq P'$ or $P' \bullet\geq P$ completeness

for all P, P', P'' $\in$ **P**.

In /ROBE79/, p.110, we find the following theorem which we can apply directly to flowgraphs.

Theorem 2.1:
Suppose (**P**, $\bullet\geq$) is an empirical relational system, where **P** is a non-empty countable set of flowgraphs and where $\bullet\geq$ is a binary relation on **P**. Then there exists a function $\mu: P \to \Re$, with

$$P \bullet\geq P' \iff \mu(P) \geq \mu(P'),$$

for all P, P' $\in$ **P**, iff (**P**, $\bullet\geq$) is a weak order. If such a μ exists, then

$$((\mathbf{P},\bullet\geq),(\Re,\geq),\mu)$$

is an ordinal scale.
♦

Additive Ratio Scale

We want to introduce the following notation.

$P \approx P'$ iff $P \bullet\geq P'$ and $P' \bullet\geq P$,
$P \bullet> P'$ iff $P \bullet\geq P'$ and not $P' \bullet\geq P$.

Definition 2.2 *(Extensive Structure /KRAN71/, p.73):*
Let **P** be a non-empty set, $\bullet\geq$ a binary relation on **P**, and o a closed binary operation on **P**. The relational system (**P**, $\bullet\geq$, o) is an **closed extensive structure** if and only if the following axioms hold for all P1,..,P4 $\in$ **P**:

A1: (**P**,$\bullet\geq$)   is a weak order

A2: P1 o (P2 o P3)$\approx$(P1 o P2) o P3,
    axiom of weak associativity

A3: P1 $\bullet\geq$ P2 <=> P1 o P3 $\bullet\geq$ P2 o P3 <=> P3 o P1$\bullet\geq$ P3 o P2
    axiom of monotonicity

A4: If P1 $\bullet$> P2 then for any P3, P4, there exists a natural number n, such that
    nP1 o P3 $\bullet\geq$nP2 o P4,   Archimedian Axiom
♦

The meaning of the notation nP is: We define 1P to be P. Having nP, we define (n+1)P to be P o nP.

Theorem 2.2 /KRAN71/, p. 74:
Suppose **P** is a non empty set, $\bullet\geq$ is a binary relation on **P**, and o is a closed binary operation on **P**.
Then there is a real-valued function μ:**P** $\rightarrow\Re$ satisfying:

$$a \ \bullet\geq \ b <=> \mu(a) \geq \mu(b)$$
and
$$\mu(a \ o \ b) = \mu(a) + \mu(b)$$

if and only if (**P**, $\bullet\geq$,o) is an extensive structure.
If another function μ' fulfills these properties then there exists a positive real-value α that

$$\mu'(a) = \alpha\mu(a)$$

holds.
♦

We see that Theorem 2.2 gives us conditions for the additive ratio scale (Definition of scales in Figure 2.2). In Bollmann et al. /BOLL85/, Zuse et al. /ZUSE89/ and Zuse /ZUSE91/ these concepts were applied to static software complexity measures on flowgraphs. We want to explain the approach in Section 2.3.

2.3 Measurement Theory and Complexity Measures

There are more than one hundred software measures for intra-modular complexity (flowgraphs and source code), about fifty software measures for software design and modularity, and about fifty measures for software maintenance in /IEEE88/. If we want to use one of them we need criteria for their proper use. This leads to questions as:

- Does a measure match the real complexity of the software?
- Under which conditions may a measure be used as ordinal or ratio scale?

This leads to our approach where we specialize the general measurement theory approach for software complexity. We consider the empirical relational system (**P**, •≥, o) where **P** is the set of flowgraphs, •≥ the binary relation "equally or more complex", and o is a binary operation (BSEQ: sequential, BALT: if-then-else, see below) on flowgraphs as defined in /BOLL85/, /ZUSE89/ and /ZUSE91/. We interpret •≈ as being equally complex and •> as being more complex than.

As binary operations we introduce the sequential combination of flowgraphs and the if-then-else combination of flowgraphs (Binary operations BSEQ and BALT).

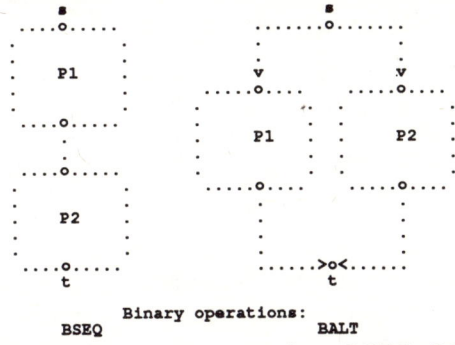

```
         s                         s
    ....o......            ......o......
    .   P1    .            .           .
    .         .            v           v
    ....o.....             ....o....  ....o....
    .         .            .       .  .       .
    .         .            .   P1  .  .   P2  .
    .         .            .       .  .       .
    ....o.....             ....o....  ....o....
    .   P2    .            .                  .
    .         .            .                  .
    ....o.....             ......>o<..........
         t                         t
       BSEQ          Binary operations:    BALT
```

Figure 2.2: The binary operations BSEQ=P1 o P2 of two arbitrary flowgraphs P1 and P2 and BALT=P1 • P2, s and t are the start- and exit-node of the combined flowgraph.

Our approach is the application of measurement theory to software complexity measures. In /ZUSE89/ we choose the Measure of McCabe with $\mu=|E|-|N|+2$ /MCCA76/ to demonstrate our method. We consider the hypothetical empirical relational system

$$(\mathbf{P}, •≥ , o),$$

where **P** is the set of flowgraphs, o the sequential combination BSEQ of flowgraphs of programs as defined in /ZUSE89/, and $\mu: \mathbf{P} \to \Re$ is the Measure μ of McCabe (In /BOLL85/ and /ZUSE89/ the hypothetical relation •≥ of a measure was called "viewpoint" of a measure). We ask the following questions:

1. Which qualitative conditions have to hold for •≥ in order to have

   $P •≥ P' <=> \mu(P) \geq \mu(P')$,

   for all P,P' ∈ **P** or equivalently which empirical conditions have to hold in order to use the Measure of McCabe as an ordinal scale?

2. If •≥ fulfills these conditions empirically is then (**P**, •≥ ,o) an extensive structure or equivalently can we then have an additive ratio scale for (**P**, •≥, o)?

The answer for the first question, given in /ZUSE89/ and /ZUSE91/, is as follows: Under the assumption of reflexivity and transitivity, the Measure of McCabe can be used as an ordinal scale, if and only if for all flowgraphs P,P' ∈ **P**, the following three conditions hold:

e1: If P results from P' by inserting an edge then P is more complex than P'.

e2: If P results from P' by inserting an edge and a node then P and P' are equally complex.

e3: If P results from P' by transfering an edge from one location to another location then P and P' are equally complex.

In order to understand the ordinal properties of the Measure of McCabe the user needs little mathematical knowledge when our approach is used.

For the second question we get: If o is the sequential combination (BSEQ) of flowgraphs, if complexity is reflexive and transitive, and if the conditions e1, e2 and e3 hold empirically, then (**P**, •≥, o) is a closed extensive structure. In this case ((**P**, •≥, o), ($\Re$, ≥, +), μ - 1), where $\mu = |E|-|N|+2$ is the Measure of McCabe, is an additive ratio scale.

We now see the benefits of our approach. If we want to investigate software measures we have to talk about reality and we have to talk about the measures. Both can be accomplished if we derive hypothesises about the empirical relational system. Such hypothesises could be:

- If P results from P' by inserting an edge and a node then P and P' are equally complex.
- For the binary operation BSEQ the axiom of monotonicity holds.

Hence, we can talk about software complexity without having any mapping into the real numbers. At the same time we can talk about the measures because the hypothesises are conditions for their proper use. This is also useful in order to design experiments. If we would find out by empirical testing that we had to reject monotonicity we had to reject all measures that assume just this.

2.4 Scales on Flowgraphs and Scales on Programs

We consider the complexity of flowgraphs. The reason is that most of the measures are based on flowgraphs. To measure the complexity of flowgraphs was already proposed by McCabe /MCCA76/. In the following we give an empirical interpretation of (**P**, •≥, o).

We assume that the complexity relation on programs implies a complexity relation on flowgraphs. This complexity relation was partially discussed by many authors when comparing the real complexity on flowgraphs with the complexity given by some measure. For example, Sagri /SAGR89/ compares flowgraphs directly with respect to complexity without reference to any program in the source code. Harrison et al. /HARR81/ compare flowgraphs with respect to complexity by comparing programs with the given flowgraphs. For each flowgraph they consider just one program hence assuming that all programs with the same flowgraph are equally complex.

If we investigate software measures based on flowgraphs the question is whether it is sufficient to discuss them on flowgraphs. If **P*** are all programs written in a given language, like PL/1, C, PASCAL or ADA, let o* be a partial operation of combining programs such as the sequence (BSEQ) or if-then-else (BALT). Let •≥* be the complexity relation on **P*** and φ:**P*** -> φ(**P***)=**P** be the mapping that maps every program on its flowgraph.

We consider the following conditions F1-F4 for (**P***, •≥*, o*) and φ.

- **F1:** For all P*, P1*, P'*, P1'* ∈ **P***:
  If φ(P*)= φ(P1*) and φ(P'*)= φ(P1'*) and P* •≥* P'* then P1* •≥* P1'*.

  F1 means that programs with the same flowgraph may be substituted for each other with respect to the complexity relation •≥*.

- **F2:** For all P*, P'* ∈ **P***:

  φ(P*)= φ(P'*) => P* ≈* P'*.

  F2 means that programs with the same flowgraph are equally complex.

  If •≥* is transitive and F2 holds then F1 holds. If •≥* is reflexive and F1 holds then F2 holds.

- **F3:** For all P*, P1*, P'*, P1'* ∈ **P***:
  If φ(P*)= φ(P'*), φ(P1*)= φ(P1'*) and P* o* P1* and P'* o* P1'* both exist, then φ(P* o* P1*)= φ(P'* o* P1'*).

  F3 means that the flowgraph of two combined programs only depends on the flowgraphs of each program.

- **F4:** For all P, P'∈ **P** there exist P* and P'*∈ **P*** with P=φ(P*), P'=φ(P'*) and P* o* P'* exists.

  F4 requires that the programming language is sufficiently rich. F4 requires that for any two flowgraphs there exist programs with just these flowgraphs, such that the programs can be combined.

The proofs of the following five theorems can be found in the Appendix I. The next two theorems give conditions that a complexity scale on programs corresponds to a scale on flowgraphs.

Theorem 2.3:
Let $((\mathbf{P^*}, \bullet\geq^*), (\Re, \geq), \psi)$ be a scale. There exists a relation $\bullet\geq$ on $\mathbf{P}$ with $P^* \bullet\geq^* P'^* <=> \phi(P^*) \bullet\geq \phi(P'^*)$ for all $P^*, P'^* \in \mathbf{P^*}$ and a mapping $\mu: \mathbf{P} \to \Re$ with $\psi = \mu \phi$ such that $((\mathbf{P}, \bullet\geq), (\Re, \geq), \mu)$ is a scale and both scales have the same admissible transformations iff F1 and F2 hold.

Theorem 2.4:
Let $((\mathbf{P^*}, \bullet\geq^*, o^*), (\Re, \geq, \bullet), \psi)$ be a scale ($\bullet$ is some binary operation on $\Re$). If F1, F2, F3 and F4 hold then there exist $\bullet\geq$ and o on $\mathbf{P}$ with $P^* \bullet\geq^* P'^* <=> \phi(P^*) \bullet\geq \phi(P'^*)$ for all $P^*, P'^* \in \mathbf{P^*}$ and with $\phi(P^* o^* P'^*) = \phi(P^*) o \phi(P'^*)$ for all $P^*, P'^* \in \mathbf{P^*}$ whenever $P^* o^* P'^*$ exists and a mapping $\mu: \mathbf{P} \to \Re$ such that $\psi = \mu\phi$, $((\mathbf{P}, \bullet\geq, o), (\Re, \geq, \bullet), \mu)$ is a scale and both scales have the same admissible transformations.

The next two theorems give sufficient criteria that a measurement theoretical investigation of flowgraph measures may be done just on flowgraphs.

Theorem 2.5:
If F1 holds then there exists a relation $\bullet\geq$ on $\mathbf{P}$ with $P^* \bullet\geq^* P'^* <=> \phi(P^*) \bullet\geq \phi(P'^*)$ for all $P^*, P'^* \in \mathbf{P^*}$ such that for every $\mu: \mathbf{P} \to \Re$ the following holds: $((\mathbf{P^*}, \bullet\geq^*), (\Re, \geq), \mu\phi)$ is an ordinal scale iff $((\mathbf{P}, \bullet\geq), (\Re, \geq), \mu)$ is an ordinal scale.

Theorem 2.6:
If F1, F3 and F4 hold then there exist $\bullet\geq$ and o on $\mathbf{P}$ with $P^* \bullet\geq^* P'^* <=> \phi(P^*) \bullet\geq \phi(P'^*)$ for all $P^*, P'^* \in \mathbf{P^*}$ and with $\phi(P^* o^* P'^*) = \phi(P^*) o \phi(P'^*)$ for all $P^*, P'^* \in \mathbf{P^*}$ whenever $P^* o^* P'^*$ exists such that for every $\mu: \mathbf{P} \to \Re$ the following holds: $((\mathbf{P^*}, \bullet\geq^*, o^*), (\Re, \geq, +), \mu\phi)$ is a ratio scale iff $((\mathbf{P}, \bullet\geq, o), (\Re, \geq, +), \mu)$ is a ratio scale.

The main advantage of our approach, where we assume flowgraphs to be empirical objects, is that the theorems of measurement theory can be applied directly because the binary operations are closed. For an additive ratio scale there are measurement theoretic theorems where we either need closed binary operations or partial binary operations with properties that are not fulfilled for programs (see Krantz /KRAN71/, Chapter 3). We could obtain some necessary conditions for programs but we do not see a straight forward way to show that they are also sufficient. If we instead consider flowgraphs with binary operations measurement theory can be applied directly. Under the given assumptions such as F1, F2, F3, and F4 we get the same scales and the same admissible transformations. Hence nothing is lost by our approach. If on the other hand we have reason to believe that some of these assumptions do not hold, flowgraph complexity does not make sense anyway.

The following question is now: If we want to test the hypotheses on flowgraphs do we not have to go back to the programs? Let us consider the axiom of weak associativity.

Theorem 2.7:
Assume F1, F2, F3 and F4 hold. Then there exist •≥ and o on **P** with P* •≥* P'* <=> φ(P*) •≥ φ(P'*) for all P*, P'*∈ **P*** and with φ(P* o* P'*)= φ(P*) o φ(P'*) for all P*, P'*∈ **P*** whenever P* o* P'* exists such that the following statements are equivalent.

1. For all P*, P'*∈ **P*** if there exist Q, Q1, Q2∈ **P** with φ(P*)=Q o (Q1 o Q2) and φ(P'*)=(Q o Q1) o Q2) then P* ≈* P'*.

2. For all Q, Q1, Q2∈ **P**:
   Q o (Q1 o Q2) ≈ (Q o Q1) o Q2.

♦

Proof: See Appendix II

We see that in order to test associativity we do not need to consider combined programs. It is sufficient to consider programs with combined flowgraphs. Hence we can avoid the partial operations on programs. This basically means that we only have to consider the complexity relation on flowgraphs that is given by the complexity relation on programs and the closed operations on flowgraphs.

If the conditions F1, F2, F3 and F4 hold, then the complexity relation on programs implies a complexity relation on flowgraphs. Then scales on programs correspond to scales of the same scale type on flowgraphs and vice versa. On the other hand hypothetical complexity relations on flowgraphs imply equivalent hypothetical relations on programs. With this empirical interpretation (**P**, •≥) and (**P**, •≥, o) are considered as empirical relational systems.

3 Operations

In this Section we discuss combination rules of objects. These rules can be easily applied to software measures.

We have seen that the Measure of McCabe requires an extensive structure on flowgraphs, which implies the existence of an additive measure if the flowgraphs are combined sequentially by the binary operation BSEQ. However, it might be that the axioms of an extensive structure (weak associativity, monotonicity and Archimedian axiom) are too strong assumptions for complexity measurement. If we cannot have additivity, the question is whether there exists any numerical operation such that the complexity of the combination of two programs/flowgraphs/designs is a function of the complexity of the single programs/flowgraphs/designs.

Furthermore if we have a unary operation T we can ask whether the complexity of T(P) is a function of the complexity of P. The answer to the questions is important in the following cases:

- If a program consists of several modules is it possible to compute the overall complexity from the complexity of the single modules?

- If a module is substituted by a less complex module does this imply that the overall complexity decreases or at least does not increase?

Let us assume (A, •≥, o) is an empirical relational system where •≥ is a weak order and o is a closed binary operation on A. Let us assume further that

$$((A, \bullet\geq), (\Re, \geq), \mu)$$

is an ordinal scale. We want to discuss the question whether there exists a binary operation • on $\mu(A) \subseteq \Re$ such that

$$\mu(a \, o \, b) = \mu(a) \bullet \mu(b)$$

for all a, b ∈ A.

The answer is given in the following theorems:

1. **Theorem C1:** There exists such a • iff

    a ≈ b => a o c ≈ b o c, and a ≈ b => c o a ≈ c o b,

    for all a, b, c ∈ A.

2. **Theorem C2:**
   There exists • which is one to one in each variable iff

    a ≈ b <=> a o c ≈ b o c <=> c o a ≈ c o b,

    for all a, b, c ∈ A.

3. **Theorem C3:**
   There exists • which is not decreasing in each variable iff

    a •≥ b => a o c •≥ b o c, and a •≥ b => c o a •≥ c o b,

    for all a, b, c ∈ A.

4. **Theorem C4:**
   There exists • which is strictly monotonic increasing in each variable iff

    a •≥ b <=> a o c •≥ b o c <=> c o a •≥ c o b,

    for all a, b, c ∈ A.

The proof of these theorems can be found in the Appendix II. The consequences for software measurement will be discussed in Section 4. The next figure illustrates the combination rules C1-C4 in a more transparent way.

C1: A Concatenation exists:

$$a \approx b \Rightarrow a \circ c \approx b \circ c$$
$$a \approx b \Rightarrow c \circ a \approx c \circ b$$

C2: Concatenation is one to one

$$a \approx b \Leftrightarrow a \circ c \approx b \circ c$$
$$a \approx b \Leftrightarrow c \circ a \approx c \circ b$$

C3: Concatenation is not decreasing

$$a \bullet{\geq} b \Rightarrow a \circ c \bullet{\geq} b \circ c$$
$$a \bullet{\geq} b \Rightarrow c \circ a \bullet{\geq} c \circ b$$

C4: Concatenation is strictly monotonic increasing in each argument

$$a \bullet{\geq} b \Leftrightarrow a \circ c \bullet{\geq} b \circ c$$
$$a \bullet{\geq} b \Leftrightarrow c \circ a \bullet{\geq} c \circ b$$

Figure 3.1: An overview of the combination rules of objects for a binary operation o. Condition C1 is the weakest condition for a concatenation/combination operation. If the condition C1 holds a concatenation operation exists. The conditions C2, C3 and C4 are stronger conditions for the behaviour of the measure. The list of measures for the properties C3 and the extensive structure which includes C4 is given in /ZUSE91/.

We now consider a unary operation T:A->A and we assume again that $((A, \bullet{\geq}), (\Re, \geq), \mu)$, is an ordinal scale. Then the question is whether there exists a function f such that

$\mu(T(a)) = f(\mu(a))$,

for all $a \in A$.

The following theorems hold:

Theorem O1:
There exists such a function f iff

$a \approx b \Rightarrow T(a) \approx T(b)$,

for all $a, b \in A$.

Theorem O2:
There exists a function f that is one to one iff

$a \approx b \Leftrightarrow T(a) \approx T(b)$,

for all $a, b \in A$.

Theorem O3:
There exists a function f that is non-decreasing iff

a •≥ b => T(a) •≥T(b),

for all a,b∈ A.

Theorem O4:
There exists a function f that is strictly monotonic increasing iff

a •≥ b <=>T(a) •≥T(b),

for all a,b∈ A.

The proofs of the Theorems O1-O4 are similar to those of the theorems C1-C4.

4 Operations and Complexity

Composition and decomposition are major strategies to construct or to modularize programs. The description of the composition of programs, software design, etc. is an essential operation in software development. For example, during the design phase in the software life-cycle, the whole design is composed of many smaller designs which can be developed in distributed software engineering departments.

We proposed concatenation operations related to programs/flowgraphs already in /BOLL85/, /ZUSE89/ and /ZUSE91/. These were the concatenation operations BSEQ and BALT. Additionally concatenation operations for structure charts can be defined.

4.1 Concatenation Operations in Literature

In order to make the strategy of concatenation operations more clear, we will cite some of the proposed composition and decomposition operations in the literature:

- In /PAGE88/, Chapter 3, a sequential concatenation of sub-structure charts and an alternative concatenation of sub-structure charts to a structure chart are defined. For this types of concatenation operations our approach can be used, too.

- In /URBA84/, p.186, among others, the following control structures are introduced:

    — The sequence of two D-structures (Djikstra structures). This is our concatenation operation BSEQ.

    — The alternative construction, which is denoted with "if then else". This is our concatenation operation BALT.

- In Yourdon et al. /YOUR79/ in Chapter 2: "Basic Concepts of Structured Design" and in Chapter 3: "The Structure of Computer Programs", program composition and decomposition are explained and discussed.

- Weyuker /WEYU85/ and /WEYU88/ also uses concatenation operations of programs. She points out:
  One way to think of a program is an object made up smaller programs. Certainly this is the perspective used in our definition of a program body, or any recursive definition. Using this point of view, the basic operation in constructing programs is composition. Since each of the programming language constructs is single entry and single exit, it makes sense to speak of concatenation of two program bodies. P;Q is the program body formed by appending the program body Q immediately following the last statement of P. We shall say that P;Q is composed from P and Q.

- Bache /BACH87/ also proposes the concatenation of flowgraphs. He proposes the sequential concatenation of flowgraphs, as similar proposed by Zuse /BOLL85/, /ZUSE89/ and /ZUSE91/.

- Jayaprakash et al. /JAYA87/ and Lakshmanan /LAKS91/ (Property 5) also propose the BSEQ concatenation operation of programs. They require additivity of software measures related to a sequential concatenation operation (BSEQ), that means the additive ratio scale. See also the discussion in /ZUSE91/ (Section 6).

- The method of Structured Charts and the Constantine Design Method /LAWR81/ also contain the sequential and if-then-else concatenation operations. It is called there the sequence and the selection (p.61 and 154).

- Prather /PRAT84/ also proposes the concatenation of programs. He requires for his software complexity Measure NTC the following properties:

S,S1,S2,..,Sn	Simple Statements
NTC(S)	=1
NTC(begin S1, S2,..,Sn end)	= ΣNTC(Si)
NTC(if P then S1 else S2)	=2 max (NTC(S1), NTC(S2))

- Preiser et al. also propose the two concatenation operations BSEQ and BALT. For the operation BSEQ they require additivity and for the concatenation operation BALT they require:

  M(If c1 then s1 else s2)=M(c1) + 1/2 (M(s1), M(s2)), where M is the complexity Measure of Preiser et al. That means there exists no binary concatenation rule because the complexity also depends of the complexity of the decision node. Cases with different weights of decision nodes are not covered by our discussion.

- In /FENT91/ many software measures, which are based on prime decomposition, are proposed. Many of them are defined by additivity related to a sequential concatenation operation, like BSEQ.

The citations above show that composition and decomposition of programs/flowgraphs and designs are essential methods in software engineering. We mean, that it is also very important, to consider the behaviour of software measures related to the discussed concatenation operations.

In software departments of the industry and research centers, software is not developed by one person, but by many programmers. They measure the complexity of the pieces of the modules and the design. Combining the pieces of design to the entire system it is very important to know the contribution of the small pieces to the entire system using software complexity measures.

4.2 Operations on Flowgraphs

Interesting is the question whether for the following four cases for the concatenation operations should hold:

$$\mu(P1 \circ P2) = \mu(P1) \bullet \mu(P2),$$
or
$$\mu(T(P)) = f(\mu(P)).$$

That means, it is the question whether the complexity of the concatenated flowgraphs can be determined by a function of the single flowgraphs P1 and P2 or P.

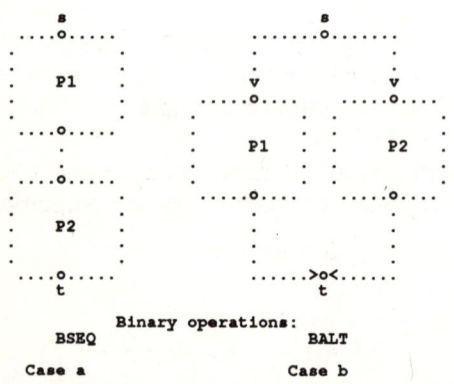

Figure 4.1: Cases a and b: Concatenation operations BSEQ and BALT for single programs as proposed by many authors (see above).

```
              o
              .
              o.........
              .        .
        ....o.....     .
        .         .    .
        .         .    .
        .   P     .    .
        .         .    .
        .         .    .
        ....o.....     .
              .        .
              .        .
              o<........
              .
              o

Operation IFTH
```

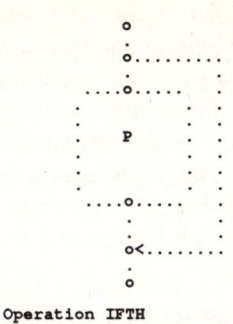

Figure 4.2: If-then operation (IFTH).

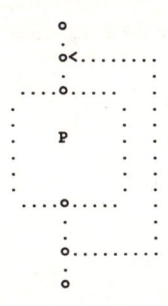

```
              o
              o<........
              .        .
        ....o.....     .
        .         .    .
        .         .    .
        .   P     .    .
        .         .    .
        .         .    .
        ....o.....     .
              .        .
              o.........
              .
              o

Operation DOU
```

Figure 4.3: Do-until operation (DOU).

4.3 Consequences of the Theorems C1-C4 and O1-O4 for Software Complexity Measurement

We now discuss some consequences of the Theorems C1-C4 for software complexity measurement. We say that an axiom or a condition or a property holds for a measure iff it holds for its hypothetical relational system. In the following examples complexity means the numerical complexity computed by some measure.

Discussion of C1:
If the assumptions of Theorem C1 are fulfilled and a program is the combination of two other programs then the overall complexity remains unchanged if we substitute one module by an equally complex one. The assumptions of Theorem C1 are independence assumptions.

There is a controversial discussion whether the assumptions of Theorem C1 hold. Fenton /FENT91/ and Prather /PRAT84/ require that complexity of a sequential flowgraph should be uniquely determined by the complexity of the components. Hence they assume C1 holds.

Weyuker /WEYU88/ claims that for the sequential combination of programs because of dependencies there exist programs P,Q,R such that for a complexity measure μ, with $\mu(P)=\mu(Q)$ holds: $\mu(PoR) \neq \mu(QoR)$. This implies $P \approx Q$ but not $PoR \approx QoR$. Hence Weyuker's hypothesis means that for sequential combinations the overall complexity can never be computed from the single complexities of the modules. This hypothesis has severe implications. If a program system or a software design is developed at different locations the local complexities cannot be used to compute the overall complexity. In the cases of the operation BALT and IFTH (Figure 4.1, Case b, and Figure 4.2) we can expect less dependencies. Hence we suppose that the assumptions of Theorem C1 and Theorem O1 could be satisfied in these cases.

It is interesting to note that for many software measures /ZUSE91/ (Section 9) we have a combination rule in the case of sequential combination. However, often we do not have a combination rule in the case of the BALT concatenation nor in the case of the unary operation IFTH the overall complexity as a function of the complexity of flowgraph P.

Let us consider for example the Measure N-MCCABE /ZUSE91/ (p.177) and (Appendix III) for the sequential concatenation BSEQ:

```
A: P1X          A: P1           A: GSEQ10
N: P1X          N: P1           N: GSEQ10
R: Author       R: Author       R: Author
C: Example      C: Example      C: Sequence
SU: S           SU: S           SU:
        1 s             1 s             1 s
        v               .               v
        2               v               2
        v               2               v
       ...3...          .               3
        .               v               v
     v     v          ...3...           4
     4     5            .               v
      ..>6<..         v     v           5
        v             4     5           v
      ...7...          ..>6<..          6
        .               .               v
     v     v            v               7
     9     8          ...7...           v
      .>10<..           .               8
        v             v     v           v
       11             9     8           9
        v              .>10<..          v
       12               .              10 t
        v               v
       13              11
        v               .
       14               v
        v              12 t
      ..15...
        .     .
     v           v
    16          17
      .>18<..
        v
      ..19...
        .     .
     v           v
    20          21
      .>22<..
        v
       23
        v
       24 t
```

```
Concatenation exists: P1X eq. P1 => P1X o GSEQ10 eq. P1 o GSEQ10
................and: P1X eq. P1 => GSEQ10 o P1X eq. GSEQ10 o P1
-------------------------
Binary operation BSEQ:

A1 = P1X o GSEQ10
A2 = P1 o GSEQ10
A3 = GSEQ10 o P1X
```

A4 = GSEQ10 o P1

	RESULTS OF THE MEASURE(S)						
	P1X	P1	GSEQ10	A1	A2	A3	A4
N-MCCABE	0.17	0.17	0.00	0.12	0.09	0.12	0.09

Figure 4.4: This example of the Measure N-MCCABE=($|E|-|N|+1$)/$|N|$ shows that there exist no combination rule for the Measure N-MCCABE and the BSEQ concatenation operation (eq. means ≈). The conditions of C1 are not fulfilled for the Measure N-MCCABE (Theorem C1: There exists such a • iff a ≈ b => a o c ≈ b o c, and a ≈ b => c o a ≈ c o b for all a, b, c ∈ A).

As the example above shows the following does not hold (μ is the the Measure N-MCCABE): μ(P1X) ≈ μ(P1) => μ(P1X) o μ(GSEQ10) ≈ μ(P1) o μ(GSEQ10), and μ(P1X) = μ(P1) => μ(GSEQ10) o μ(P1X) = μ(GSEQ10) o μ(P1). In our example above the values of the Measure N-MCCABE for the flowgraphs P1X and P1 are identical (N-MCCABE(P1X)=N-MCCABE(P1). However the values of the combined flowgraphs A1/A2 and A3/A4 are different.

In order to determine the complexity of a software design, Gilb /GILB77/ proposed a software design complexity Measure CS (Definition see Appendix III). This measure is similar to the Measure N-MCCABE. For the Measure CS does not exist a combination rule, either. That means, there is no predescription (Predescriptiveness as required by Kearney /KERN86/) possible when measuring the complexity of a piece of the software design to the complexity of the entire design using the sequentially concatenation operation as defined by Lawrence /LAWR81/ (p.61).

Another example for C1 is the Measure EJ-ISC, which was proposed in 1985 by Ejiogu /EJIO85/ as a "Simple Complexity Measure" /ZUSE91/ (p. 333).

```
A: P1           A: P2           A: P1
N: P1           N: P2           N: P1
R: Author       R: Author       R: Author
C: Example      C: Example      C: Example
SU: S           SU: S           SU: S

       1 s             1 s             1 s
       .               .               .
       v               v               v
       2               2               2
       .               .               .
       v               v               v
      ...3...         ...3......      ...3...
       .   .           .     .   .     .   .
       v   v           v     .   .     v   v
       4   5          ...4...  .       4   5
       .   .           .   v   v       .   .
      ..>6<..          v   5   8      ..>6<..
       .               6   .   .       .
       v              ..>7<...         v
      ...7...          .   .   .      ...7...
       .   .           .  ..>9<....    .   .
       v   v           v   .           v   v
       9   8           v   .           9   8
      .>10<..         10   .          .>10<..
       .               .   .           .
       v              11   .           v
      11               .   .          11
       .               v   .           .
       v              12 t             v
      12 t                             12 t
```

```
Concatenation exists: P1 eq. P2 => P1 o P1 eq. P2 o P1
AND..................: P1 EQ. P2 => P1 O P1 EQ. P1 O P2
------------------------
Binary operation BSEQ:

A1 = P1 o P1
A2 = P2 o P1
A3 = P1 o P1
A4 = P1 o P2
```

	RESULTS OF THE MEASURE(S)						
	P1	P2	P1	A1	A2	A3	A4
EJ-ISC	2.00	2.00	2.00	4.00	6.00	4.00	6.00

Figure 4.5: For the Measure EJ-ISC does not exist a combination rule for the binary operation BSEQ. See the explanation in Figure 4.4.

A further interesting example is the Measure DMAX /ZUSE91/ (p.169) which captures the maximal nesting depth of nodes in a flowgraph. For this measure the conditions of Theorems C1 and C3 hold, but the conditions of the Theorems C2, C4 and the extensive structure do not hold.

```
A: P1           A: P2           A: MNA
N: P1           N: P2           N: Max.-Nested-Alt.
R: Author       R: Author       R: HOWA86
C: Example      C: Example      C: 7 max. nest. Alt.
SU: S           SU: S           SU: S

    1 s             1 s             1 s
    .               .               v
    2               2               2
    .               .               .>3
    v               v               . .>4
 ...3...         ....3.....         . . .>5
    .               .               . . . .>6
  v   v             v               . . . . .>7
  4   5         ...4....            . . . . . .>8
  .>6<..         v  v   v           . . . . . . v>9
    .            6  5   8           . . . . . . v 10
    .           ..>7<...            . . . . . v 11
    v               .               . . . . v 12
 ...7...            .               . . . v 13
  v   v          ...>9<....         . . v 14
  9   8             .               . 15
 .>10<..            10              v
    .               .               16 t
    v               v
    11              11
    .               .
    v               v
    12 t            12 t
```

```
Concatenation is one to one: P1 eq. P2 <=> P1 o MNA eq. P2 o MNA
and..........................: P1 eq. P2 <=> MNA o P1 EQ. MNA o P2
------------------------
Binary operation BSEQ:

A1 = P1 o MNA
A2 = P2 o MNA
A3 = MNA o P1
A4 = MNA o P2
```

	RESULTS OF THE MEASURE(S)						
	P1	P2	MNA	A1	A2	A3	A4
DMAX	1.00	2.00	7.00	7.00	7.00	7.00	7.00

Figure 4.6: A counter-example demonstrating that the conditions for Theorem C2 do not hold. For the Measure DMAX a combination rule C1 exists, that means the conditions of Theorem C1 hold. The interpretation of this example is analogous to Figure 4.4.

Without a proof we mention, that for the Measure DMAX the combination rule C1 holds, the combination rule C2 does not hold, the combination rule C3 holds and combination rule C4 does not hold. Furthermore, the Measure DMAX does not assume an extensive structure, either.

Discussion of O1:

The next example shows Theorem O1 applied to the If-Then Operation in Figure 4.2 (IFTH) using the Measure SCOPE.

```
A: P1          A: GSEQ16
N: P1          N: GSEQ16
R: Author      R: Author
C: Example     C: Sequence
SU: S          SU:

       1 s                1 s
       .                  v
       v                  2
       2                  v
       .                  3
       v                  v
    ...3...               4
     .   .                v
     v   v                5
     4   5                v
     .   .                6
    ..>6<..               v
       .                  7
       .                  v
       v                  8
    ...7...               v
     .   .                9
     v   v                v
     9   8                10
    .>10<..               .
       .                  .
       v                  v
       11                16 t
       .
       v
      12 t

Theorem O1:
.....................: P1 eq. GSEQ16 => IFTH ( P1 ) eq. IFTH ( GSEQ16 )
------------------------
Binary operation BSEQ:

A1 = IFTH ( P1 )
A2 = IFTH ( GSEQ16 )
```

```
                     RESULTS OF THE MEASURE(S)
---------------------------------------------------------------------
                                    P1     GSEQ16      A1        A2
---------------------------------------------------------------------
SCOPE                              16.00    16.00    26.00     30.00
```

Figure 4.7: The example above shows that the conditions of Theorem O1 does not hold for the Measure SCOPE.

A1=IFTH(P1) shows the unary operation IFTH applied to flowgraph P1. It holds for the values of the Measure SCOPE: SCOPE(P1)=SCOPE(GSEQ16). However, the values of the modified flowgraphs (by the unary operation IFTH) A1 and A2 (A1=SCOPE(IFTH(P1)) and A2=SCOPE(IFTH(GSEQ16))) are different. This shows that the Measure SCOPE does not fulfill the conditions of O1.

The next two examples show the behaviour of the Measure CSG of Schmidt and Gong /ZUSE91/ (p. 375) related to the Theorem O1 and the operations IFTH and DUO.

```
A: SCHMMON1        A: SCHMMON2
N: SCHMMON1        N: SCHMMON2
R: Author          R: AUTHOR
C: Monotonicity    C: Example
SU:                SU:
            s                          s
        ....1......              .......1.......
        .   .     .              .     .       .
        .   .     .              .     v       .
        2   .     .              .....2   ...3    ...4
        .   .     .              .   .    .   .    .  .
        .   .     .              v   .    v   .    v  .
        ..>3....  .              5   .    6   .    7  .
        .   .     .              .   .    .   .    .  .
        4   :    11.             .   .    .   .    .  .
        .   .     .              v   .    v   .    v  .
        ..>5<....                .....8   ...9    ...10
        .   .     .              .   .    .   .    .  .
        6   .     7              .   .    .   .    .  .
        .   .     .              .   .    v   .    .  .
        ..>8<..                  .........11......
        .   .                    .   .    .
        .   .                    v   .    .
        9   .                    12  .    .
        .   .                    .   .    .
        .   .                    ...13   .
        ...>10<..                .   .    .
             t                   v   .    .
                                 14  .    .
                                 .   .    .
                                 .   v    .
                                 ....15
                                     t
```

```
Theorem O1:
O1:................: SCHMMON1 eq. SCHMMON2 => IFTH ( SCHMMON1 ) eq. IFTH ( SCHMMON2 )
------------------------------------------------------------------------
Binary operation BSEQ:

A1 = IFTH ( SCHMMON1 )
A2 = IFTH ( SCHMMON2 )
```

	RESULTS OF THE MEASURE(S)			
	SCHMMON1	SCHMMON2	A1	A2
CSG	8.13	8.13	9.19	9.14

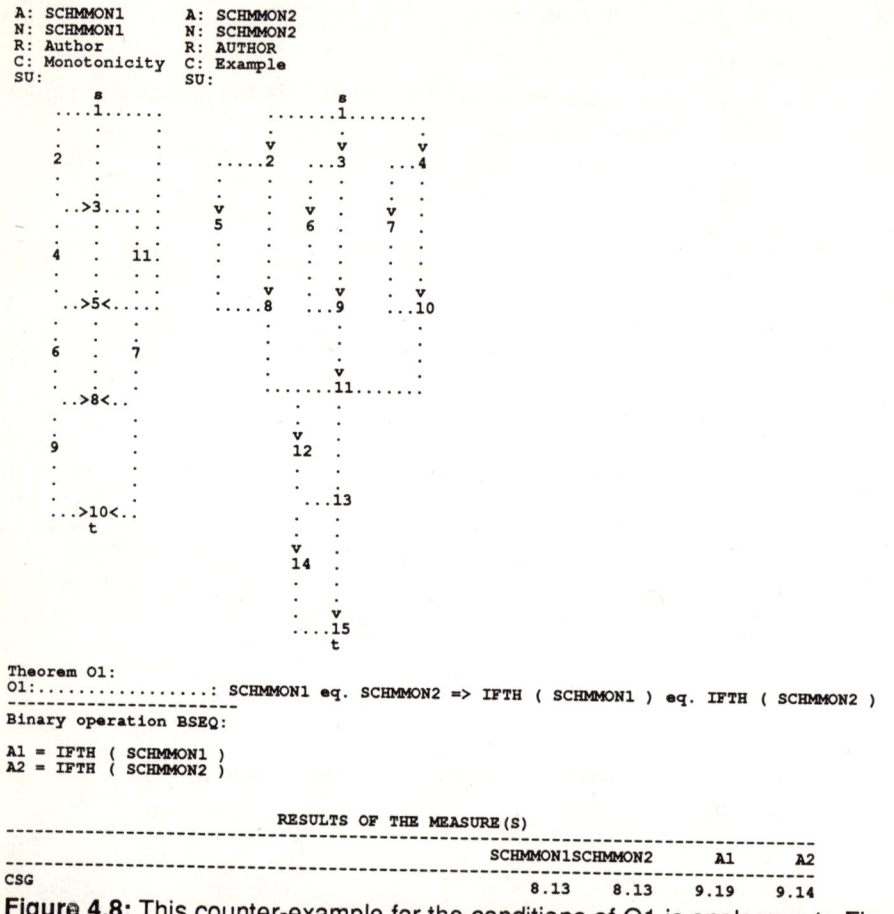

Figure 4.8: This counter-example for the conditions of O1 is analogous to Figure 4.7. The conditions of Theorem O1 do not hold for the Measure CSG of Schmidt and Gong related to the if-then-operation (IFTH). The reason is that the values of CSG(SCHMMON1)=CSG(SCHMMON2), but applying the operation IFTH, the values become different (CSG(A1)≠ CSG(A2)).

Let us consider the behaviour of the Measure CSG related to the DOU-operation and the Theorem O1.

```
A: SCHMMON1        A: SCHMMON2
N: SCHMMON1        N: SCHMMON2
R: Author          R: AUTHOR
C: Monotonicity    C: Example
SU:                SU:
         s                      s
    ....1......            .......1........
    .        .             .      .       .
    .        .             v      v       v
    2        .             .....2    ...3    ....4
    .        .             .      .       .
    .        .             v      v       v
    ...>3....             5      6       7
    .        .             .      .       .
    .        .             .      .       .
    4        11.           .      .       .
    .        .             v      v       v
    ...>5<....             ....8    ...9    ....10
    .        .             .      .       .
    6        7             .      .       .
    .        .             v
    .        .             .......11......
    ...>8<..              .
    .                      v
    9                      12
    .                      .
    .                      ...13
    ...>10<..              .
       t                   v
                           14
                           .
                           v
                           ....15
                              t
```

```
Theorem O1:
O1:................: SCHMMON1 eq. SCHMMON2 => DOU ( SCHMMON1 ) eq. DOU ( SCHMMON2 )
-----------------------
Binary operation BSEQ:

A1 = DOU ( SCHMMON1 )
A2 = DOU ( SCHMMON2 )
```

```
                    RESULTS OF THE MEASURE(S)
-----------------------------------------------------------------
                                    SCHMMON1 SCHMMON2    A1    A2
-----------------------------------------------------------------
CSG                                   8.13     8.13     9.13  9.13
```

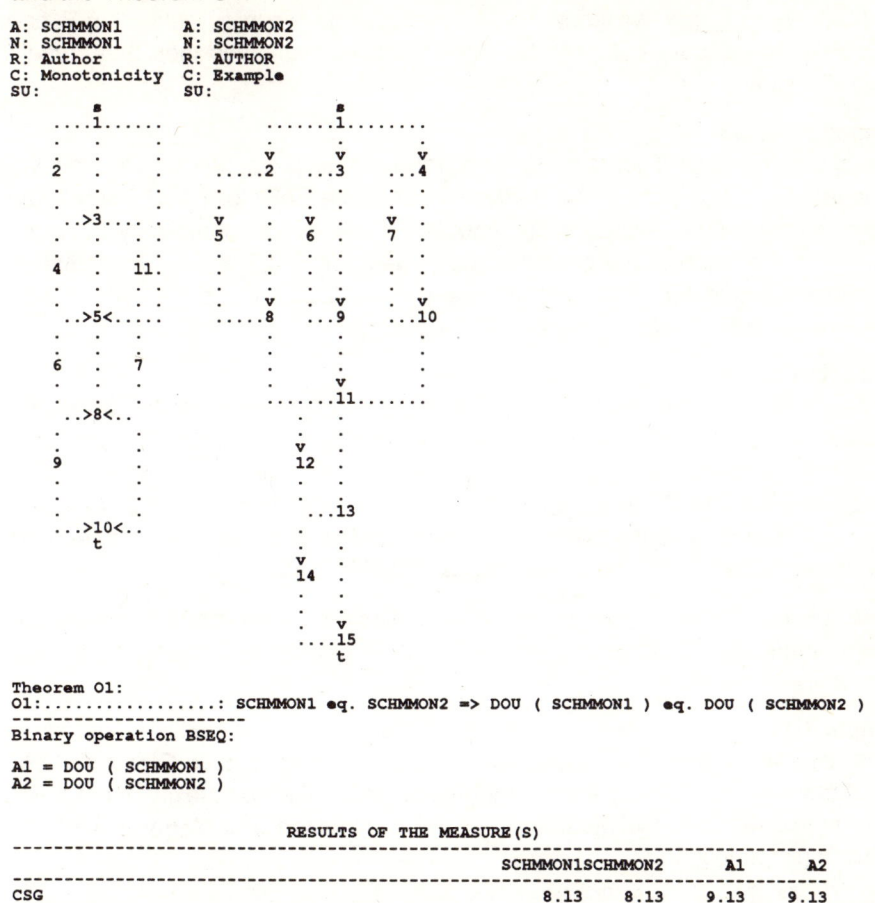

Figure 4.9: This example is analogous to Figure 4.8. The difference is the application of the unary operation DOU instead of IFTH.

Without a proof we mention that the conditions of Theorem O1 hold for the Measure CSG in the case of the unary operation DOU. The reason is that the Measure CSG is based on a dominance tree and the structure of the dominance tree is invariant to adding loops /HECH77/.

The Figures 4.8 and 4.9 show very clearly the different behaviour of the Measure CSG related to the unary IFTH and DOU operations. The reason for this behaviour of the Measure CSG is the normalization of the values (see Appendix III) and the structure of the dominance tree related to loops.

In the cases of the sequence BSEQ and DOU dependencies might occur. In these cases one might expect that the assumptions of Theorem C1 and Theorem O1 are not satisfied in reality.

Discussion of C2:

If the assumptions of Theorem C2 hold, then the assumptions of Theorem C1 also hold. Additionally we know the following. If in two programs P1 o P and P2oP which are equally complex the same module is removed then they remain equally complex.

Discussion of C3:

If the assumptions of Theorem C3 hold, then the assumptions of Theorem C1 also hold. Additionally we know that if in a program PoP1 or P1oP the module P1 is substituted by a less complex module P2, the overall complexity does not increase. In the case of the concatenation operation BALT such a combination rule was proposed by other authors. See Zuse /ZUSE91/, p.300 and p.320. There Prather /PRAT84/ requires μ (PoP')=2max (μ (P), μ (P')).

Discussion of C4:

The assumption of Theorem C4 is the monotonicity axiom of the extensive structure. If the assumptions of Theorem C4 hold, then the assumptions of Theorem C1, C2 and C3 also hold. Furthermore we know that if in a program PoP1 or P1oP the module P1 is substituted by a less complex module P2, then the overall complexity is decreasing. Such combination rules where proposed by many authors. See Zuse /ZUSE91/, pages 179, 206, 345, 383.

If there is no combination rule for the complexities then it is difficult to control the overall complexity of a program. We want to illustrate this by considering the following artificial example.

Example 4.1:

Let us assume a program is composed of two program bodies CP1 and CP2 each of them is produced by a different programmer. The complexity of the modules is measured with the Measure SCOPE of Harrison and Magel /HARR81/, /ZUSE91/ (Appendix III).

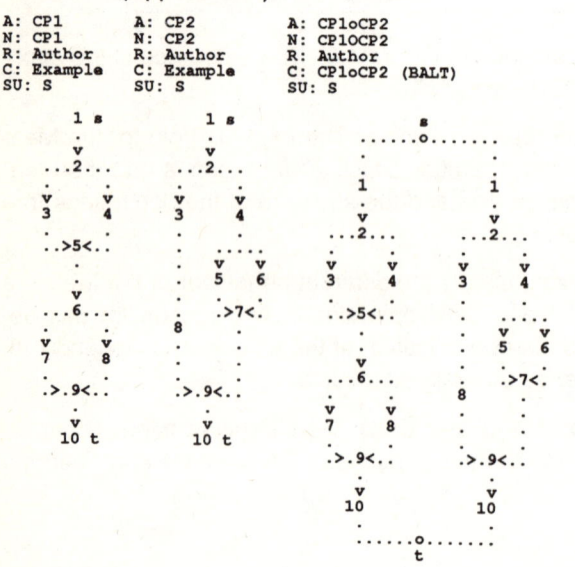

```
A: CP1              A: CP2              A: CP1oCP2
N: CP1              N: CP2              N: CP1oCP2
R: Author           R: Author           R: Author
C: Example          C: Example          C: CP1oCP2  (BALT)
SU: S               SU: S               SU: S

      1 s                 1 s                          s
       .                   .                   ......o........
       v                   v                   .             .
     ...2...             ...2...               1             1
      . .                 . .                  .             .
      v v                 v v                  v             v
      3 4                 3 4               ...2...       ...2...
      .                   .                  . .           . .
      v                   .....              v v           v v
    ...5<..                . v v              3 4           3 4
      .                    . 5 6              .             .....
      v                    .                  v             . v v
    ...6...                .>7<.            ...5<..         . 5 6
      .                    . 8                .             .
      v v                  .                  v           .>7<.
      7 8                  .                ...6...         . 8
      .                    .                  . .           .
    .>.9<..              .>.9<..              v v           .
      .                    .                  7 8           .
      v                    v                  .           .>.9<..
     10 t                 10 t              .>.9<..         .
                                              .             v
                                              v            10
                                             10             .
                                              .          ......o........
                                                                t
```

```
                          RESULTS OF THE MEASURE(S)
------------------------------------------------------------------
                                              CP1     CP2  CP1oCP2
------------------------------------------------------------------
SCOPE                                       14.00   23.00    59.00
```

Figure 4.10: The flowgraphs CP1 and CP2 are combined by the concatenation operation BALT.

The overall complexity of the program is 59. Let us assume that the manager decides that this is too complex and demands a less complex version of the program. According to this each programmer tries to find a less complex version of his program body. After some time those solutions are given. The overall complexity of the program is computed again and is 61. The manager is upset and wants to find out who is guilty. What has happened? The structure of the new program CP3oCP4 is shown in Figure 4.11.

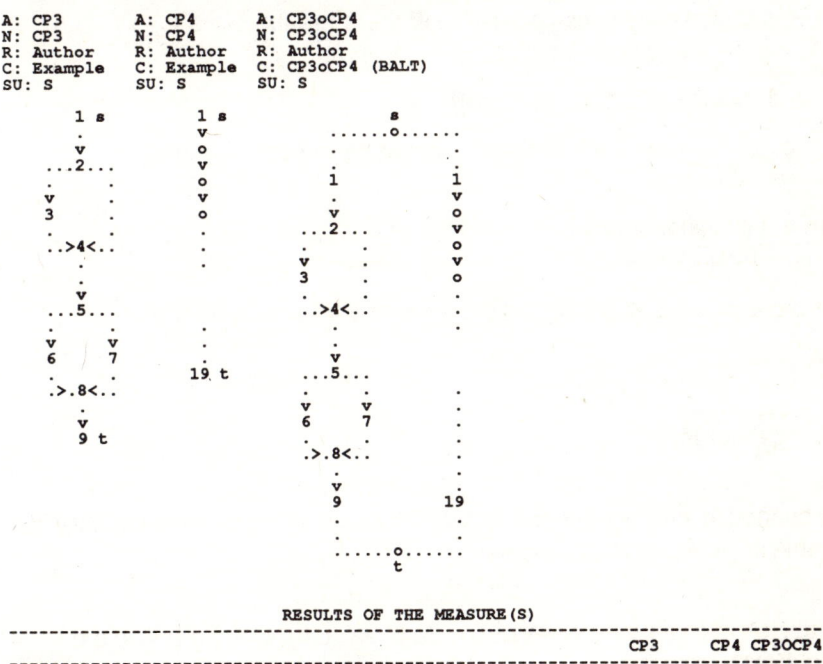

```
A: CP3         A: CP4         A: CP3oCP4
N: CP3         N: CP4         N: CP3oCP4
R: Author      R: Author      R: Author
C: Example     C: Example     C: CP3oCP4 (BALT)
SU: S          SU: S          SU: S

      1 s            1 s                   s
       .              v             ......o......
       v              o             .           .
      ...2...         v             .           .
       .              o             1           1
       v              v             .           v
       3              .             v           o
       .              .            ...2...      v
      ..>4<..         .             .           o
       .              v             3           v
       v              .             .           o
      ...5...         .            ..>4<..      .
       .              .             .           .
       v    v         .             v           .
       6    7        19 t          ...5...      .
      .>.8<..                       .           .
       .                             v    v     .
       v                             6    7     .
       9 t                          .>.8<..     .
                                     .          .
                                     v         19
                                     9          .
                                     .          .
                                    ......o......
                                          t
```

```
                          RESULTS OF THE MEASURE(S)
------------------------------------------------------------------
                                              CP3     CP4  CP3oCP4
------------------------------------------------------------------
SCOPE                                       12.00   19.00    61.00
```

Figure 4.11: The flowgraphs CP3 and CP4 are combined by the concatenation operation BALT.

The programmers created new solutions of the programs CP1 and CP2 and gave them the names CP3 and CP4. It holds that SCOPE(CP1)>SCOPE(CP3) and SCOPE(CP2)>SCOPE(CP4). But for the overall complexity it holds: SCOPE(CP1oCP2)<SCOPE(CP3oCP4). The reason for this result is that the Measure SCOPE for the concatenation operation BALT does not have the property of the Theorem C3 (Even C1 does not hold).

4.4 Decomposition and Independance

In measurement theory weaker concepts of independance are proposed than that of Weyuker /WEYU88/. In analogy to Roberts /ROBE79/, p.232, $(A, \bullet\geq, o)$ is **decomposeable** iff there are functions f: $A \to \Re$ and g: $A \to \Re$ and a function F: $f(A) \times g(A) \to \Re$, with

$$a \circ b \bullet\geq c \circ d \iff F(f(a),g(b)) \geq F(f(c),g(d)),$$

for all a, b, c, d $\in$ A. According to Roberts this representation exists in many cases. Hence general decomposeability is of no great practical value. In the context of software measurement monotonic decomposeability /KRAN71/, p.371, is of interest.

Definition 4.1 *(Monotonically Decomposeable):*
$(A, \bullet\geq, o)$ is monotonically decomposeable iff there are functions $f:A\to\Re$, $g:A\to\Re$, and $F: f(A) \times g(A) \to \Re$, with

$a \circ b \bullet\geq c \circ d \iff F(f(a),g(b)) \geq F(f(c),g(d)),$

for all a, b, c, d $\in$ A and where F is strictly increasing in each variable.
♦

Definition 4.2 *(Independence):*
$(A, \bullet\geq, o)$ is independent iff

$a \circ c \bullet\geq b \circ c \iff a \circ d \bullet\geq b \circ d$, and $c \circ a \bullet\geq c \circ b \iff d \circ a \bullet\geq d \circ b$,

for all a, b, c, d $\in$ A.
♦

The following theorem holds.

Theorem 4.1:
Let A be countable and $\bullet\geq$ a weak order. Then $(A, \bullet\geq, o)$ is monotonically decomposeable iff $(A, \bullet\geq, o)$ is independent.

Proof:
We consider $(A \times A, \bullet\geq')$ where we define $(a,b) \bullet\geq' (c,d) \iff a \circ b \bullet\geq c \circ d$. We now follow /KRAN71/ (Chapter 7).
♦

Let us reconsider the example in Figures 4.10 and 4.11 where μ is the Measure SCOPE of Harrison and Magel and the binary operation BALT is used. Let n_i be the number of nodes of P_i. Then we get $\mu(P1 \circ P2) = \mu(P1) + n1 + \mu(P2) + n2 + c$, where c is a constant independant of P_i. Hence we get

$\mu(P1 \circ P2) = F(f(P1),f(P2))$, with $f(P_i) = \mu(P_i) + n_i$ and $F(x,y)=x+y+c$.

Hence for the hypothetical empirical system $(P, \bullet\geq, o)$ of the Measure SCOPE independence holds. Hence in our example the programmers could have minimized the overall complexity by minimizing $\mu(P_i)+n_i$ instead of $\mu(P_i)$ separately. It is important to note that this minimization could be done by each programmer independently. A drawback of this approach appears if the structure of the programs is more complex. For example consider P=P1 o (P2 o P3), where o is the binary operation BALT. Then

μ (P)=μ (P1 o (P2 o P3))=μ (P1) + n1 + μ (P2 o P3) + n23 + c,

where n2,3 is the number nodes in P2 o P3, and n2,3 = n2 + n3 + 2.
Hence

μ (P)= μ (P1)+n1 + (μ (P2)+n2 + μ (P3) + n3 + c) + (n2 + n3 + 2) + c

μ (P)= (μ (P1)+n1) + (μ (P2)+ 2n2) + (μ (P3) + 2 n3) + 2c + 2.

Hence the programmer in charge of P1 has to minimize μ (P1) + n1, whereas for P2 and P3 μ (P2)+2n2, and μ (P3)+2n3 have to be minimized. The minimization can still be done independently but with respect to different functions according the location of the program body in the combined program.

We see that there are several concepts of independence. Basically one concept means that if a program system P consists of several program bodies P1,..,Pn, then there exist functions f1,...,fn where fi depends on the location of Pi in P such that the overall complexity μ (P) of P is minimized if the fi(Pi), i=,1...,n are minimized independently. The other concept which is rejected by Weyuker basically means that fi= μ, for all i=,1..,n. We see that it is still an open problem which kind of independence for concatenation operations holds in reality. This has to be investigated empirically. The outcome of this investigation will have consequences on the usefulness of software measurement for modular designs.

5 Summary

In this paper we have shown the benefits of the measurement theoretic approach in software metrics. If we want to make experiments we need hypotheses. The measurement theoretic approach yields these hypotheses. Moreover we can use these hypotheses to talk about complexity even without having any mapping into the real numbers. Additionally we can talk about the measures and can compare them because these hypotheses are conditions for their proper use. We have illustrated how this approach can be applied to the Metric of McCabe by deriving conditions for its use as an ordinal and ratio scale. Furthermore we discussed several independence conditions for concatenation operations. The hypothetical empirical relational systems of different measures have different independence properties. These independence conditions are empirical criteria for i.e. predescriptiveness - which is an required property for software metrics -, whether or how the complexity of simple programs or subdesigns influences the overall complexity of a program or design. Hence they are important because composition and decomposition operations are major strategies in software engineering. We see, that, for example predescriptiveness is an empirical property and it is not yet known whether it holds in reality.

Our overall conclusion is that measurement theory is an extremely useful tool in order to investigate software complexity and software complexity measures.

6 References

/ALVE88/ Edited by: Elliott, J.J; Fenton, N.E.; Linkman, S.; Markham, G.; Whitty, R.:
Structure-Based Software Measurement, Alvey Project SE/069, 1988, Department of Electrical Engineering, South Bank, Polytechnic, Borough Road, London, SE1 OAA, UK.

/BACH87/ Bache, R.:
Structural Metrication within an Axiomatic Framework In: ALVE88.

/BASI86/ Basili; Selby; Hutchens:
Experimentation in Software Engineering IEEE Transactions on Software Engineering, Vol. SE-12, No. 7, July 1986

/BOLL85/ Bollmann, P; Zuse, H.:
An Axiomatic Approach to Software Complexity Measures, Third Symposium on Empirical Foundations of Information and Software Science III Edited by Jens Rasmussen and Pranas Zunde Plenum Press, New York Roskilde, Denmark, October 21-24, 1985

/CONT86/ Conte, S.D.; Dunsmore, H.E.; Shen, V.Y.:
Software Engineering Metrics and Model, Benjamin/Cummings Publishing Company, Menlo Park, 1986.

/EJIO85/ Ejiogu, Lem O.:
A Simple Measure of Software Complexity Sigplan Notices, V20 #3, March 1985.

/FENT91/ Fenton, N.:
Software Metrics: A Rigorous Approach City University, London, Chapman & Hall, 1991

/GILB77/ Gilb, T.:
Software Metrics, Winthrop Publishers, Cambridge, Massachusetts, 1977

/HARR81/ Harrison, Warren; Magel Kenneth:
A Topological Analysis of the Complexity of Computer Programs with less than th ree binary Branches, ACM SIGPLAN Notices, Vol. 16, No. 4, pp. 51-63, 1981.

/HARR82/ Harrison, Warren; Magel Kenneth; Kluczny Raymond; DeKock Arlan:
Applying Software Complexity Metrics to Program Maintenance, Computer, No. 9, 1982.

/HECH77/   Hecht, M.S:
            Flow Analysis of Computer Programs, Elsevier, New York, 1977

/JAYA87/   Jayaprakash, S.; Lakshmanan, K.B.; Sinha, P.K.:
            MEBOW: A Comprehensive Measure of Control Flow Complexity COMPSAC 87, pp. 238-244, 1987

/IEEE88/   IEEE Sdt 982.1-1988:
            Standard Dictionary of Metrics to Produce Reliable Software The Institute of Electrical and Electronics Engineers, Inc 345 East 47th Street, New York, NY 10017-2394, USA IEEE Standard Board, 1988.

/KEAR86/   Kearney, Joseph K.; Sedlmeyer, Robert L.; Thompson, William:
            Software Complexity Measurement, CACM Vol. 29,No. 11, 1986

/KRAN71/   Krantz, David H.; Luce, R. Duncan; Suppes; Patrick; Tversky, Amos:
            Foundations of Measurement, Vol 1, Academic Press, 1971

/LAWR81/   Lawrence, J. Peters:
            Software Design: Methods and Techniques, Yourdon Press, 1981

/LI87/   Li, H.F.; Cheung, W.K.:
            An Empirical Study of Software Metrics, IEEE Transactions on Software Engineering, Vol. Se-13, NO. 6, June 1987.

/LAKS91/   Lakshmanan, K.B.; Jayaprakash, S.; Sinha, P.K.:
            Properties of Control-Flow Complexity Measures, IEEE Transactions on Software Engineering, Vol. 17, No.12, December, 1991, p.1289-1295 (Very similar to /JAYA87/).

/LUCE90/   Luce, R. Duncan; Krantz, David H.; Suppes; Patrick; Tversky, Amos:
            Foundations of Measurement, Vol 3, Academic Press, 1990

/MAYR90/   Mayrhauser, Anneliese von:
            Software Engineering - Methods and Management, Academic Press, Inc., 1990

/MCCA76/   McCabe, T.:
            A Complexity Measure, IEEE Transactions of Software Engineering Vol. SE-1, No. 3, pp. 312-327, 1976

/PAGE88/   Page-Jones, Meilir:
            The Practical Guide to Structured Systems Second Edition, Yourdon Press, 1988

/PRAT84/ Prather, Ronald E:
An Axiomatic Theory of Software Complexity Measure. The Computer Journal, Vol. 27, No. 4, 340-347, 1984

/PREI79/ Preiser, S.; Storm, I.L:
An Index of Complexity for Structured Programming IEEE Proceedings of the Workshop on Quantitative Software Models, New York, 1979, pp.130-133.

/ROBE79/ Roberts, Fred S.:
Measurement Theory with Applications to Decisionmaking, Utility, and the Social Sciences, Encyclopedia of Mathematics and its Applications Addison Wesley Publishing Company, 1979.

/SAGR89/ Sagri, M.M.:
Rated and Operating Complexity of Program - An Extension to McCabe's Theory of Complexity Measure. SIGPLAN Notices, Vol. 24, No. 8, 1989, p.8-12.

/SCHM85/ Schmidt, Monika:
A Complexity Measure Based on Selection and Nesting, ACM SIGMETRICS-Performance Evaluation Review, V13, No. 1, June 85

/URBA84/ Urban, Joseph, E.:
Computer Languages. In: Vick, C.R.; Ramamoorthy, C.V.; Handbook of Software Engineering, p.184-200, Van Nostrand Reinhold Company, 1984.

/WEYU85/ Weyuker, Elaine J:
Evaluating Software Complexity Measures Januar 85 Technical Report #149 Courant Institute of Mathematical Sciences 251 Mercer Street, New York, N.Y. 10012

/WEYU88/ Weyuker, Elaine J:
Evaluating Software Complexity Measures IEEE Transactions of Software Engineering Vol. 14, No. 9, Sep. 88.

/YOUR79/ Yourdon, E; Constantine, L:
Structured Design Fundamentals of a Discipline of Computer Programs and Design Prentice-Hall, 1979

/ZUSE89/ Zuse, H.; Bollmann, P.:
Using Measurement Theory to Describe the Properties and Scales of Static Software Complexity Metrics, SIGPLAN Notices, Vol. 24, No. 8, pp.23-33, August 89.

/ZUSE91/ Zuse, H:
Software Complexity - Measures and Methods, DeGruyter Publisher 1991, Berlin, New York.

Appendix I

Definition

Let $\mathbf{A^*} = (A^*, R_1^*, \ldots, R_n^*, o^*_1, \ldots, o^*_m)$, and $\mathbf{A} = (A, R_1, \ldots, R_n, o_1, \ldots, o_m)$ be two relational systems. The operations o^*_j, $j=1,\ldots,m$ may be partial operations on A^*. $\mathbf{A}$ is the **homomorphic image of** $\mathbf{A^*}$ iff there exists $\phi: A^* \to A$ such that $\phi(A^*)=A$, and for all $a^*_1,\ldots,a^*_{ki}, a^*, b^* \in A^*$, and all $i=1,\ldots,n$, $j=1,\ldots,m$, and for all $a, b \in A$ the following three conditions hold.

i) $R_i^*(a^*_1,\ldots,a^*_{ki}) \iff R_i(\phi(a^*_1),\ldots,\phi(a^*_{ki}))$.

ii) Whenever $a^* o^*_j b^*$ exists then
$\phi(a^* o^*_j b^*) = \phi(a^*) o_j \phi(b^*)$

iii) For all $a, b \in A$ there exist $a^*, b^* \in A^*$ with $a = \phi(a^*)$, $b = \phi(b^*)$, and $a^* o^*_j b^*$ exists.

Lemma 1:

Let $\mathbf{A^*} = (A^*, R_1^*, \ldots, R_n^*, o^*_1, \ldots, o^*_m)$, and $\mathbf{A} = (A, R_1, \ldots, R_n, o_1, \ldots, o_m)$ be two relational systems. For $\phi: A^* \to A$ let $\mathbf{A}$ be a homomorphic image of $\mathbf{A^*}$ and let $\mathbf{B} = (B, S_1, \ldots, S_n, \bullet_1, \ldots, \bullet_m)$ be a formal relational system. Then $(\mathbf{A^*}, \mathbf{B}, \mu\phi)$ is a scale iff $(\mathbf{A}, \mathbf{B}, \mu)$ is a scale.

Proof:

i) Let $(\mathbf{A}, \mathbf{B}, \mu)$ be a scale. Because ϕ and μ are homomorphisms so is $\mu\phi$ a homomorphism. Hence $(\mathbf{A^*}, \mathbf{B}, \mu\phi)$ is a scale.

ii) Let $(\mathbf{A^*}, \mathbf{B}, \mu\phi)$ be a scale. We have to show that for all $a_1,\ldots,a_{ki}, a, b \in A$ and all $i=1,\ldots,n$, $j=1,\ldots,m$

$$R_i(a_1,\ldots a_{ki}) \iff S_i(\mu(a_1),\ldots,\mu(a_{ki}))$$

and
$$\mu(a \, o_j \, b) = \mu(a) \bullet_j \mu(b)$$

Let $a_1,\ldots,a_{ki} \in A$. Because ϕ is onto there exist $a^*_1,\ldots,a^*_{ki}$ such that $a_k = \phi(a^*_k)$, $k=1,\ldots,ki$. Because $\mathbf{A}$ is a homomorphic image of $\mathbf{A^*}$ we obtain

$$R_i(a_1,\ldots,a_{ki}) \iff R_i(\phi(a^*_1),\ldots,\phi(a^*_{ki}))$$
$$\iff R_i^*(a^*_1,\ldots,a^*_{ki}) \iff S_i(\mu(\phi(a^*_1)),\ldots,\mu(\phi(a^*_{ki})))$$
$$\iff S_i(\mu(a_1),\ldots,\mu(a_{ki})).$$

Let $a, b \in A$. Then there exists a^* and b^* with $a=\phi(a^*)$ and $b=\phi(b^*)$, $a^* o^* b^*$ defined and $\phi(a^*) o_j \phi(b^*) = \phi(a^* o^*_j b^*)$.

Hence

$\mu(a \, o_j \, b) \quad = \mu(\phi(a^*) \, o_j \, \phi(b^*))$

$$= \mu(\phi(a^* o^*j\, b^*))$$
$$= \mu(\phi(a^*)) \bullet j\, \mu(\phi(b^*))$$
$$= \mu(a) \bullet j\, \mu(b).$$

Hence (**A**, **B**, μ) is a scale.

Corollary 1:
Let **A** be a homomorphic image of **A*** under the homomorphism φ. Let (**A**, **B**, μ) and (**A***, **B**, μφ) be scales. Then every admissible transformation of (**A**, **B**, μ) is an admissible transformation of (**A***, **B**, μφ) and vice versa.
♦

Lemma 2:
Let **A** the homomorphic image of **A*** under φ and let (**A***, **B**, ψ) be a scale such that for all $a^*, b^* \in A^*$, $\phi(a^*) = \phi(b^*) \Rightarrow \psi(a^*) = \psi(b^*)$. Then there exists μ: A->B such that μ φ = ψ.

Proof:
We define μ: A->B for $a = \phi(a^*)$ as $\mu(a) = \psi(a^*)$. Because φ is onto such an a* always exists. μ is well defined. Let be $a = \phi(a^*) = \phi(b^*)$. Then $\mu(a) = \psi(a^*) = \psi(b^*)$. Hence for all $a^* \in A^*$ $\mu(\phi(a^*)) = \psi(a^*)$
♦

Lemma 3:
For φ:**P*** -> **P** there exists •≥ on **P** such that (**P**, •≥) is the homomorphic image of (**P*** •≥*) iff F1 holds.

Proof:
i) Assume F1 holds. φ is onto by definition of **P**. We define for all P, P'∈ **P** with $P = \phi(P^*)$, $P = \phi(P'^*)$, P •≥ P' <=> P* ≥* P'*. •≥ is well defined. Let $P = \phi(P^*) = \phi(P1^*)$ and $P' = \phi(P'^*) = \phi(P1'^*)$. Because of F1 we have P* •≥* P'* <=> P1* •≥* P1'*. Hence we have φ(P*) •≥ φ(P'*) <=> P* •≥* P'* for all P*, P'* ∈ **P***.

ii) Assume (**P**, •≥) is the homomorphic image of (**P***, •≥*) under φ. Hence for all P*, P'* ∈ **P*** φ(P*) •≥ φ(P'*) <=> P* •≥* P'*. Let P* •≥* P'* and φ(P*) = φ(P1*) and φ(P'*) = φ(P1'*). Then φ(P*) •≥ φ(P1'*). Hence φ(P1*) •≥ φ(P1'*) and finally P1* •≥* P1'*.
♦

Lemma 4:
For φ:**P*** -> **P** there exists o on **P** such that (**P**, o) is the homomorphic image of (**P***, o*) iff F3 and F4 hold.

Proof:
i) Assume F3 and F4 hold. φ is onto by definition of **P**. Let be $P = \phi(P^*)$, $P' = \phi(P'^*)$ and because of F4 we assume that P* o* P'* exists. We now define P o P' = φ(P* o* P'*). o is well defined. Let be $P = \phi(P^*) = \phi(P1^*)$, $P' = \phi(P'^*) = \phi(P1'^*)$ and P* o* P'* and P1* o* P1'* both exist. Then
φ(P*) o φ(P'*)   = φ(P* o* P'*)
                              = φ(P1* o* P1'*) because of F3

$$=\phi(P1^*) \text{ o } \phi(P1'^*).$$

Because of F4 o is closed. Because of the definition of o we have $\phi(P^* \text{ o } P'^*)=\phi(P^*) \text{ o}^* \phi(P'^*)$. Hence (P, o) is the homomorphic image of (P^*, o^*).

ii) Assume (P, o) is the homomorphic image of (P^*, o^*) under the homomorphism of ϕ. F4 holds because of the definition of the homomorphic image. Assume further that there exist $P^*, P1^*, P'^*, P1'^* \in P^*$ with $\phi(P^*)=\phi(P'^*)$, $\phi(P1^*)=\phi(P1'^*)$ and $P^* \text{ o}^* P1^*$ and $P'^* \text{ o}^* P1'^*$ both exist. Then

$\phi(P^* \text{ o } P1^*)$ $=\phi(P^*) \text{ o } \phi(P1^*)$
  $=\phi(P'^*) \text{ o } \phi(P1'^*)$
  $=\phi(P'^* \text{ o}^* P1'^*)$.

Hence F3 holds.
♦

Lemma 5:
For $\phi: P^* \to P$ there exist $\bullet\geq$ and o on P such that $(P, \bullet\geq, o)$ is the homomorphic image of $(P^*, \bullet\geq^*, o^*)$ iff F1, F3 and F4 hold.

Proof:
By combining Lemma 3 and Lemma 4.

Theorem 2.3:
Let $((P^*, \bullet\geq^*), (\Re, \geq), \psi)$ be a scale. There exists a relation $\bullet\geq$ on P with $P^* \bullet\geq^* P'^* <=> \phi(P^*) \bullet\geq \phi(P'^*)$ for all $P^*, P'^* \in P^*$ and a mapping $\mu: P \to \Re$ with $\psi = \mu \phi$ such that $((P, \bullet\geq), (\Re, \geq), \mu)$ is a scale and both scales have the same admissible transformations iff F1 and F2 hold.

Proof:
i) Assume F1 and F2 hold. Because F1 holds there exists $\bullet\geq$ on P such that $(P, \bullet\geq)$ is the homomorphic image of $(P^*, \bullet\geq^*)$ under ϕ (See Lemma 3). Because of F2 we have for all $P^*, P'^* \in P^*$ $\phi(P^*)= \phi(P'^*) => P^* \approx^* P'^* => \psi(P^*)= \psi(P'^*)$.
Because of Lemma 2 there exists $\mu: P \to \Re$ such that $\mu \phi = \psi$.
Hence $((P^*, \bullet\geq^*), (\Re, \geq), \mu \phi)$ is a scale. Because of Lemma 1 $((P, \bullet\geq), (\Re, \geq), \mu)$ is also a scale. Because of Corollary 1 the scales have the same admissible transformations.

ii) Assume $((P^*, \bullet\geq^*), (\Re, \geq), \mu \phi)$ is a scale with $\mu: P \to \Re$.

Proof of F1:
Let $\phi(P^*)= \phi(P1^*)$ and $\phi(P'^*)= \phi(P1'^*)$ and $P^* \bullet\geq^* P'^*$. Then $\mu \phi(P^*)=\mu \phi(P1^*)$, $\mu \phi(P'^*)= \mu \phi(P1'^*)$, $\mu \phi(P^*) \bullet\geq \mu \phi(P'^*)$. Then $\mu \phi(P1^*) \geq \mu \phi(P1'^*)$ and finally $P1^* \bullet\geq^* P1'^*$.

Proof of F2:
Let $\phi(P^*)=\phi(P'^*)$. Then $\mu \phi(P^*)= \mu \phi(P'^*)$ and finally $P^* \approx^* P'^*$.
♦

Theorem 2.4:
Let $((\mathbf{P^*}, \bullet\geq^*, o^*), (\Re, \geq, \bullet), \psi)$ be a scale ($\bullet$ is some binary operation on $\Re$). If F1, F2, F3 and F4 hold then there exist $\bullet\geq$ and o on $\mathbf{P}$ with $P^* \bullet\geq^* P'^* \iff \phi(P^*) \bullet\geq \phi(P'^*)$ for all $P^*, P'^* \in \mathbf{P^*}$ and with $\phi(P^* o^* P'^*) = \phi(P^*) o \phi(P'^*)$ for all $P^*, P'^* \in \mathbf{P^*}$ whenever $P^* o^* P'^*$ exists and a mapping $\mu: \mathbf{P} \to \Re$ such that $\psi = \mu\phi$, $((\mathbf{P}, \bullet\geq, o), (\Re, \geq, \bullet), \mu)$ is a scale and both scales have the same admissible transformation.

Proof:
Because of Lemma 5 there exist $\bullet\geq$ and o on $\mathbf{P}$ such that $(\mathbf{P}, \bullet\geq, o)$ is the homomorphic image of $(\mathbf{P^*}, \bullet\geq^*, o^*)$. Because of F2 $\phi(P^*) = \phi(P'^*)$ implies $\psi(P^*) = \psi(P'^*)$. Because of Lemma 2 there exists $\mu: \mathbf{P} \to \Re$ such that $\psi = \mu \phi$. Because of Lemma 1 $((\mathbf{P}, \bullet\geq, o), (\Re, \geq, \bullet), \mu)$ is a scale. Because of Corollary 1 both scales have the same admissible transformations.

Theorem 2.5:
If F1 holds then there exists a relation $\bullet\geq$ on $\mathbf{P}$ with $P^* \bullet\geq^* P'^* \iff \phi(P^*) \bullet\geq \phi(P'^*)$ for all $P^*, P'^* \in \mathbf{P^*}$ such that for every $\mu: \mathbf{P} \to \Re$ the following holds: $((\mathbf{P^*}, \bullet\geq^*), (\Re, \geq), \mu\phi)$ is an ordinal scale iff $((\mathbf{P}, \bullet\geq), (\Re, \geq), \mu)$ is an ordinal scale.

Proof:
Because F1 holds there exists $\bullet\geq$ on $\mathbf{P}$ such that $(\mathbf{P}, \bullet\geq)$ is the homomorphic image of $(\mathbf{P^*}, \bullet\geq^*)$ (see Lemma 3). Now we apply Lemma 1 and Corollary 1.

Theorem 2.6:
If F1, F3 and F4 hold then there exist $\bullet\geq$ and o on $\mathbf{P}$ with $P^* \bullet\geq^* P'^* \iff \phi(P^*) \bullet\geq \phi(P'^*)$ for all $P^*, P'^* \in \mathbf{P^*}$ and with $\phi(P^* o^* P'^*) = \phi(P^*) o \phi(P'^*)$ for all $P^*, P'^* \in \mathbf{P^*}$ whenever $P^* o^* P'^*$ exists such that for every $\mu: \mathbf{P} \to \Re$ the following holds: $((\mathbf{P^*}, \bullet\geq^*, o^*), (\Re, \geq, +), \mu\phi)$ is a ratio scale iff $((\mathbf{P}, \bullet\geq, o), (\Re, \geq, +), \mu)$ is a ratio scale.

Proof:
Because F1, F3 and F4 hold there exist $\bullet\geq$ and o on $\mathbf{P}$ such that $(\mathbf{P}, \bullet\geq, o)$ is the homomorphic image of $(\mathbf{P^*}, \bullet\geq^*, o^*)$ (See Lemma 5). Now we apply Lemma 1 and Corollary 1.

Proof for Weak Associativity:

Theorem 2.7:
Assume F1, F2, F3 and F4 hold. Then there exist $\bullet\geq$ and o on $\mathbf{P}$ with $P^* \bullet\geq^* P'^* \iff \phi(P^*) \bullet\geq \phi(P'^*)$ for all $P^*, P'^* \in \mathbf{P^*}$ and with $\phi(P^* o^* P'^*) = \phi(P^*) o \phi(P'^*)$ for all $P^*, P'^* \in \mathbf{P^*}$ whenever $P^* o^* P'^*$ exists such that the following statements are equivalent.

1. For all $P^*, P'^* \in \mathbf{P^*}$ if there exist $Q, Q1, Q2 \in \mathbf{P}$ with $\phi(P^*) = Q o (Q1 o Q2)$ and $\phi(P'^*) = (Q o Q1) o Q2$ then $P^* \approx^* P'^*$.

2. For all Q, Q1, Q2 ∈ **P**:
Q o (Q1 o Q2) ≈ (Q o Q1) o Q2.

Proof:
If F1, F3 and F4 hold then there exist •≥ and o on **P** such that (**P**, •≥, o) is the homomorphic image of (**P***, •≥*, o*) under φ.

Assume i) holds. Let be Q, Q1, Q2 ∈ **P**. There exist P* and P'* with φ(P*)=Q o (Q1 o Q2) and φ(P'*)=Q o (Q1 o Q2). Because of i) P* ≈* P'*
=> φ(P*) ≈ φ(P'*)
=> Q o (Q1 o Q2) ≈ (Q o Q1) o Q2

Assume ii) holds. Let φ(P*)=Q o (Q1 o Q2) and φ(P'*)=(Q o Q1) o Q2. Then
Q o (Q1 o Q2) ≈ (Q o Q1) o Q2
=> φ(P*) ≈ φ(P'*)
=> P* ≈* P'*

♦

Appendix II (Proofs of Theorems C1-C4):

Throughout Appendix II we assume that ((**A**, •≥),(ℜ, ≥), μ) is an ordinal scale.

Lemma A.1:
If a ≈ b => a o c ≈ b o c, and a ≈ b => c o a ≈ c o b

for all a,b,c ∈ A,

then a ≈ b and c ≈ d => a o c ≈ b o d, for all a,b,c,d ∈ A.

Proof:
a ≈ b => a o c ≈ b o c

c ≈ d => b o c ≈ b o d

Because of transitivity we obtain

a o c ≈ b o d.

Lemma A.2:
There exists a binary operation •with μ (a o b) = μ (a) • μ (b), for all a,b ∈ A, if a≈b and c≈d imply a o c ≈ b o d , for all a,b,c,d ∈ A.

Proof:
We define μ (u) • μ (v)= μ(u o v), for all for all u,v ∈ A. We have to show that • is well defined. Let us assume μ (a)= μ (b) and μ (c)= μ (d). This implies a≈b, and c≈d, and a o c ≈ b o d.
Hence μ (a) • μ (c)= μ (a o c)= μ (b o d)= μ (b) • μ (d)
♦

Lemma A.3:

If there exists a binary operation • then

a≈b => a o c ≈ b o c, and a≈b => c o a ≈ c o b, for all a, b, c ∈ A.

Proof:
Let us assume a≈b. That implies $\mu(a) = \mu(b)$.

Hence
$\mu(a) \bullet \mu(c) = \mu(b) \bullet \mu(c)$, and $\mu(c) \bullet \mu(a) = \mu(c) \bullet \mu(b)$.

This yields $\mu(a \circ c) = \mu(b \circ c)$, and $\mu(c \circ a) = \mu(c \circ b)$, and finally we obtain a o c ≈ b o c, and c o a ≈ c o b.

♦

Theorem C1:
There exists a binary operation • iff a≈b => a o c ≈ b o c, and

a≈b => coa ≈ cob, for all a,b,c ∈ A.

Proof:

The existence of • is shown by the application of Lemma A.1 and Lemma A.2. The converse statement is shown by application of lemma A.3.

♦

Theorem C2:
There exist a binary operation • that is one to one in each variable iff

a ≈ b <=> a o c ≈ b o c <=> c o a ≈ c o b, for all a,b,c ∈ A.

Proof:

1. We assume a ≈ b <=> a o c ≈ b o c <=> c o a ≈ c o b

    Then there exists • such that $\mu(a \circ b) = \mu(a) \bullet \mu(b)$, for all a, b ∈ A. We have to show that • is one-to-one in each variable. Let
    $\mu(a) \bullet \mu(c) = \mu(b) \bullet \mu(c)$

    => $\mu(a \circ c) = \mu(b \circ c)$

    => a o c ≈ b o c

    => a ≈ b

    => $\mu(a) = \mu(b)$.

    ♦

For the right variable the proof is similar.

2. Let $\bullet$ be a binary operation that is one to one in each variable.
$a \approx b \Leftrightarrow \mu(a) = \mu(b)$.

$\Leftrightarrow \mu(a) \bullet \mu(c) = \mu(b) \bullet \mu(c)$

$\Leftrightarrow \mu(a \circ c) = \mu(b \circ c)$

$\Leftrightarrow a \circ c \approx b \circ c$.

For $c \circ a \approx c \circ b$ the proof is similar.

♦

Theorem C3:
There exists a binary operation $\bullet$ that is non-decreasing in each variable iff

$a \bullet \geq b \Rightarrow a \circ c \bullet \geq b \circ c$, and $a \bullet \geq b \Rightarrow c \circ a \bullet \geq c \circ b$, for all $a, b, c \in A$.

Proof:
1. Assume
$a \bullet \geq b \Rightarrow a \circ c \bullet \geq b \circ c$, and $a \bullet \geq b \Rightarrow c \circ a \bullet \geq c \circ b$, for all $a, b, c \in A$.

This implies that there exists a binary operation $\bullet$. Assume $\mu(a) \geq \mu(b)$. Hence $a \bullet \geq b$, $a \circ c \bullet \geq b \circ c$, and $\mu(a \circ c) \geq \mu(b \circ c)$.

$\mu(a) \bullet \mu(c) = \mu(a \circ c)$

$\mu(b) \bullet \mu(c) = \mu(b \circ c)$

Hence
$\mu(a) \bullet \mu(c) \geq \mu(b) \bullet \mu(c)$.

$\mu(c) \bullet \mu(a) \geq \mu(c) \bullet \mu(b)$ is shown similarly.

2. Assume that there exists $\bullet$ and $\bullet$ is non-decreasing in each variable. Let $a \bullet \geq b$, hence $\mu(a) \geq \mu(b)$. This implies

$\mu(a) \bullet \mu(c) \geq \mu(b) \bullet \mu(c)$

$\Rightarrow \mu(a \circ c) \geq \mu(b \circ c)$

$\Rightarrow a \circ c \bullet \geq b \circ c$.

$c \circ a \bullet \geq c \circ b$ is shown similarly.

♦

Theorem C4:
There exists a binary operation $\bullet$ that is strictly monotonic increasing in each variable iff $a \bullet \geq b \Leftrightarrow a \circ c \bullet \geq b \circ c \Leftrightarrow c \circ a \bullet \geq c \circ b$ for all $a, b, c \in A$.

Proof:

1. Let • be a binary operation that is strictly monotonic increasing in each variable.

   $a \bullet \geq b \iff \mu(a) \geq \mu(b)$.

   $\iff \mu(a) \bullet \mu(c) \geq \mu(b) \bullet \mu(c)$.

   $\iff \mu(a \circ c) \geq \mu(b \circ c)$,

   $\iff a \circ c \bullet \geq b \circ c$.

   The proof for $c \circ a \bullet \geq c \circ b$ is similar.

2. We assume
   $a \bullet \geq b \iff a \circ c \bullet \geq b \circ c \iff c \circ a \bullet \geq c \circ b$.

   Then there exists • such that $\mu(a \circ b) = \mu(a) \bullet \mu(b)$, for all $a, b \in A$. We have to show that • is strictly monotonic increasing in each variable. Let

   $\mu(a) \bullet \mu(c) \geq \mu(b) \bullet \mu(c)$

   $\iff \mu(a \circ c) \geq \mu(b \circ c)$

   $\iff a \circ c \bullet \geq b \circ c$

   $\iff a \bullet \geq b$

   $\iff \mu(a) \geq \mu(b)$.

The proof for the right variable is similar.

♦

Appendix III:

In Appendix III the definitions of the used software measures are given. More informations of this measures can be found in Zuse /ZUSE91/. The discussed measures are based on flowgraphs. $G=(E,N,s,t)$ is a flowgraph where E is the set of edges, N the set of nodes, s the start-node and t the exit-node. Every node $n \in N$ has to be reachable from the start-node s and every node $n \in N$ has to reach the exit-node. We only consider measures for intra-modular complexity.

Measures MCC-V and MCC-V2:

The Measures MCC-V and MCC-V2 /MCCA76/, /ZUSE91/, p.151, were define by McCabe. The measures are defined as:

MCC-V = $|E| - |N| + 2$, and

MCC-V2 = |E| - |N| + 1.

Measure N-MCCABE:
The Measure N-MCCABE /ZUSE91/, p.176, is defined as:

N-MCCABE(G) = (|E|=|N|+1)/|N|.

Measure SCOPE:
The Measure SCOPE /HARR81/, /HARR82/, /ZUSE91/, p.413, is equally to the Measure LOC in the case of a sequence. The Measure SCOPE is defined by the sum of the adjusted complexity of the nodes. It is sensitive to nested structures in unstructured and structured flowgraphs. An disadvantage is that structured flowgraphs can be less complex than unstructured flowgraphs. For that case see Zuse /ZUSE91/. The change of a forward edge to an backward edge increases the complexity. We give an example for the flowgraph P1:

```
A: P1
N: P1
R: Author
C: Example
SU: S

        1 s
        .
        v
        2
        .                GRAPH: P1
        v                 N   NDSC(N)
     ...3...             ---------------
     .     .              1      1
     v     v              2      1
     4     5              3      1
     .     .              4      2
     ..>6<..              5      2
        .                 6      1
        .                 7      1
        v                 8      2
     ...7...              9      2
     .     .             10      1
     v     v             11      1
     9     8             12      1
     .     .
     .>10<..
        .
        v
       11
        .
        v
       12 t
```

Figure AIII.1: The adjusted complexities of the nodes (column NDSC(n)) of the flowgraph P1. For example, NDSC(5)=2 means, that the complexity of node 5 is 2. The sum of the adjusted complexities of the nodes is 16.

Measure EJ-ISC of Ejiogu:
The Measure EJ-ISC /EJIO85/, /ZUSE91/, p.333, bases on the prime decomposition of flowgraphs.

Ejiogu introduced the following definitions of L, E and M.

L	Level or maximum of the heights of nodes above the root node.
E	Explosion number or effect of rotation of branches of the root node.
M	Monadicity, or Totality or Leaves of a tree.

In order to count a node exactly once we constrain M=1 and L=1. Each prime p has a complexity of 1.

The Measure EJ-ISC is then defined as:

EJ-ISC = L * E * M

Measure DMAX:
The Measure DMAX /ZUSE91/, p.269, captures the maximal nesting depth of a decision node in a flowgraph.

Measure CSG of Schmidt and Gong:
The Measure CSG of Schmidt and Gong /SCHM85/, /ZUSE91/, p.374, is an extension of the Measure MCC-V of McCabe in order capture the nesting-effect in the flowgraph. The measure bases on the concept of dominators and postdominators of decision nodes as described in Hecht (Page 55) /HECH77/.

Firstly, we give the definitions of a dominator and postdominator.

If x, y∈ N and x≠y, then x forward dominates or postdominates y (x pdom y) if and only if every path in G from y to its exit-node t contains x. For convenience, we let PDOM(y)={x|pdom y, x∈ N) for each y∈ N). We say, that x directly dominates y if and only if

1. x pdom y, and
2. z∈ N, z pdom y, then z pdom x.

The Measure CSG bases on the concept of dominators and postdominators. Counted is the number of decision nodes dominated by the decision node d to the postdominator plus 1 (The decision node itself).

CSG(G) = MCC-V + e, with

MCC-V=|E|-|N|+2   The Measure MCC-V of McCabe.

CSG(G) = |E|-|N|+2 + e,

where

e   The the additional contribution of Schmidt and Gong to reflect the degree of nesting of G, with: $0 \leq e < 1$.

$e = (e_1 + e_2,... + e_n) / |D|$, and

$e_i = (1-1/d_i)$, with $1 \geq i \geq |D|$.

D   Set of decision node in G.

d_i Number of the decision nodes $d_i \in D$ plus 1 dominated by the decision node di to the postdominator of di which lies on a path to the node t in the dominance tree Td.

Measure CS of Gilb

The software design Measure CS of Gilb /GILB77/ is defined as:

$CS = |SM|/|SE|$, where

SM is the set of modules in the software design and SE is the set of connected components in the software design.

Author Index

Bieman, J.M.	38, 63
Bollmann-Sdorra, P.	219
Courtney, R.E.	145
Fenton, N.	3, 38
Fuchs, N.	84
Gustafson, D.A.	38, 145, 179
Kitchenham, B.	28
Melton, A.	38, 194
Prasad, B.	179
Rice, M.D.	108
Russell, M.	209

Published in 1990

AI and Cognitive Science '89, Dublin City University, Eire, 14–15 September 1989
A. F. Smeaton and G. McDermott (Eds.)

Specification and Verification of Concurrent Systems, University of Stirling, Scotland, 6–8 July 1988
C. Rattray (Ed.)

Semantics for Concurrency, Proceedings of the International BCS-FACS Workshop, Sponsored by Logic for IT (S.E.R.C.), University of Leicester, UK, 23–25 July 1990
M. Z. Kwiatkowska, M. W. Shields and R. M. Thomas (Eds.)

Functional Programming, Glasgow 1989, Proceedings of the 1989 Glasgow Workshop, Fraserburgh, Scotland, 21–23 August 1989
K. Davis and J. Hughes (Eds.)

Persistent Object Systems, Proceedings of the Third International Workshop, Newcastle, Australia, 10–13 January 1989
J. Rosenberg and D. Koch (Eds.)

Z User Workshop, Oxford, 1989, Proceedings of the Fourth Annual Z User Meeting, Oxford, 15 December 1989
J. E. Nicholls (Ed.)

Formal Methods for Trustworthy Computer Systems (FM89), Halifax, Canada, 23–27 July 1989
Dan Craigen (Editor) and Karen Summerskill (Assistant Editor)

Security and Persistence, Proceedings of the International Workshop on Computer Architecture to Support Security and Persistence of Information, Bremen, West Germany, 8–11 May 1990
John Rosenberg and J. Leslie Keedy (Eds.)

Printing: Weihert-Druck GmbH, Darmstadt
Binding: Theo Gansert Buchbinderei GmbH, Weinheim